A Day at elBulli

Foreword

When this book was first released, it was a faithful testimony of the processes that took place at the restaurant every single day for six months of the year. As the opening lines announced: 'Not every day is the same, but there are many like this…' The book you have in your hands is an accurate reflection of the comings and goings of the daily work of the chefs and waiting staff during elBulli's active summer months. Today, now that the activities it describes belong to the past, the book has a different feel and holds additional value as a record of the restaurant's workings – the fruit of many years of perfecting, effort, creativity and passion.

elBulli closed its doors on 30 July 2011, but that did not signify an end – rather, it was a sign of transformation. We now understand it as just another change in the way elBulli operates, just another among the many that have taken place over the last twenty-five years. In 1987, we made the decision to close for six months of the year. This action allowed us to come back refreshed every year and to offer a completely renewed catalogue of creations. In 2001, we decided to have only one service, which would enable us to attend to our diners in the way that they deserved. We did away with the à la carte menu the following year, limiting choice to a single tasting menu (another idea that we also pioneered). In 2009, elBulli opened for the first time in autumn and winter, which gave us the opportunity to work with a range of seasonal produce to which we had no access in our usual summer opening.

In short, although it is apparently more radical, in our opinion this new change is nothing more than another way forward. It is certainly a major step, because it means giving up the occupation that was the justification for our very existence. However, I insist that the change is not as great as it might seem. elBulli will become a foundation, in which we will continue to research, and where we will also archive everything we have been working on, preserving and devising in the course of almost three decades and where we will analyse the effectiveness of our creativity by collaborating with creatives not only from the kitchen, but also from other fields.

The idea of redirecting ourselves did not come to us as an impulse. It began to take shape in 2009. We felt we were reaching a point where we needed new incentives. We were clearly capable of surprising and pampering diners, but our energy and motivation were no longer the same. The team at elBulli had always been very unconventional, an aspect that has continued to bring fresh ideas to our work. However, in the last few years, the seriousness and respect that we owed the people that came to eat at elBulli had turned it into excessive discipline and routine; it was a life that no longer appealed to us. Our intention was to be able to work in a more relaxed way – and we feel that at the elBullifoundation this will be possible.

Although there is no denying that one change this transformation will require is a complete revision of our day-to-day lives. In other words, 'a day at elBullifoundation' will be different from 'a day at elBulli'. The foundation will have no strict rules, although it will have a creative team comprising four or five people and four teams made up of five people each, in addition to an 'itinerant' team, consisting of creatives from outside the foundation, such as designers or architects. We won't know what a day at elBullifoundation will be like until we begin our regular activities, but it is likely to start with a brainstorming session with all the creatives in a purpose-built space, in which everything that was done the previous day and the plans for the same day will be discussed. One important point will be communicating our creations and research. The idea is that there will be real-time dissemination, every day.

One of the questions I am most commonly asked is whether elBulli will ever go back to serving food. The answer is yes, although on a level and at a pace that will be very different from those of a restaurant. Feedback is a logical part of cooking, meaning that people will come to eat at the foundation, but without strict rules. And it may be different each year, or each time. What is clear is that there will be no bookings, and we will be open to everyone from students to the most exclusive gourmets. We don't want to feel pressured or tied, because the primary mission of the foundation will be to create, rather than to serve food.

As you can see, the day-to-day at elBullifoundation differs from that of the restaurant. But I feel that the evolution taking place at elBulli will only increase the interest and value of the document that is this book. More than the workings of a restaurant, I think it highlights the dedication and passion of people who are part of a place, a landscape in which they live in close symbiosis. This geographical setting is inseparable from what our cuisine represented. It marked us, influenced us and accompanied us from the earliest hours of the day. As the hours passed, players of a different nature joined in the daily event, for the sole purpose of providing pleasure for the guest actors that were our diners. From 7.30 onwards each evening they would see the results of what several dozen people had been preparing for their pleasure. Besides tiredness, the end of the day brought satisfaction for a job well

06:05 – 02:00

INSIGHTS, IDEAS AND METHODS

- 06:05 *Daybreak*
- 06:10
- 06:15
- 06:20
- 06:25
- 06:30
- 06:35
- 06:40
- 06:45
- 06:50
- 06:55
- **07:00**
- 07:05
- 07:10
- 07:15
- 07:20
- 07:25
- 07:30
- 07:35
- 07:40
- 07:45
- 07:50
- 07:55
- **08:00**
- 08:05
- 08:10
- 08:15
- 08:20 *The empty stage*
- 08:25
- 08:30
- 08:35
- 08:40
- 08:45
- 08:50
- 08:55
- **09:00**
- 09:05
- 09:10
- 09:15
- 09:20
- 09:25
- 09:30
- 09:35
- 09:40
- 09:45
- 09:50
- 09:55
- **10:00** *Ferran arrives*
- 10:05
- 10:10
- 10:15
- 10:20
- 10:25
- 10:30
- 10:35
- 10:40
- 10:45
- 10:50
- 10:55 *Juli arrives*
- **11:00** *Creative sessions begin*
- 11:05
- 11:10 *Starting with coffee*
- 11:15
- 11:20
- 11:25
- 11:30 *Testing gets under way*
- 11:35
- 11:40
- 11:45
- 11:50
- 11:55
- **12:00**
- 12:05
- 12:10
- 12:15
- 12:20
- 12:25
- 12:30
- 12:35 *Produce arrives*
- 12:40
- 12:45
- 12:50 *Albert gets to work*
- 12:55
- **13:00**
- 13:05
- 13:10
- 13:15
- 13:20
- 13:25
- 13:30 *Order sheets made*
- 13:35
- 13:40 *Reservations checked*
- 13:45 *Lunch time*
- 13:50
- 13:55
- **14:00**
- 14:05
- 14:10
- 14:15
- 14:20
- 14:25
- 14:30 *Kitchen team arrives*
- 14:35
- 14:40 *Afternoon meeting*
- 14:45
- 14:50
- 14:55 *Cooking begins*
- **15:00**
- 15:05 *The sweet world*
- 15:10 *A moment for reflection*
- 15:15
- 15:20
- 15:25
- 15:30 *Waiters start work*
- 15:35 *Dining rooms prepared*
- 15:40
- 15:45
- 15:50
- 15:55
- **16:00**
- 16:05
- 16:10 *Checking the wine stocks*
- 16:15 *Checking the cigar stocks*
- 16:20
- 16:25
- 16:30 *More produce arrives*
- 16:35
- 16:40
- 16:45
- 16:50
- 16:55
- **17:00**
- 17:05 *Checking the logistics*
- 17:10
- 17:15
- 17:20
- 17:25
- 17:30 *Last-minute changes*
- 17:35 *Dining rooms ready*
- 17:40
- 17:45
- 17:50 *Staff family meal*
- 17:55
- **18:00**
- 18:05
- 18:10
- 18:15
- 18:20 *A ten-minute break*
- 18:25
- 18:30 *Kitchen ready*
- 18:35
- 18:40
- 18:45
- 18:50 *Final order sheets*
- 18:55
- **19:00** *Car park opens*
- 19:05
- 19:10 *Front of house meeting*
- 19:15 *Fifteen minutes to go*
- 19:20
- 19:25
- 19:30 *The doors are opened*
- 19:35
- 19:40
- 19:45 *First guests arrive*
- 19:50 *Act one begins*
- 19:55
- **20:00** *Chefs make cocktails*
- 20:05
- 20:10
- 20:15 *Juli welcomes the guests*
- 20:20
- 20:25
- 20:30
- 20:35
- 20:40
- 20:45 *The table in the kitchen*
- 20:50
- 20:55 *Wine is served*
- **21:00**
- 21:05
- 21:10 *Last guests arrive*
- 21:15
- 21:20 *Act two begins*
- 21:25
- 21:30
- 21:35
- 21:40
- 21:45
- 21:50
- 21:55
- **22:00**
- 22:05
- 22:10
- 22:15
- 22:20
- 22:25
- 22:30
- 22:35
- 22:40
- 22:45
- 22:50
- 22:55
- **23:00**
- 23:05
- 23:10
- 23:15
- 23:20
- 23:25
- 23:30
- 23:35 *A dangerous moment*
- 23:40 *Act three begins*
- 23:45
- 23:50
- 23:55
- **24:00** *Act four begins*
- 00:05
- 00:10
- 00:15
- 00:20
- 00:25
- 00:30
- 00:35
- 00:40 *Preparations for tomorrow*
- 00:45
- 00:50 *Savoury service is over*
- 00:55
- **01:00** *Guests start to leave*
- 01:05
- 01:10
- 01:15
- 01:20 *Kitchen lights out*
- 01:25
- 01:30
- 01:35
- 01:40
- 01:45
- 01:50
- 01:55
- **02:00** *The curtain comes down*

06:05

—

Not every day is the same,
but there are many like this...

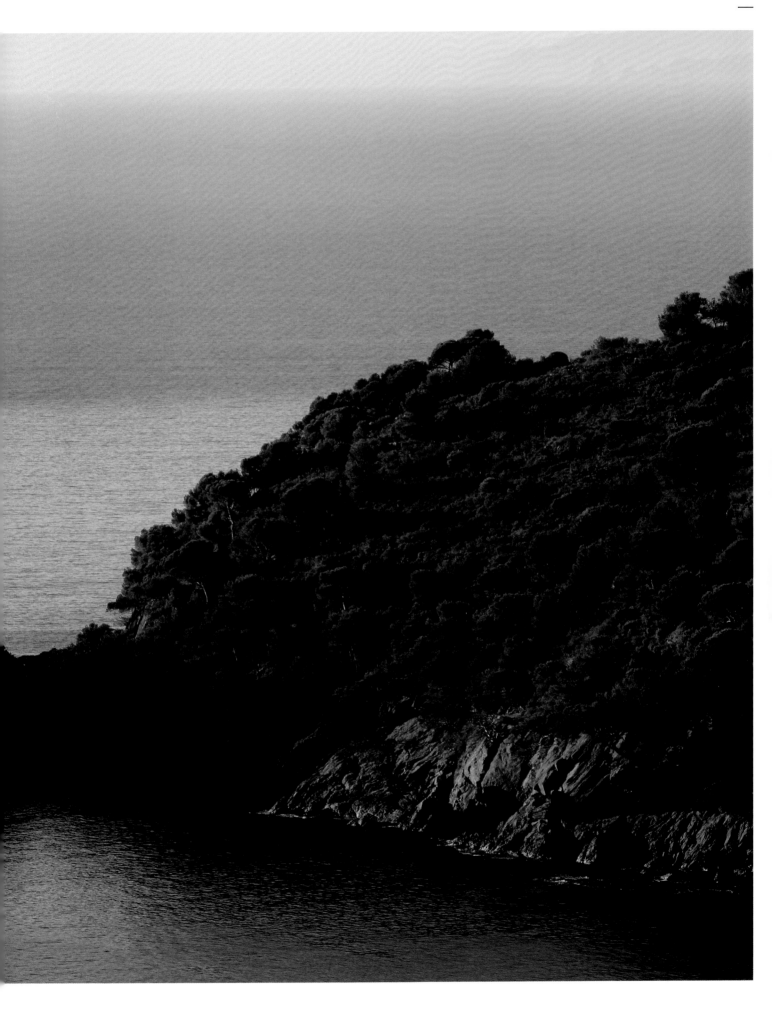

07:30

—

The elBulli garden

The Cap de Creus natural park spans eight districts of Girona (Cadaqués, Llançà, Palau-Saverdera, Pau, el Port de la Selva, Roses, la Selva de Mar and Vilajuïga). In 1998, 3.5 square miles (9 square kilometres) of it was declared a nature reserve, and 3.2 square miles (8.4 square kilometres) of the surrounding sea became a marine reserve.

The site is 450 million years old and of great geological importance.

And here we are...

Your questions about elBulli

WHAT…

…IS ELBULLI?

elBulli is a restaurant owned by Ferran Adrià and Juli Soler. Ferran Adrià is the most innovative chef working in the world today, and Juli Soler has run the front of house operations since 1981. elBulli is famous around the world for its avant-garde cuisine, and every year there is overwhelming demand for reservations. It has been voted 'Best Restaurant in the World' four times by an international panel of chefs and food critics for *Restaurant* magazine, one of the most sought-after accolades in the restaurant industry.

WHERE…

…IS ELBULLI?

At Cala Montjoi, a beautiful and secluded bay near the town of Roses in the province of Girona, northern Spain, a few hours from Barcelona and not far from Perpignan.

WHEN…

…IS THE RESTAURANT OPEN?

For six months of each year, from around 1 April to 30 September.

WHY…

…IS ELBULLI OPEN FOR ONLY SIX MONTHS OF THE YEAR?

Years ago it was because most people who ate at elBulli were visitors to Cala Montjoi on their summer holidays. But since 1987 the only way to carry out all the work needed to create the menu has been to open for six months during the summer, and to spend the rest of the year in the workshop in Barcelona developing dishes for the next season.

…IS THERE ONLY ONE SERVICE PER DAY?

The complexity of the menu, the number of courses, the amount of work that goes into each dish and the style of service all mean that it would be impossible to open for both lunch and dinner.

HOW…

…MANY MICHELIN STARS DOES ELBULLI HAVE?

Three. The first and second stars were awarded in 1976 and 1983; when Ferran Adrià joined in 1984, the second star was removed because of the change of head chef, in accordance with Michelin Guide practice. Under Ferran Adrià, elBulli regained the second star, and won a third and final star in 1997.

…MANY PEOPLE EAT AT ELBULLI EVERY YEAR?

Approximately 8,000. That is, about 50 people a day for about 160 days a year.

…MANY RESERVATIONS REQUESTS ARE RECEIVED EVERY YEAR?

About two million.

HOW…

…MANY PEOPLE WORK AT ELBULLI?
Between sixty and seventy, depending on the time of year, which means that there are actually more staff than guests.

…ARE STAFF RECRUITED?
Advertisements are posted on the elBulli website, and the best applicants are chosen from the thousands of responses received from all over the world.

…MANY HOURS ARE WORKED BY STAFF AT ELBULLI?
The chefs usually work twelve-hour shifts. Those who take part in the morning creative session, in which the new dishes are developed, start three hours earlier. The front of house team works for about ten hours a day.

WHAT…

…IS ON THE MENU?
Rather than choosing dishes from a menu, each guest is served a tasting menu of between twenty-eight and thirty-five dishes, comprising cocktails, snacks, tapas-dishes, avant-desserts, desserts and morphings.

…ARE SNACKS?
Designed to provide a more interesting alternative to bread and butter, snacks are little mouthfuls (such as black olive madeleines) that are served at the start of the meal, just after the cocktail and before the main tapas-dishes.

…ARE AVANT-DESSERTS?
Served after the tapas-dishes and before the desserts, these small dishes make the transition from the savoury world to the sweet world; they might include spherical mango ravioli or a sweet vanilla potato purée.

…ARE MORPHINGS?
These are an elBulli invention that replace petits fours at the end of the meal.

…IF A GUEST WANTS TO TRY A DISH FROM A PREVIOUS YEAR?
At elBulli the menu changes completely at the end of every season, so a guest will never eat the same dish twice.

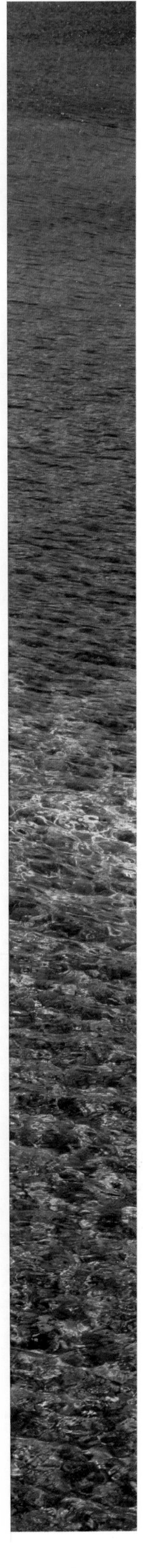

08:10

—

Nature's textures

The colours and textures of elBulli's remote and beautiful setting have provided a rich source of inspiration.

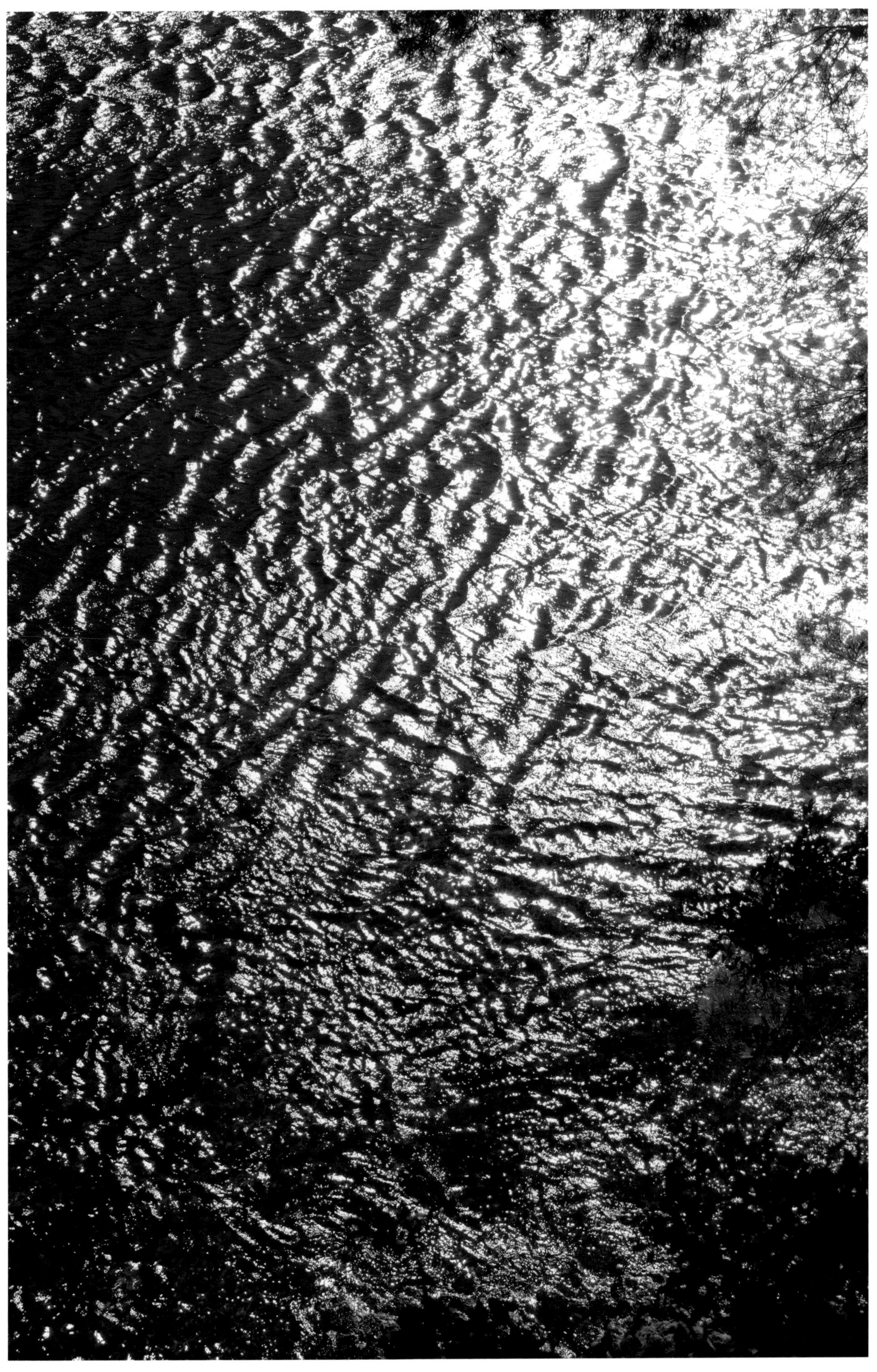

08:20

—

The empty stage

08:40

The restaurant is in the beautiful bay of Cala Montjoi on the Costa Brava. The small white building is hidden in lush Mediterranean vegetation, and there is a spectacular view of the sea from the terrace and garden.

'A good dinner is inseparable from good scenography.'

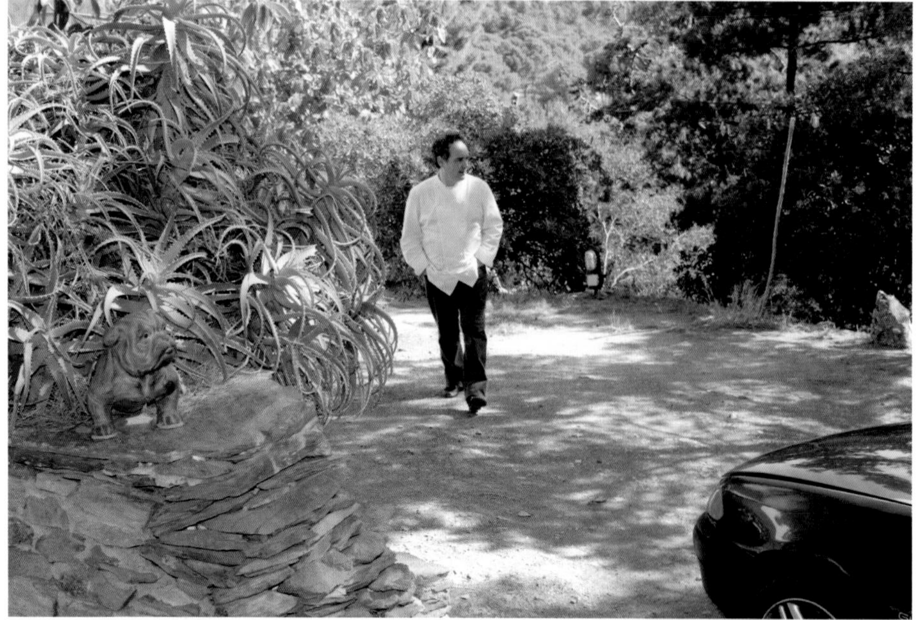

Ferran arrives at the secret workshop

When they hear about the elBulli workshop, most people think of the one on Calle Portaferrissa in Barcelona where most of the creative work takes place during the winter. However, the real workshop, Ferran's secret laboratory, is near the restaurant at Cala Montjoi.

The initial research into techniques and concepts takes place at the Barcelona workshop, but the dishes themselves are created in the kitchens at elBulli. For more than twenty years the main ideas and strategies have been decided here.

Creativity involves coming up with something that has not been done before, but novelty alone is not enough. It takes many hours of experimentation to create something that is both new and interesting.

'New, creative and unique are not the same thing.'

The early years of Ferran Adrià

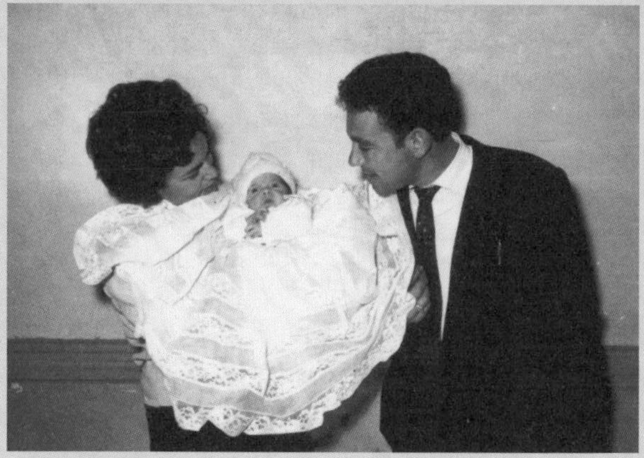

With his father and godmother on the day
of his baptism, 1962

Young Ferran playing with a new pet

At dinner with his younger brother, Albert

Aged 12, with the local soccer team

With his family in 1977

During his military service, 1982–3

With the kitchen team at Castell Arnau restaurant, Barcelona, in 1981

Historia

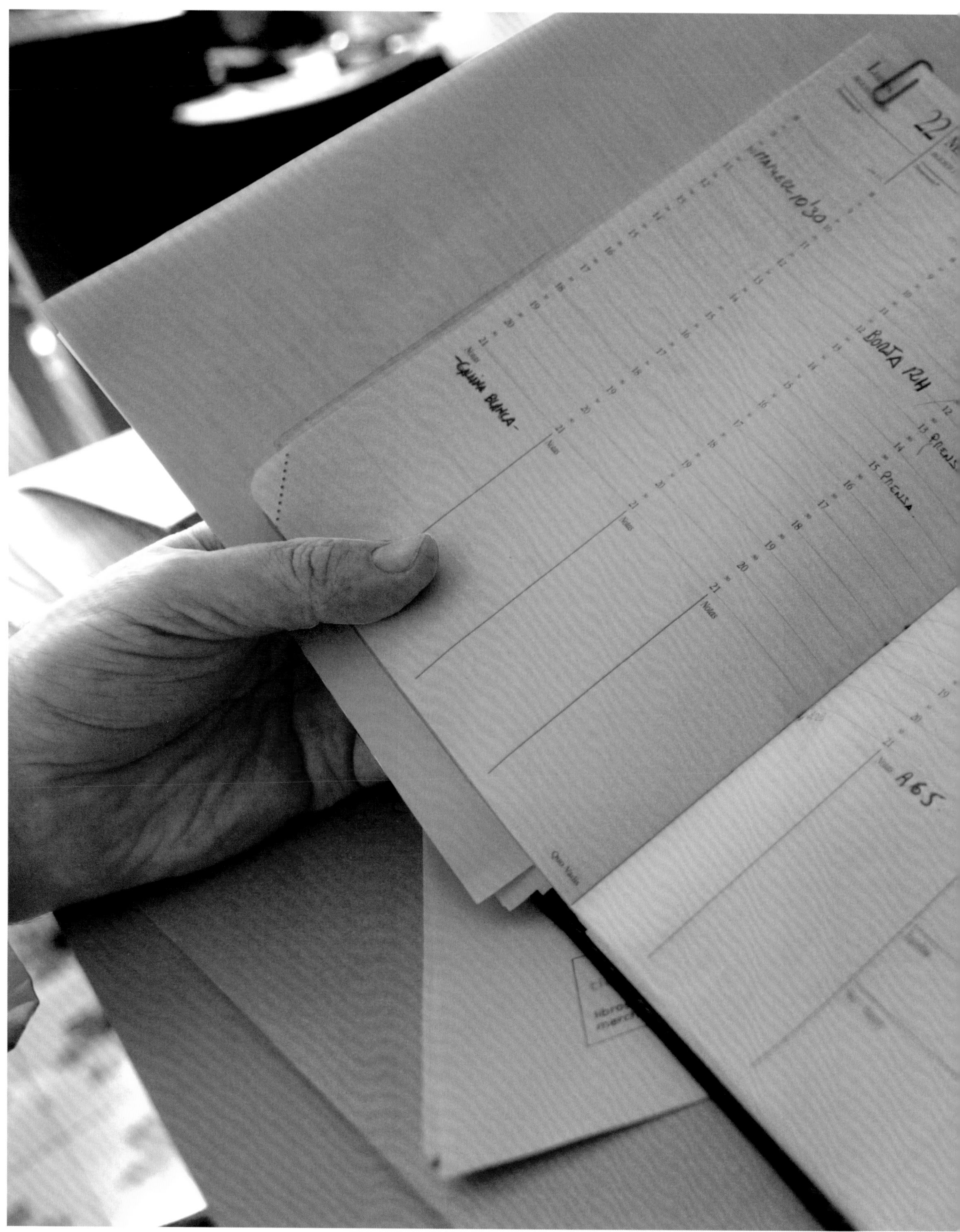
BORJA 12H
PRENSA
A65
Notas
Quo Vadis

23 Miércoles
24 Jueves
25
26 Sábado
AGOSTO (08)
27 Domingo
AGOSTO (08)
28
Semana 34
Tercer Trimestre
del
22 de agosto
al
28 de agosto
Teléfonos
Fax
Email

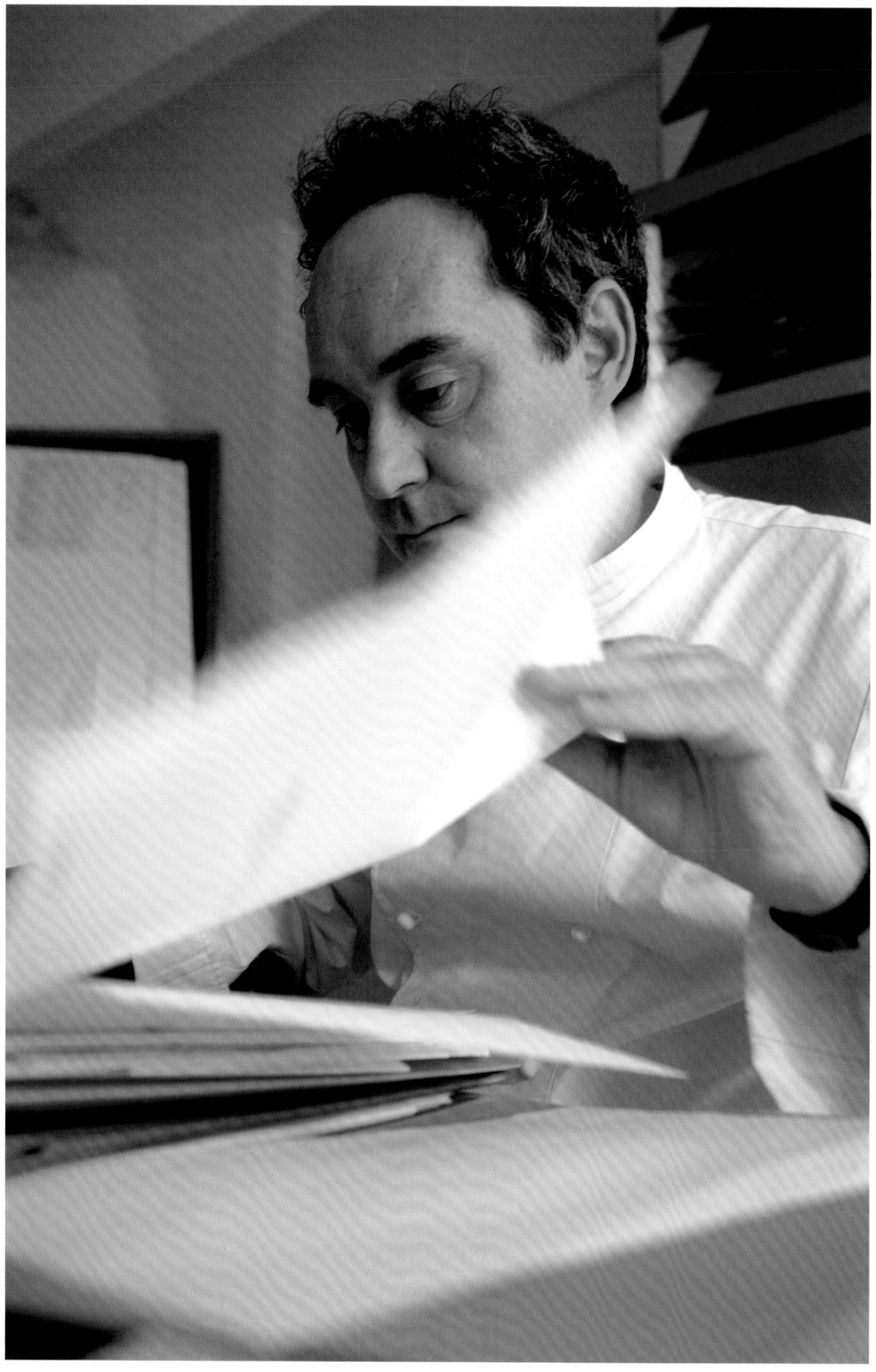

It is impossible to be creative without good organization

An hour of solitude and concentration is essential in order to ensure that everything is well organized and runs smoothly. During the season at elBulli this is the only hour of the day that Ferran dedicates to business matters and administration.

Ferran is constantly curious and never stops looking for new ideas, no matter where he is or what he is doing. He is so busy setting himself challenges that he does not have the time to stop and see them as problematic. In fact, solving them is essential to help him keep an active and creative mind. Seen in this way, his 'problems' are not really problems at all.

'You don't have problems if new ones arrive every minute.'

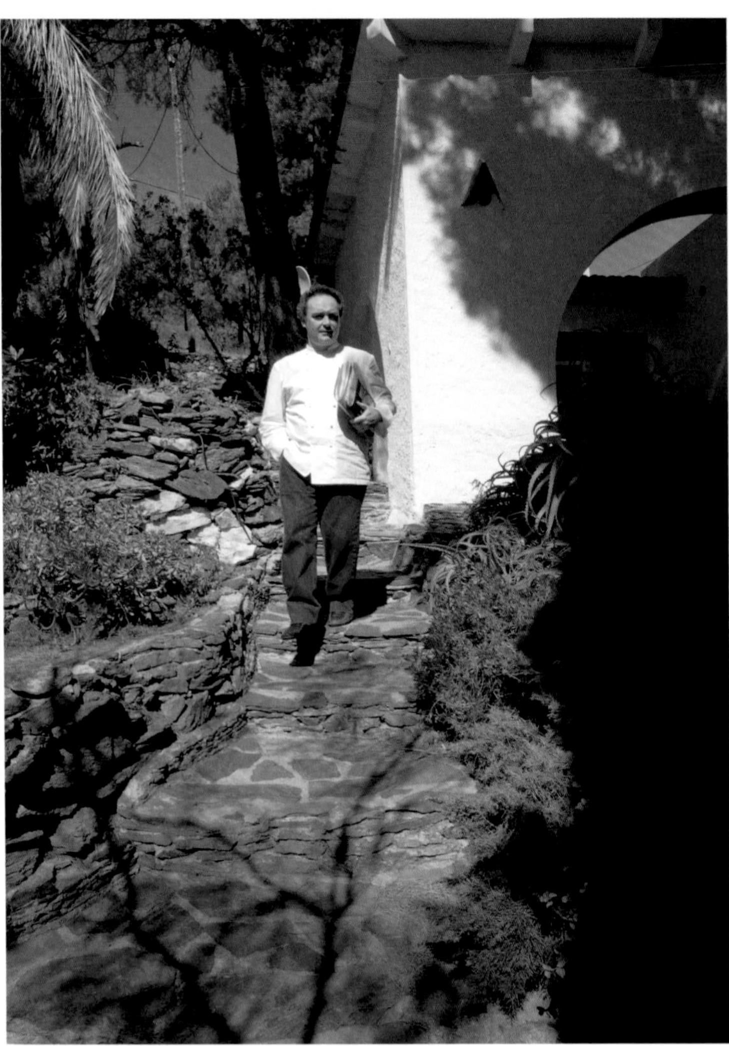

Ambition without patience is a dangerous thing

After spending an hour on paperwork, Ferran leaves his secret workshop to walk to the restaurant kitchens, where the creative sessions will take place.

Forcing things gets you nowhere, and patience is essential: this is the attitude elBulli has tried hard to adopt over the last twenty years. There is a painstaking process of trial and error behind the development of every dish, and the creative process cannot be hurried.

‘Creativity means not copying’

Ferran and Albert have been trying to define creativity for many years, and they have expressed it in thousands of different ways. But the best definition is still the simple statement, 'Creativity means not copying', made by the celebrated French chef Jacques Maximin in February 1987.

Before 1987, the style of elBulli's food was based on the tenets of nouvelle cuisine, and Ferran and Christian Lutaud (the co-head chef at that time) produced their own versions of dishes by classic French chefs such as Jacques Pic. Then, at a 1987 conference in Nice, Maximin's answer to the question 'What is creativity?' inspired Ferran's resolution to leave the cookbooks behind and create a unique identity for elBulli. In the same year, the extension of the winter closing period allowed six months to be devoted purely to creating new dishes. The combination of these two factors marked the beginning of the creative journey at elBulli.

The creative process has evolved over time. Throughout the months when the restaurant is closed, new concepts, techniques and preparations are investigated during sessions led by Ferran, Albert and Oriol at the elBulli workshop in Barcelona. They work not on specific dishes, but on developing new techniques that will later be used to create dishes. This is the heart of the development process, and it is in inventing techniques that have never been used before in cookery – such as spherification, using siphons to create foams or the new gelling agents – that elBulli is truly creative. At the sessions held in the restaurant kitchens shortly before they open for the season, the new techniques and concepts are used to develop the new collection of dishes, and the menu for the year is finalized. The process goes on throughout the summer season, and new dishes are continually added to the menu.

DECEMBER

Creative sessions come to a close, and the season is assessed. The ideas that have accumulated during the season are evaluated, and the starting points for next year's research are determined. A rough schedule is produced for the sessions in which the new techniques, concepts and dishes for the next season will be created. Trips and courses are planned, and organizational issues such as finding new suppliers or products are discussed.

JANUARY

The restaurant closes. The creative team begin investigations for the following season at the elBulli workshop in Barcelona.

FEBRUARY – JUNE

During the winter months, new products are investigated and sourced, potential new suppliers are contacted and new techniques are tested and photographed daily. Chefs attend specialist courses and visit food and drink trade fairs. Inspiration comes not only from visits to restaurants and food markets around the world, but might also come from local hardware shops (where new tools not previously used in cookery might be discovered), museums and art galleries, and walks in the countryside. The chocolate dusts and powders of the dessert *Earth*, for example, were inspired in 2003 by the colours and textures of the earth in the Australian bush.

Collaboration with industrial designers and manufacturers also takes place during these months. This might involve developing a new plate or piece of cutlery for a particular dish, such as the wide glass straws in which shots are served, or the scent spoons, which have a point onto which an aromatic herb can be attached, so that a fragrance is released while the food on the spoon is eaten. Specialist equipment might be designed for the kitchen to make a new technique more efficient. For example, when the spherification technique was developed, in which tiny droplets from a syringe were made to congeal to form 'caviar', it quickly became apparent that producing fifty portions for one evening's service at the restaurant would be very time-consuming. To make it more efficient, industrial designer Luki Huber built a rack to hold twenty syringes that could be activated simultaneously.

JULY

The creative team moves to Cala Montjoi and continues to develop dishes for the new season throughout the day, right up until service begins. For the first few weeks, the previous year's menu is served alongside a few new recipes. New dishes are added gradually, as testing is completed (this may take a few days or two weeks, depending on the dish). By the end of July, there is a whole new menu.

AUGUST – NOVEMBER

Finishing touches continue to be added to the dishes, and the search for new concepts and techniques goes on. As new seasonal ingredients become available, new dishes are developed and added to the menu.

The stage manager

Juli Soler has been the manager of elBulli since 1981. Having entered the restaurant business at the age of thirteen as an assistant waiter in Terrassa (near Barcelona), he built up a wealth of experience in restaurant service before deciding to pursue his other love – music. In fact, Juli ran a record shop for many years before Hans and Marketta Schilling, the previous owners of elBulli, tempted him back into restaurants when they offered him the position of general manager. With their support, he spent time studying the restaurant business and visiting the best restaurants in Europe in order to fulfil his dream of creating an avant-garde restaurant in Spain. In 1984 he quickly recognized the talent in Ferran Adrià and, when Ferran was considering whether to leave to open a restaurant of his own, Juli persuaded him to stay, making him co-head chef of the restaurant with Christian Lutaud.

With his knowledge and experience, Juli set a new high standard for front of house service that had never been seen before in Spain. In 1981, upon hearing that elBulli had lost its Michelin star, he travelled to Paris to ask the publishers for an explanation. It turned out that they thought the restaurant had closed down when the previous head chef had left. Juli insisted that they visit the restaurant again, and sure enough elBulli was back in the Guide with one star the following year. Together with Ferran, Juli has transformed the experience of eating at elBulli into the unforgettable pleasure that it is today.

At elBulli, Juli's work begins very early, although he is rarely to be seen. What he does is hidden, little recognized and little noticed. He might only be glimpsed once or twice before 19:30, if he needs something in particular or to eat lunch with the staff. But although he is seldom seen before the restaurant opens, he and Ferran always find time to meet and discuss the issues of the day.

Juli's time is taken up with the thousands of emails received at elBulli, but his work involves much, much more. He likes to think of himself as the sixth Rolling Stone, but he is also a problem solver, a part-time publisher and a great lover of wine, a subject that he embraces with huge passion and knowledge. If a new gadget arrives at elBulli, you can be sure that it was Juli who brought it in. His unique sense of humour can be disconcerting to newcomers, but it is also enduring, like his attention and his concentration.

The creative sessions begin

Ferran arrives at elBulli for the start of the creative sessions, along with head chefs Albert Raurich, Eduard Xatruch and Oriol Castro, Albert Adrià (Ferran's brother and the creative director of the workshop) and Mateu Casañas, the head chef of the sweet world. Joining them are three young chefs chosen from the many who join elBulli every year on work experience placements, known as 'stages'.

When they first arrived, these young chefs (or 'stagers') probably never imagined they would have the chance to participate in the creative sessions. In the following weeks the other stagers will have their turn to experience the ongoing development work. The process of arriving at a new dish is as important as the dish itself, and sometimes the creative path leads in unexpected directions.

'With creativity, it is not what you look for that matters, but what you find.'

11:05

Start with a coffee

A Lavazza coffee is the best way for the team to get things going. The creative level that elBulli has reached could not have been achieved by one person alone. The core members of the creative team – Ferran, Albert, Oriol – have been working together for twelve years and the connection between the whole team is as strong as a family bond. No other restaurant produces an entirely new menu of more than one hundred new dishes every year, and without the strength of the creative team at elBulli this simply could not be done. They constantly test new ideas, which could come from anywhere, and are always searching for the next new concept or technique.

'There is a very fine line between being influenced and copying.'

Testing gets under way

By mid-morning the creative team is running like a diesel engine, solid and sure. The kitchen staff will not arrive until 14:30, and being able to enjoy the peace of the morning alone in the 3,780-square-foot (350-square-metre) workspace is a real luxury.

There are different levels of creativity in cooking. You can talk about following a recipe; following a recipe and adding a few touches of your own; inventing a new recipe of your own; or inventing a new cooking technique or language. Each of these can be creative, but the last one represents the highest level of creativity, and this is the level that elBulli strives to attain. It is built on a foundation of technical knowledge, experience, a developed palate, good organization and many hours of work. Wanting to be creative is not enough.

'A creative spirit does not necessarily lead to a creative result.'

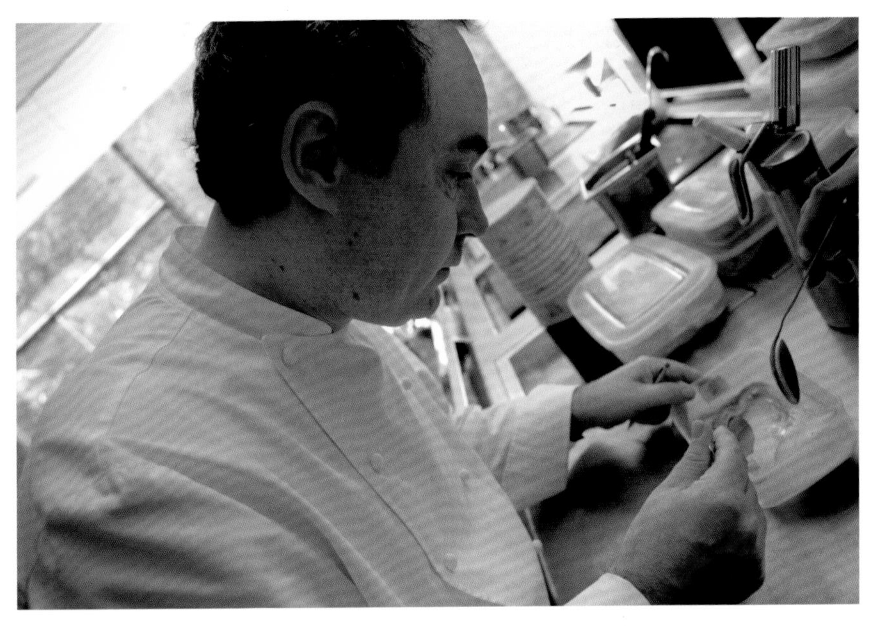

11:40

The ideas file, notebooks and archives of tested dishes are the creative records

The creative notebooks are filled with ideas, concepts, photographs and sketches for new dishes, and are used and maintained by every member of the creative team. They are compiled at the Barcelona workshop as well as at the restaurant. Each day Ferran will take an idea from the notebook as the starting point for that day's session. The chefs can easily refer to the hundreds of notebooks that have been filed away over the years to look for new ideas or to compare results.

The archives show how a dish has evolved and can provide many fruitful starting points for new dishes, but they cannot always explain the original source of inspiration.

'Every creative idea has a history, but not necessarily a reason for being.'

à la carte

entrées chaudes & froides — le ventre de thon de Saint Jean-de-Luz sur une vinaigrette aux cerises :

fromage blanc lissé & folioles anisées.

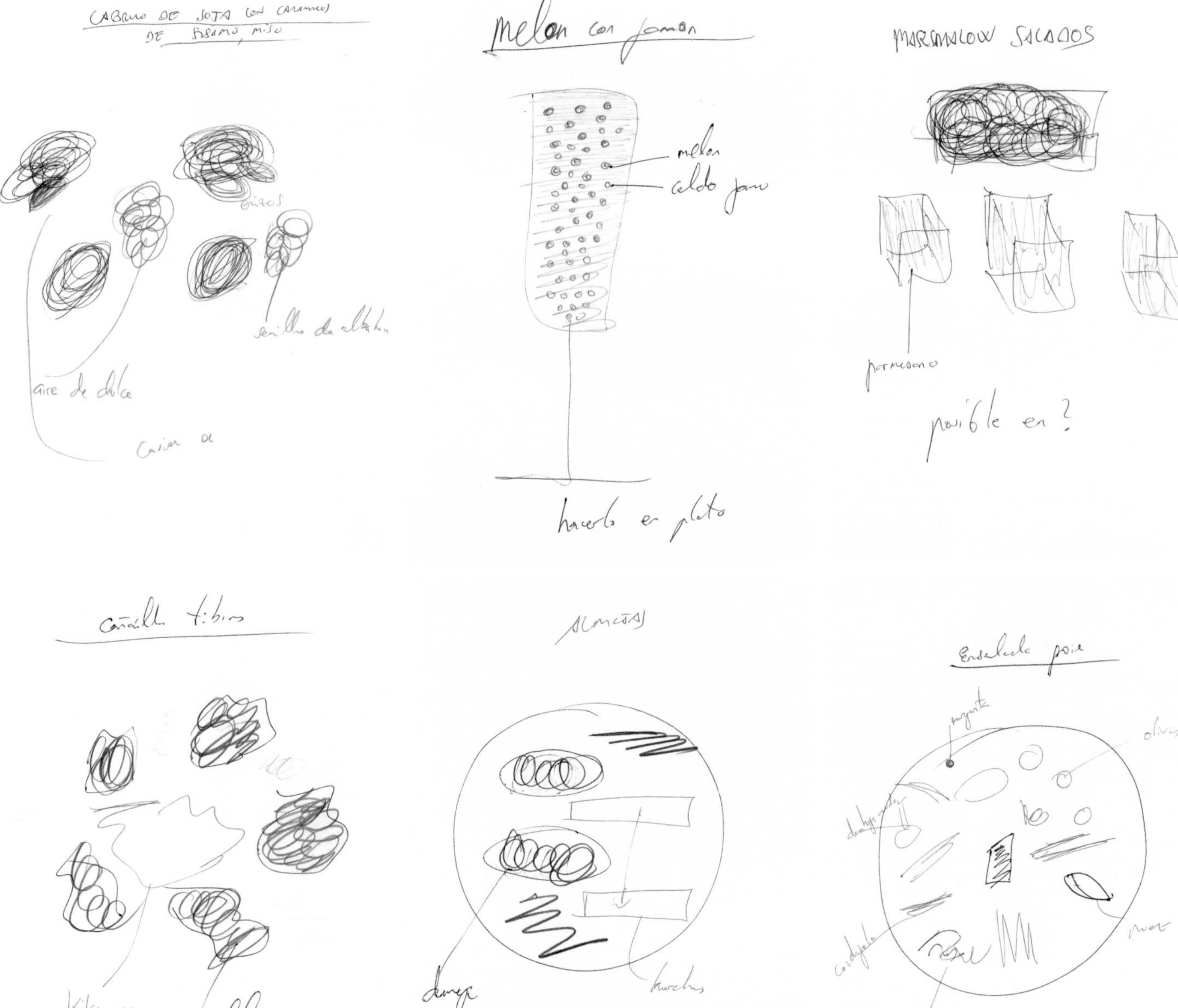
melon con jamon
melon
hacerlo en plato
parmesano
posible en ?
aire de dulce

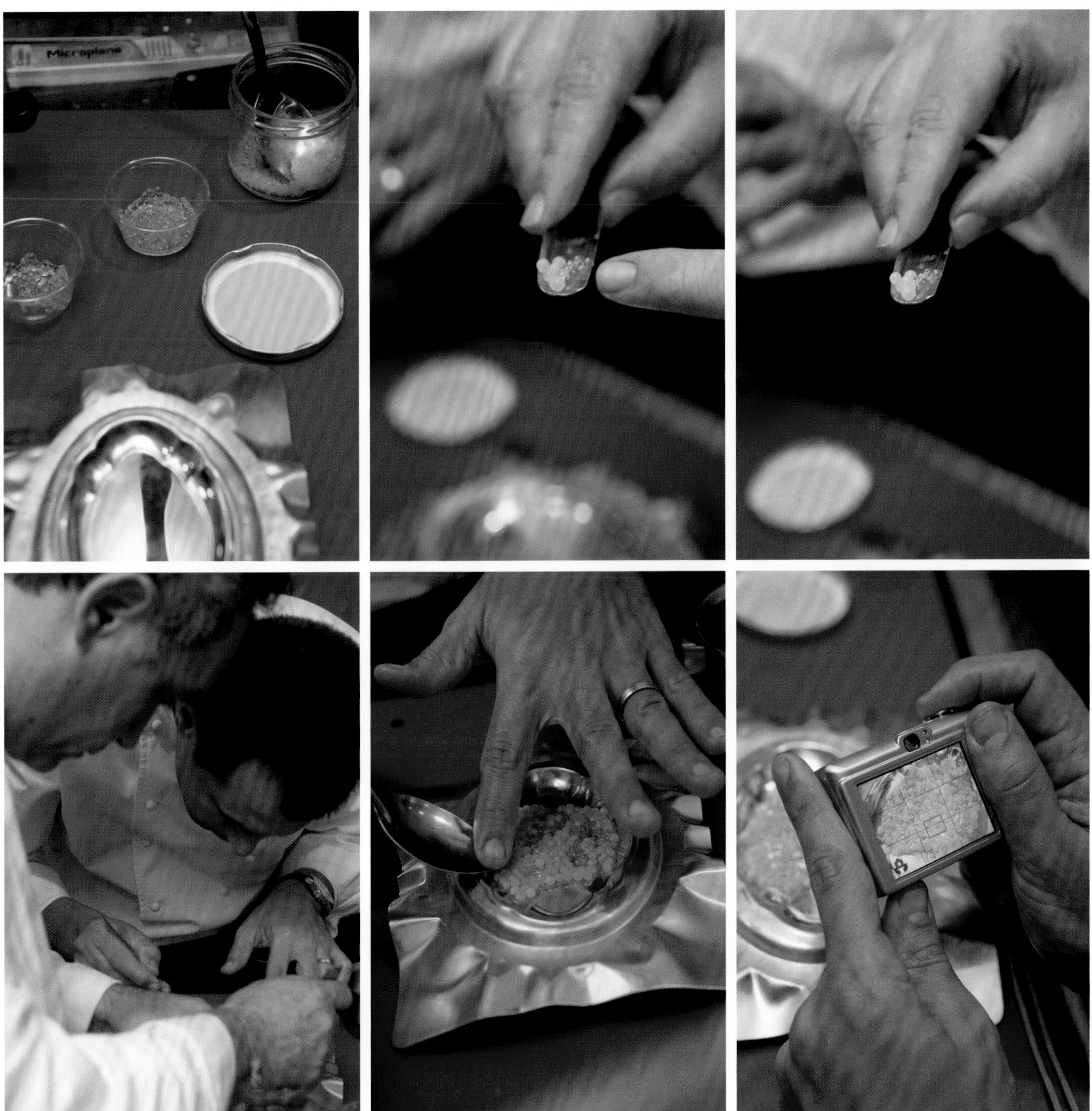

Photographs of dishes at every stage of their development form an essential part of the creative archives. During the creative sessions the preparation and presentation of the dishes are finalized, and the snapshot of the final result records another step and another achievement.

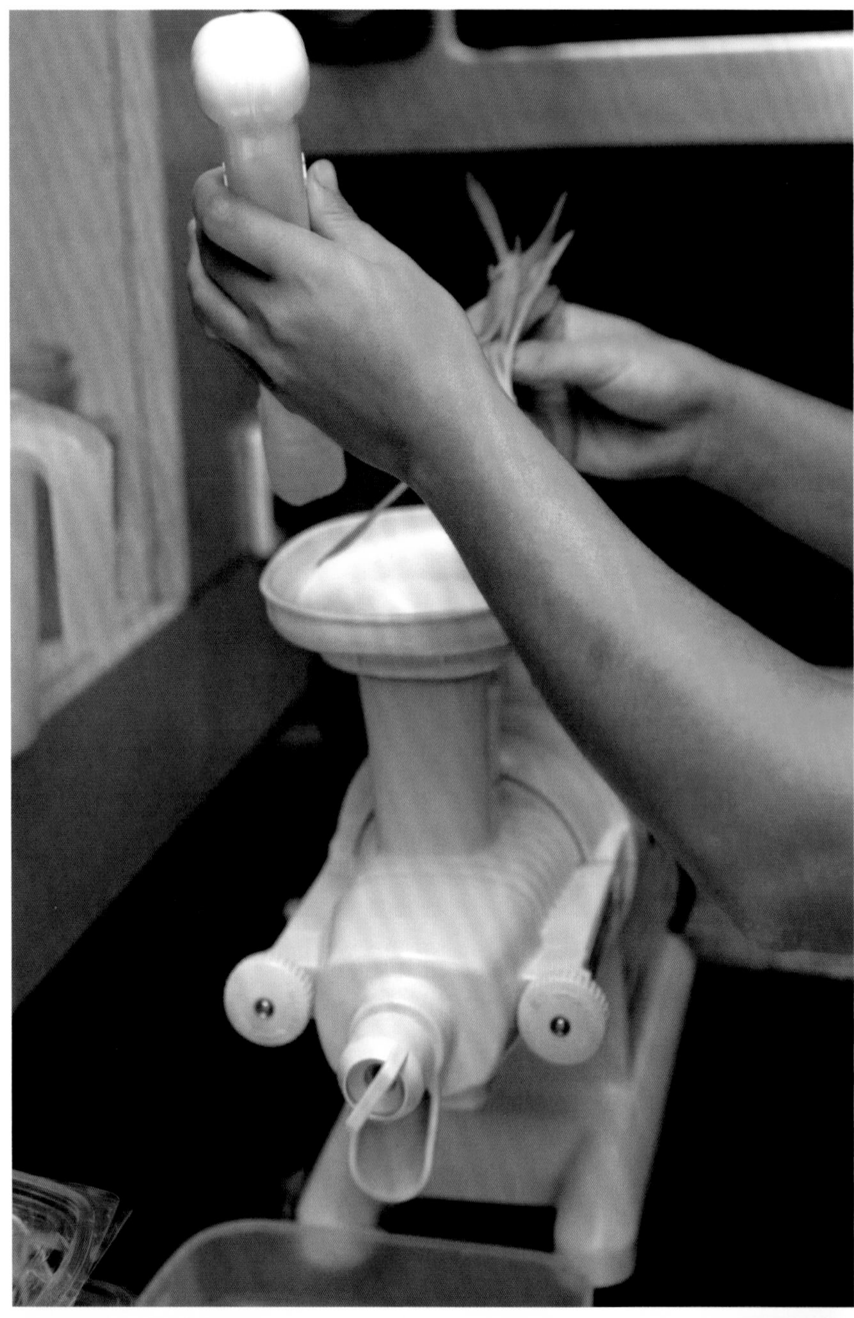

How many starting points are there to creating a dish?

From techniques, concepts, textures and new ingredients, to adapting or deconstructing existing dishes, there are many starting points from which a new dish can be created. Each year a different creative method becomes more prominent.

Every day different techniques and methods of preparation are explored. The square spaghetti that Oriol is trying allows him to test the texture of a new gelling agent, and if the results are good the technique will be used in other dishes. A special herb press is used to extract the juice from sprouted corn, which could not be done with a conventional juicer.

The stages of developing a dish

Exploring, touching, tasting, analysing: all of these open up different routes, which sooner or later result in a new dish.

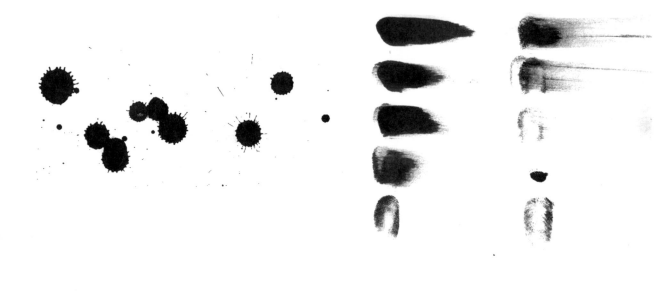

1.

At the Barcelona workshop, a member of the creative team has an idea for a new technique, concept or dish.

2.

The idea is developed by using one or more of the creative methods or by working intuitively.

3.

Tests are carried out, and the results are documented with photographs and in the creative notebooks. If the idea is for a new technique, the technique is sometimes tried first on something neutral, such as water or a starch-based ingredient.

4.

The tests are analysed using the chefs' mental palates, and the tables showing the flavour combinations of previous elBulli dishes may also be consulted.

5.

Final testing takes place and results in a prototype, which is developed into a dish in the kitchens at elBulli.

6.

The new dish is served in the restaurant. The creative team take into account the reactions or observations of the first guests in order to perfect the dish.

7.

Refinements are made. These could be intended to make the dish easier to eat, to heighten or lessen textural contrasts, or to alter the presentation.

8.

Once completed, the dish is listed in the general catalogue.

A new idea could also come from the team's experiments with proteins. In this case, Oriol is using a siphon to create a foam, which will later be frozen and then freeze-dried.

Observing an ingredient or product and working with it in different ways helps to find new ways to treat and prepare it.

Here, the pulp is extracted from tamarind, and the peel is used to make a tamarind infusion.

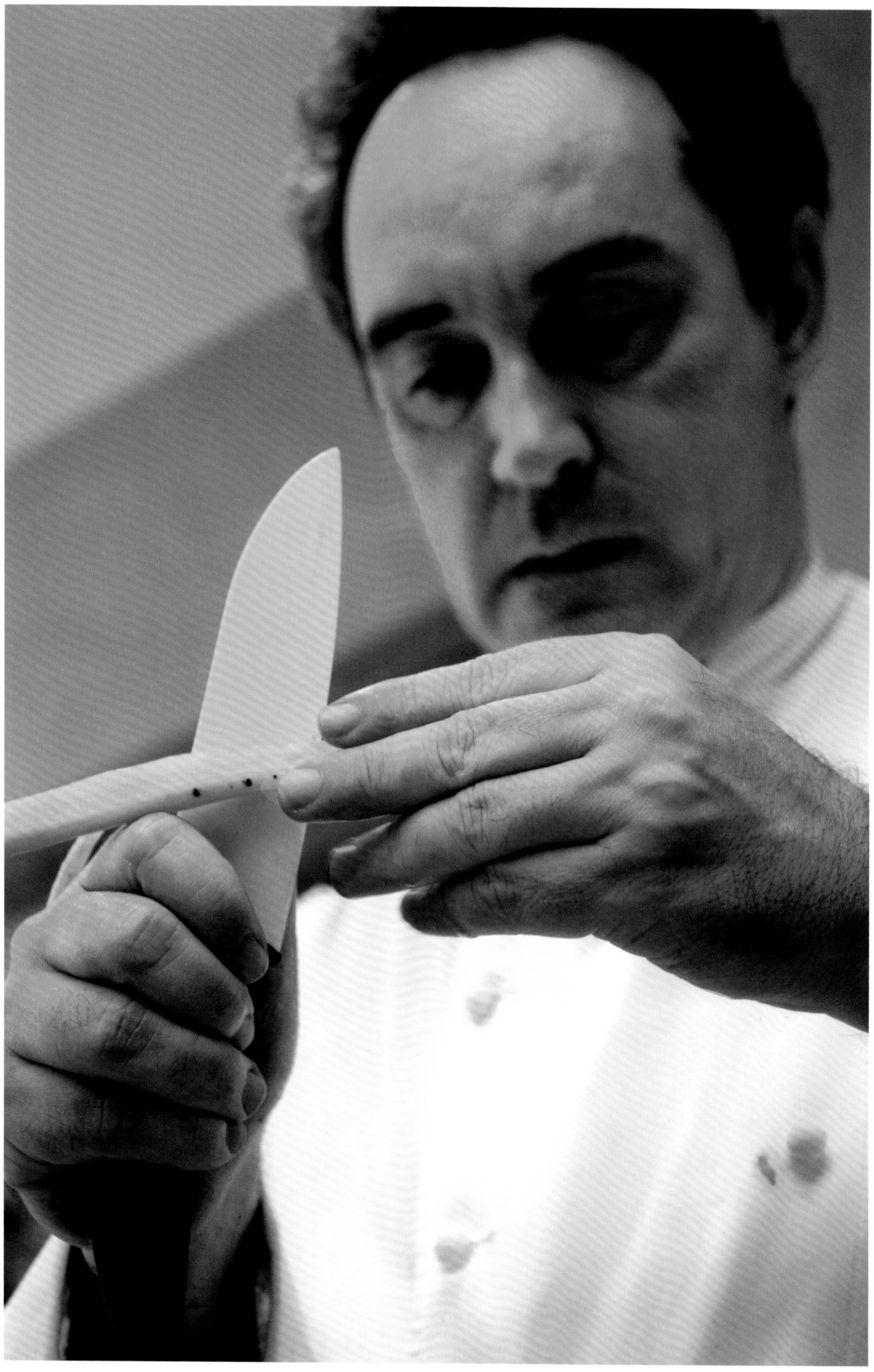

Ferran tries different methods of slicing salsify. Although apparently simple, this is one of the most fundamental ways of experimenting with a vegetable, and can lead to completely new ways of using it.

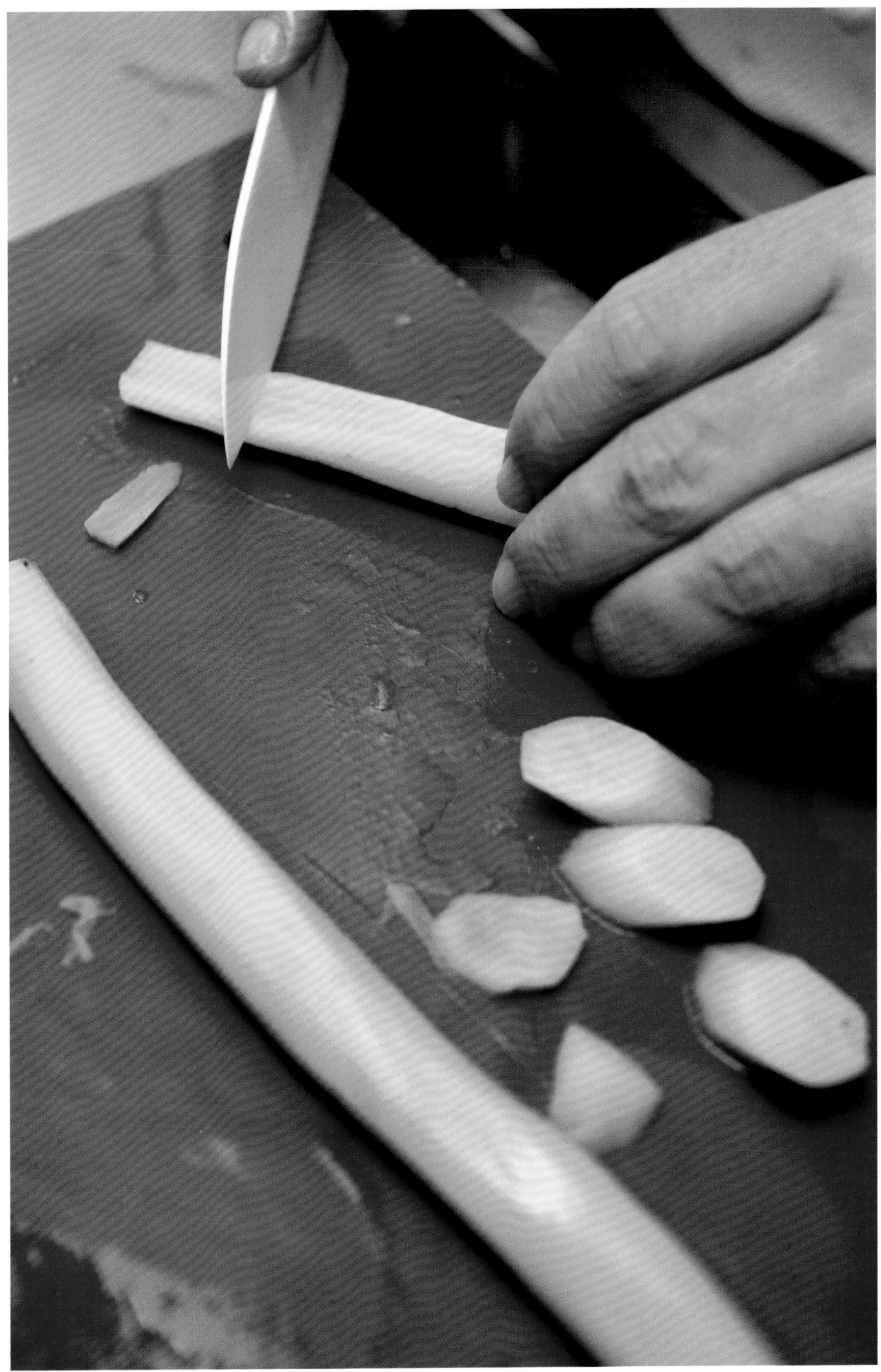

The mental palate

Years spent working in restaurants, the flavours and textures of thousands of ingredients, countless hours of cooking, tasting and experimenting with dishes all contribute to a chef's mental database.

The mental database provides short cuts that help make the experiments more efficient. It allows the chefs to use their knowledge of the flavours and textures of ingredients to imagine how they might combine with another product, and therefore cuts down on the amount of time that they need to spend on testing new combinations. Lists of the flavour combinations of every dish are kept, and these provide a reference tool, but without the mental database the testing process would be interminable.

Cooking is an act of judgement in which the mental palate is developed constantly. Chefs should be better at tasting than they are at cooking.

'Let what you like to eat tell you how you should cook.'

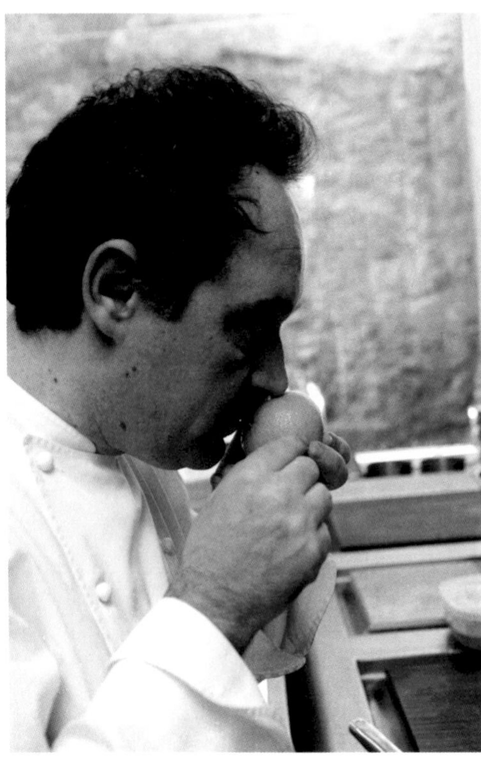

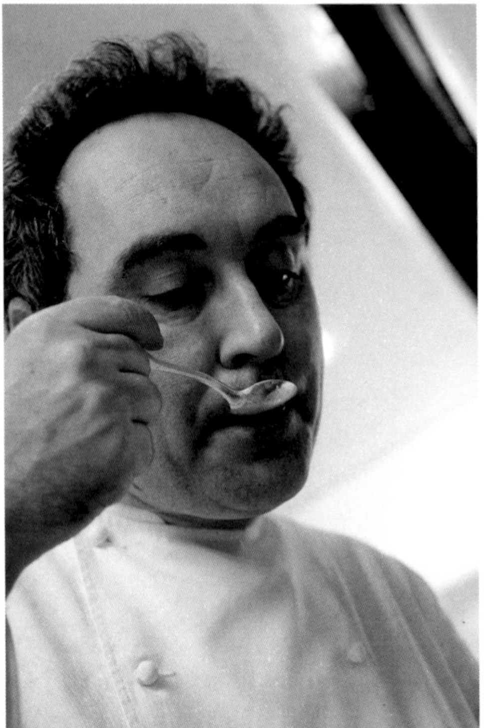

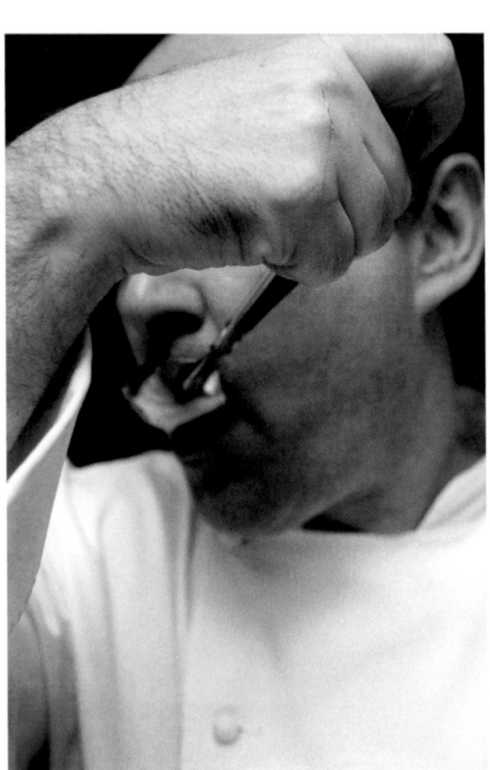

Knowledge is essential for judging the products

Ingredients are the chef's raw materials and the qualities of the dish served greatly depend on the raw materials chosen. The philosophy of elBulli is to establish a relationship with each ingredient without prejudice, and to see it for what it is. Bearing in mind its inherent qualities, the product must be studied with a fresh approach and considered with common sense.

To understand the fundamental qualities of an ingredient, the chef must be willing to return to the market and buy it, not for daily service in the restaurant, but for the purpose of study. Through this study a chef can understand all the characteristics of the ingredient and make maximum use of them. It is necessary to touch it, to turn it, to look at it from all angles – just as sushi master does with a tuna before he knows where to cut it – and in doing so, take in its shape, density, weight and size.

Reflecting on products can lead to the discarding of myths that are deeply rooted in the subconscious, not only of the consumer but also of the chefs themselves. For example, all the spices available to us are traditionally used for specific dishes. Therefore, it seems strange to us to find pepper or saffron in a dessert, or a salad with vanilla among the ingredients. If we try to see these products without the burden of tradition, we will realize that spices are neither sweet nor savoury, and that if vanilla is added to mashed potatoes the only concern should be whether the aromatic combination is coherent and effective. Similarly, if we add freshly ground pepper to a dessert we are incorporating an element that could be very interesting.

It is important to remember that until recently the importance of basic products was forgotten within high-end cuisine. Salt, water, eggs, milk and its by-products, flour and sugar are vital pillars in cookery, at least in the western tradition. If these elements were removed from the recipes in a classic or traditional cookbook, it would be impossible to make any of the dishes successfully. They are basic ingredients which chefs would rarely list among their favourites because they are taken for granted, whereas in fact they deserve the same attention as those with greater gastronomic prestige. Given their importance, one should always use the best available. A chef will always check the quality of a lobster, but will treat flour and salt as though they are all the same quality, which is not the case.

Developed over many years, elBulli's philosophy on sourcing and purchasing ingredients can be summarized as follows:

1. Everything known about an animal or vegetable species is relevant when it comes to choosing a particular item within that species.

2. Within a species there can be many different ingredients, and each of them has its own set of characteristics. It is important to recognize the limits of one's knowledge and to be curious about every new ingredient.

3. An ingredient should be considered on two levels: gastronomically (by tasting and studying it) and scientifically (by understanding its features and chemical composition).

4. Knowing and understanding an ingredient includes knowing at what temperature and under what conditions it should be stored, and when it is best eaten. For example, the flavour of sole is better the day after it is caught, but a sardine should be eaten on the same day because it is an oily fish and therefore deteriorates more quickly.

5. Ecology and respect for the environment are important factors to consider when choosing ingredients. This has been the policy at elBulli for more than twenty years.

6. At elBulli local produce is always the first choice, providing it is of top quality. However, high-quality products from other parts of the world are also used.

7. Every ingredient should be judged on its gastronomic merits, rather than on its price, and the best products are not always the most expensive. Traditionally, young green almonds, or *almendrucos*, do not have the same status as crayfish but today both products are considered to have the same culinary value; they can inspire brilliant new recipes and are therefore highly prized. So it makes sense to give the same culinary importance to a sardine as to a sea bass, to an artichoke as to a truffle, and to consider that what dictates the selection of an ingredient is its potential, and not the price or conventional prestige. This approach does not mean undervaluing expensive products such as truffles and caviar, which are exquisite whatever the cost.

8. Other than meat and fish, most ingredients can belong to either the sweet world or the savoury world. There are, of course, certain naturally sweet vegetables such as beetroot or carrots, but ingredients from almost every other food group can also have both sweet and savoury applications.

9. A new ingredient can inspire thousands of new dishes. Its characteristics might suggest new techniques and concepts, such as mango ravioli, or they might suggest a new application of an existing technique.

In 1988, as the earliest creative methods were being developed, the team came up with a system for classifying ingredients in different product families. These classifications helped extend the creative possibilities of each ingredient, because if a certain cooking or preparation method works for one ingredient in a product family, it could be applied to any of the others within that group. Later, symbols were created to represent each product family. The classifications are always made on a culinary basis, rather than a scientific one.

Waters

Gases

Fish

Crustaceans

Molluscs

Other marine products

Canned products

Sauces and condiments

Fish offal

Seaweed

Vegetables

Fruit and berries

Mushrooms and truffles

Cereals

Breads, doughs and starters

Juices and soft drinks

Dried pulses

Seeds

Flowers

Shoots and sprouts

Fresh herbs

Nuts

Smoked products

Tea, infusions and coffee

Furred game

Meat

Feathered game

Poultry

Meat and poultry offal

Eggs

Liqueurs and other alcohol

Brined and pickled products

Foie gras

Caviar and fish roe

Cocoa and cocoa products

Yeasts and raising (rising) agents

Butter and other fats

Cheese, milk and other dairy products

Wines

Dried and fresh pasta

Oils and vegetable fats

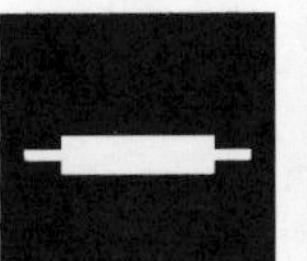

Flours, semolina and starches

Sugars

Salts

Vinegars

Stabilizers and gelling agents

Dried herbs and spices

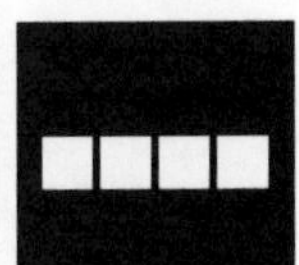

Jams and preserves

Freeze-dried and dehydrated products

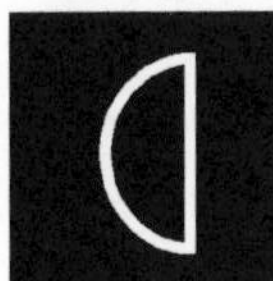

Dried and candied fruits

Sausages

Salted and dried goods

Others

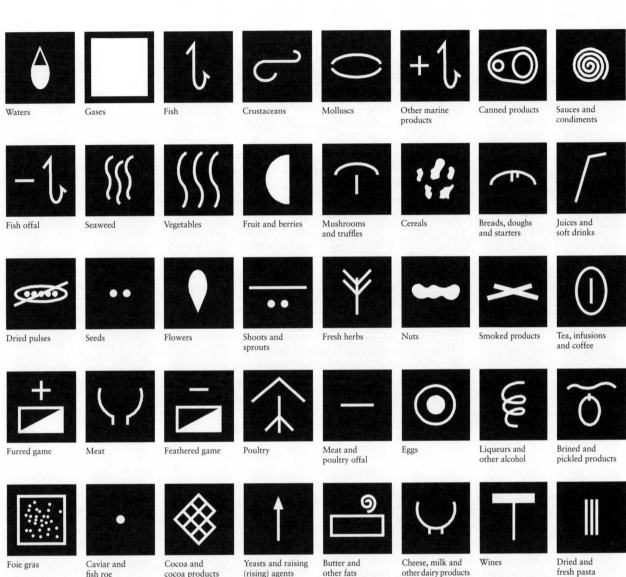

Where do the ingredients for elBulli come from?

Although there are no geographical limits when it comes to sourcing produce for elBulli, most of it comes from Catalunya. Some products even start life in the immediate surroundings of the restaurant, like the green pine cones collected from the garden (from which fresh pine nuts are harvested), the mussels and sea urchins from the Cap de Creus and the local variety of cactus.

About seventy per cent of ingredients come from Spain:

- CATALUNYA: fish, shellfish, vegetables, mushrooms and truffles, meat, eggs and dairy products, dried fruit and nuts, fruit and oil
- VALENCIA: citrus and other fruit
- ARAGÓN: olives
- ANDALUCÍA: citrus and other fruit, olives and flowers
- GALICIA: shellfish and fresh seaweed
- CASTILLA Y LEÓN: pork products
- OTHER AREAS OF SPAIN: meat, game and vegetables

About thirty per cent of ingredients come from other countries:

- FRANCE: meat, cheese and other dairy products, chocolate, spices
- ITALY: cheese and truffle oil
- HOLLAND: shoots and cresses, fruit and flowers
- GREECE: mastic
- AUSTRIA: pumpkin seed oil
- SWITZERLAND: nut oils
- RUSSIA: caviar
- INDIA: spices
- CHINA: dried fruit and vegetables, spices and Himalayan salt
- JAPAN: dried seaweed, *katsuobushi* and *yuzu*
- NORTH AFRICA: Argan oil, spices and couscous
- CENTRAL AND SOUTH AMERICA: tropical fruit pulp and ackees
- NORTH AMERICA: pickled daisy buds, flour and sugar
- AUSTRALIA: spices and miraculin

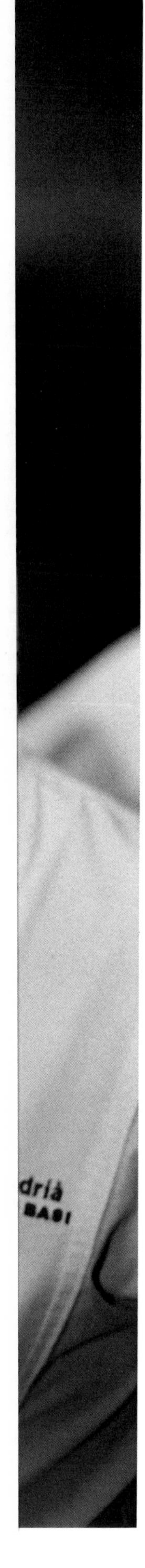

Deliveries to elBulli

To complement the shopping done locally in Roses and Barcelona, ingredients from other parts of Spain and the rest of the world are delivered directly to the restaurant. (Names in brackets refer to the source.)

- Vegetables, fruit, dairy products and organic eggs (JOSEP JULIÀ)
- Fish and shellfish (AMADEU)
- Fresh seaweed and fish from Galicia (PORTO MUIÑOS)
- Mixed groceries (GUZMÁN AND GURMALIA)
- Products from France, mostly dairy (LOMPRE)
- Truffle oil and mozzarella cheese from Italy (TOSCOBOSCO)
- Moroccan spices, couscous and vanilla (FRANCESC CULLELL)
- Spices from France (CHATILLON)
- Mushrooms and truffles from Lerida (LAUMONT)
- Nut oils from Switzerland and Morocco (GEMMA SARL)
- Pumpkin seed oil from Austria (FAMILIE ENGL)
- Citrus fruit and their flowers from Valencia (NARANJAS LOLA) and Andalucía (AGRÍCOLA ROLANDIS)
- Wild flowers from Málaga (SABOR Y SALUD)
- Frozen pulps and bakery products (SOSA)
- Chocolate (VALRHONA AND CHOCOVIC)
- White asparagus and artichokes (LUÍS SAN JOSÉ)
- Cheese (QUESOS CAÑAREJAL)
- Game (DE MIGUEL)
- Foie gras (CAN MANENT)
- Snails' eggs and Llavaneres peas (FRANCESC RABASSA AND JOAN TRABALON)
- Dried fruit and nuts (FOMENT AGRÍCOLA DE LES GARRIGUES)
- Duck products (COLLVERD)
- Bread (TRITICUM, LA TORNA AND PA TONET)
- Sea urchins and rock mussels (LINARES)
- *Jamón ibérico* and other pork products (JOSELITO)
- Oils (OLIVIAS)

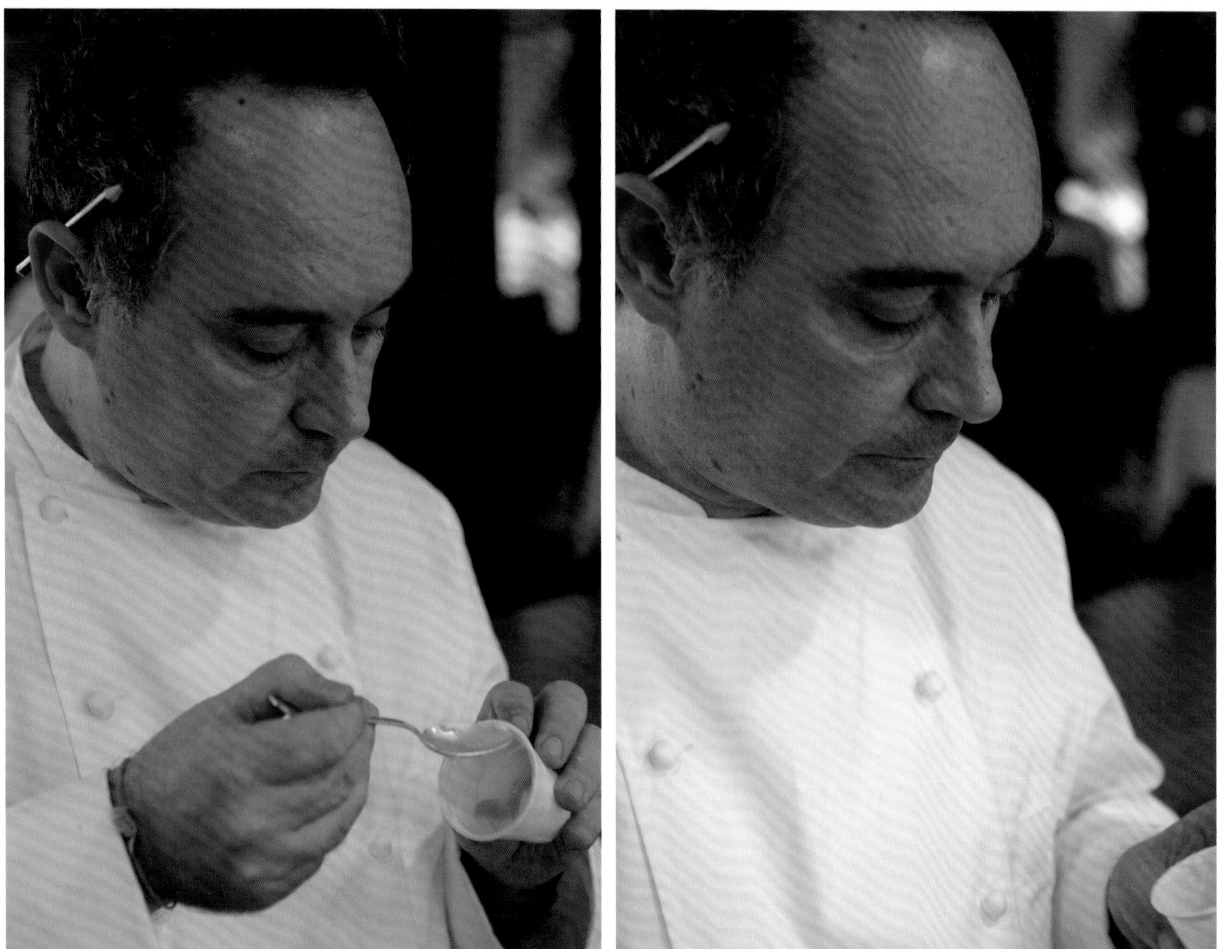

12:30

—

Deliveries are checked

Quality is very important and it is carefully monitored. However, cooking with the very best produce available and purchasing sensitively with respect for the long-term health of the environment should be a given at any fine dining restaurant. If chefs talk a lot about the quality and provenance of their ingredients it might mean that they do not have anything else to say about their food.

LAVAZZA
JORGE
ORDOÑEZ
& CO.
MALAGA

12:35

Shopping in Roses

With list in hand, logistics manager Jose Mari does the shopping that will supply most of the ingredients needed in the restaurant, whether for the main menu or the family meal for the staff. Shellfish, fish, meat, herbs, bread, vegetables, fruit and flowers are just some of the many ingredients he must examine and select.

At the post office

Jose Mari begins his daily errands at the post office, where he picks up parcels and letters for the restaurant.

Fish from Amadeu

At the market he collects the fish that has been ordered specially for elBulli from Amadeu, a fishmonger in Barcelona, and has arrived during the night. It is like having a little Mercabarna (a large wholesale food market on the outskirts of Barcelona) just a few kilometres from elBulli.

Shellfish from the Cap de Creus

Some of the shellfish served at elBulli is supplied by Manolo, a local seafood specialist who has a series of beds from which Jose Mari chooses the best molluscs and crustaceans. Manolo is one of only three local fishermen licensed to harvest shellfish around the Cap de Creus.

Bread for the family meal

Jose Mari buys three dozen loaves at the Forn Cusí bakery, enough for a lunch-time sandwich for each member of staff and to accompany their evening meal.

Meat from the Quintana brothers

The Quintana brothers are among elBulli's longest-standing suppliers. Their meat is ordered the night before and will be used to make stocks and sauces for the restaurant and to feed all the staff.

The Cervera Spar

The owners of this grocery speak several languages and serve an international clientele. Hard-to-find foreign produce is stocked here, and until very recently it was one of the few places where kombu seaweed could be purchased locally.

The Mateu garden centre

The herbs used at elBulli are bought from the garden centre and kept in pots at the restaurant so that they are completely fresh when used in the dishes.

Santiago's fruit and vegetables

Santiago's is another of elBulli's veteran suppliers. In fact, when this family business first started it did not have a shop, and the fruit and vegetables were sold from a van. The owners always do all they can to help, and will often supply special produce just for elBulli.

The history of a dish

Freeze-drying is a technique that has captured the imagination of the team. Here, experimentation begins with a pistachio foam that has been freeze-dried, which means that it has been completely dehydrated through sublimation (turning a solid substance into a gas). The foam is frozen very rapidly and then pressurized so that the ice crystals are turned directly into a vapour.

The freeze-dried pistachio foam is crumbled and mixed with liquid. Then the mixture is separated into large pieces, which look like savoury pistachio cakes.

Next, truffle is added, which is a classic flavour combination with pistachios. The truffle takes the form of juice mixed with Xantana, a natural thickening agent. Finally an acidic touch is needed, and a few days later the more unusual flavour of mandarin is settled upon, and is added to the dish in the form of an air.

The idea is developed and further tests are carried out, and the results are then analysed and considered. The decisions are influenced by the chef's senses and, later, by feedback from the guest.

Albert's sweet world

Albert Adrià joined elBulli in 1985, a year after Ferran, who instilled in him a real passion for the restaurant trade. Albert began by completing a two-year apprenticeship in each section of the kitchen, where the excitement of learning new things every day in a restaurant as unique as elBulli cemented his passion for food, and for the sweet world most of all. In order to continue his training, he worked in the kitchens of famed pastrycooks and chefs such as Francisco Torreblanca in Spain and Guy Savoy in France, during the winter season when elBulli was closed. In 1998, Albert was instrumental in setting up the very first creative workshop, which consisted of no more than a table, four books and a couple of chairs. When the workshop moved to its current premises he became its creative director, taking responsibility for the creation of a completely new menu for every season, both sweet and savoury. From this point on his professional life became inseparable from that of Ferran and Oriol. In 2006, he opened his own restaurant in Barcelona, the Inopia Classic Bar, which serves traditional tapas. At elBulli Albert is head of the sweet world, and he is the main conduit for the exchange of creativity between the two worlds.

'Creativity means changing your mind every day.'

12:55

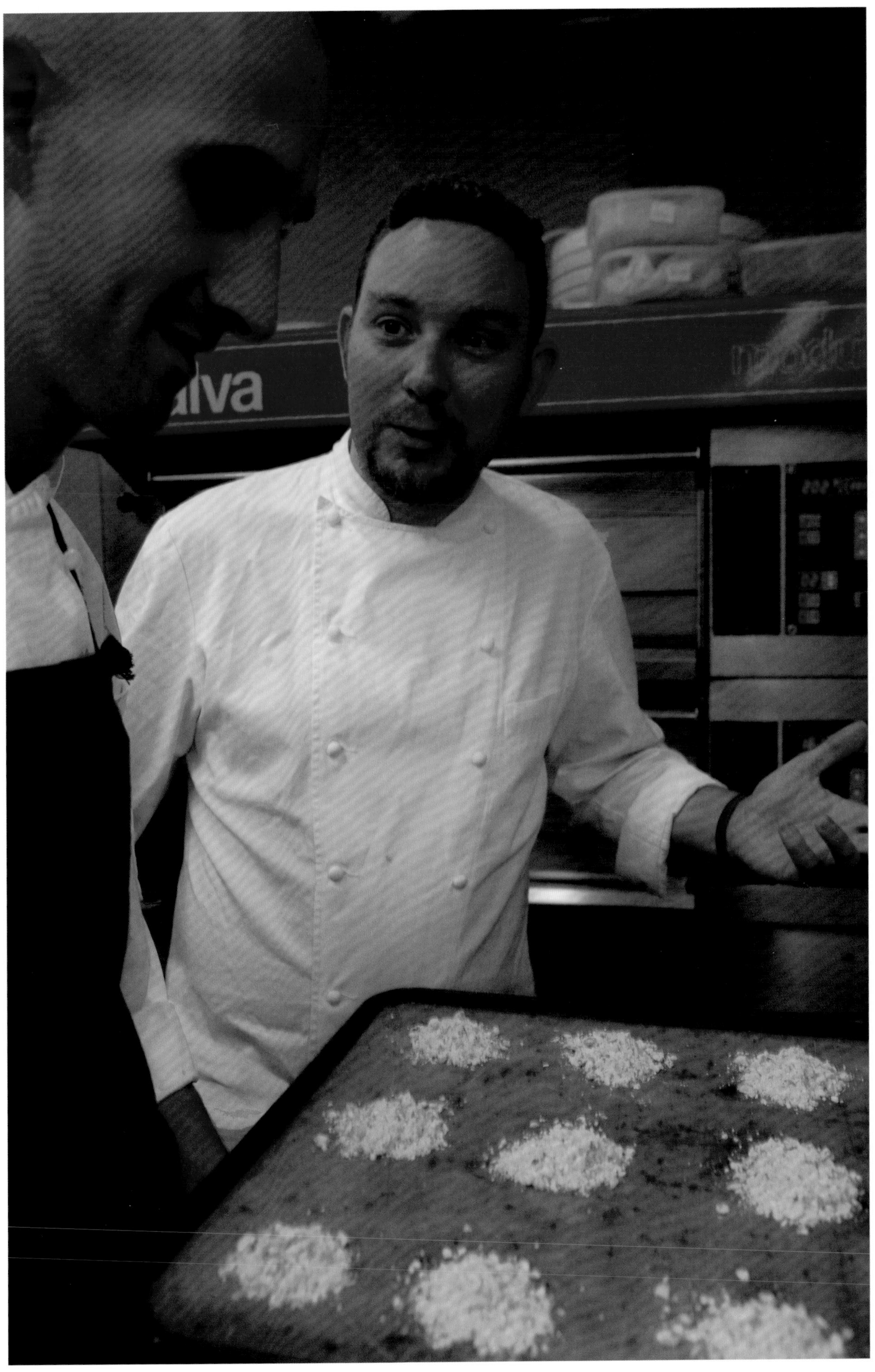
alva

—

Mateu and Albert working side by side

Mateu and Albert work independently from Ferran and Oriol, although their experiments often overlap. Their work includes cocktails, snacks (even though these are savoury), desserts and morphings.

Albert begins with a dry meringue. He adds the crisp freeze-dried passion fruit and then tries turning the mixture into a powder.

Finally, a croquanter beetroot rose is stuck into the dry meringue to create the dessert *Beetroot rose with strawberry concentrate sorbet*.

13:05

Here they are working on a giant hemisphere made of salt. Once it has set, it is hollowed out and left to dry. It might be used as a dome to cover other foods, or two of them might be connected to create a sphere.

It is impossible to say where ideas come from, but it helps to be curious all the time, and to keep on trying.

'Ideas are easy – you just need to have some.'

El Bulli

Albert tries coating marshmallows with different ingredients such as coconut, Parmesan or chopped pistachios to see which one will work best. Parmesan and pine nut are the flavours he eventually settles on.

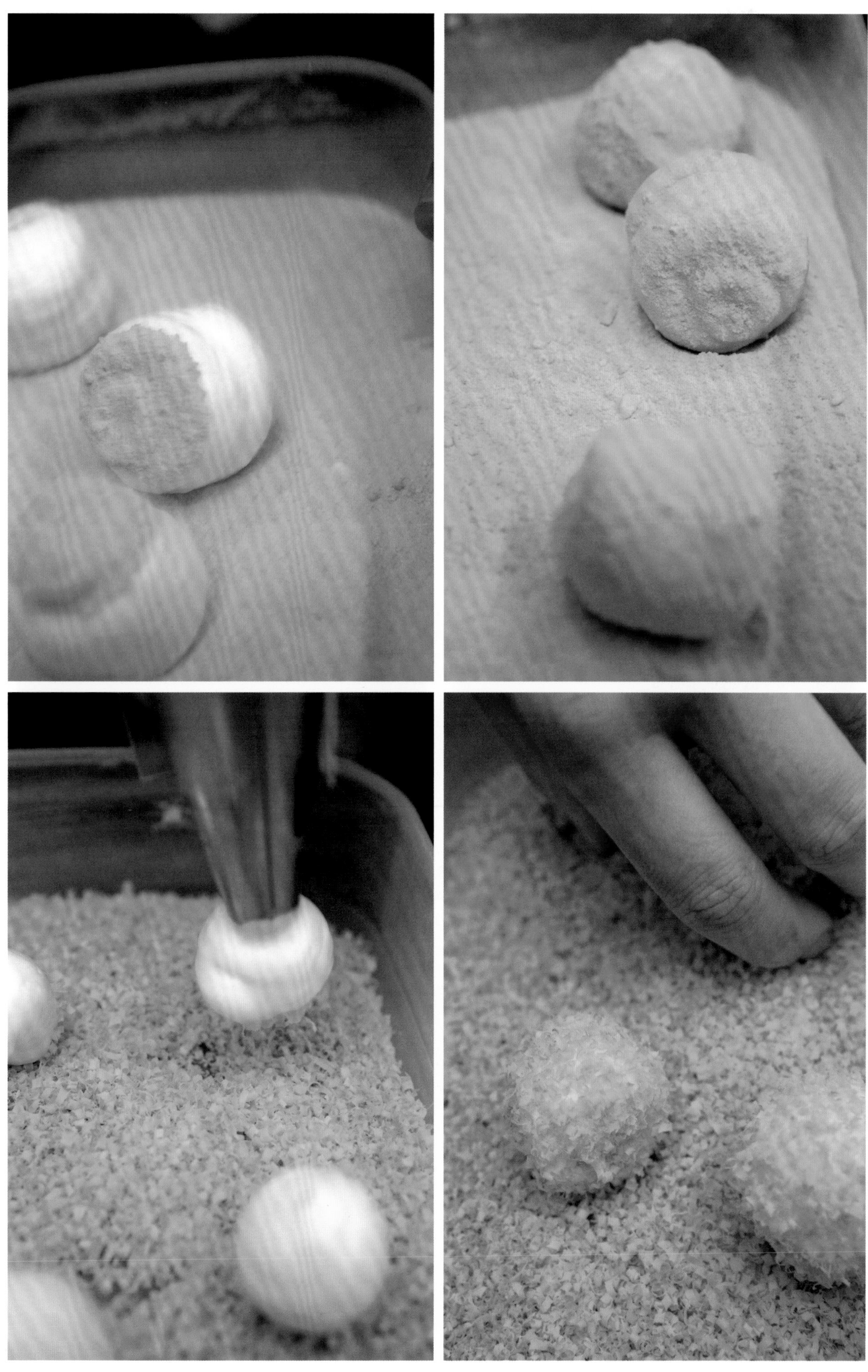

13:20

—

Here, Mateu and Albert are trying to create a new concept using liquid nitrogen to make leaves and flowers from coconut. They spread a coconut cream over a mould and dip it into a bath of liquid nitrogen at -196°C (-321°F). The coconut cream freezes rapidly and forms a frozen shape that can then be turned out of the mould. It must be served quickly before it melts.

A concept is the set of essential qualities that characterize a dish, not the recipe itself. One concept can lead to many different elaborations and new dishes.

'A concept is an idea that can open new doors.'

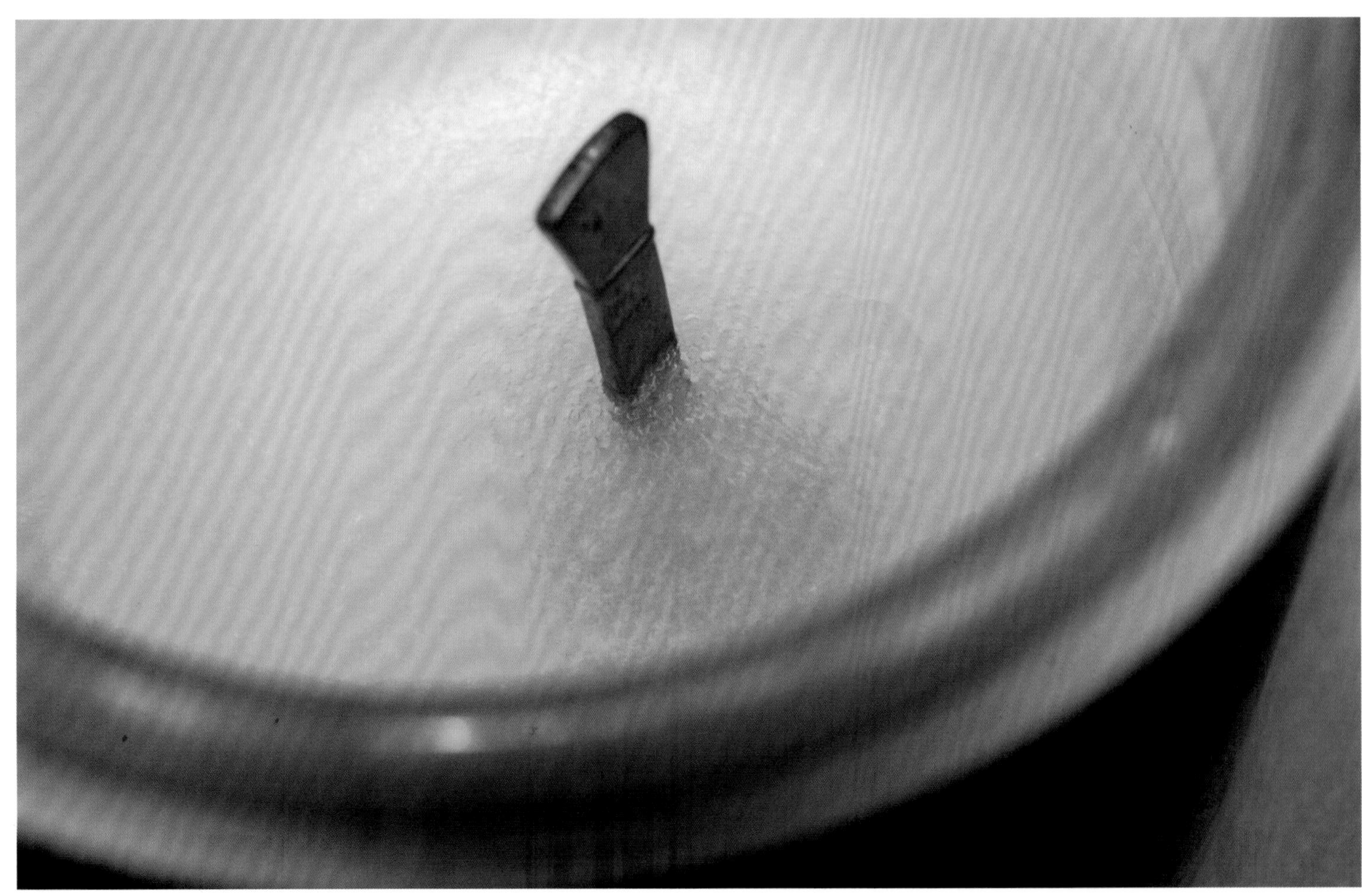

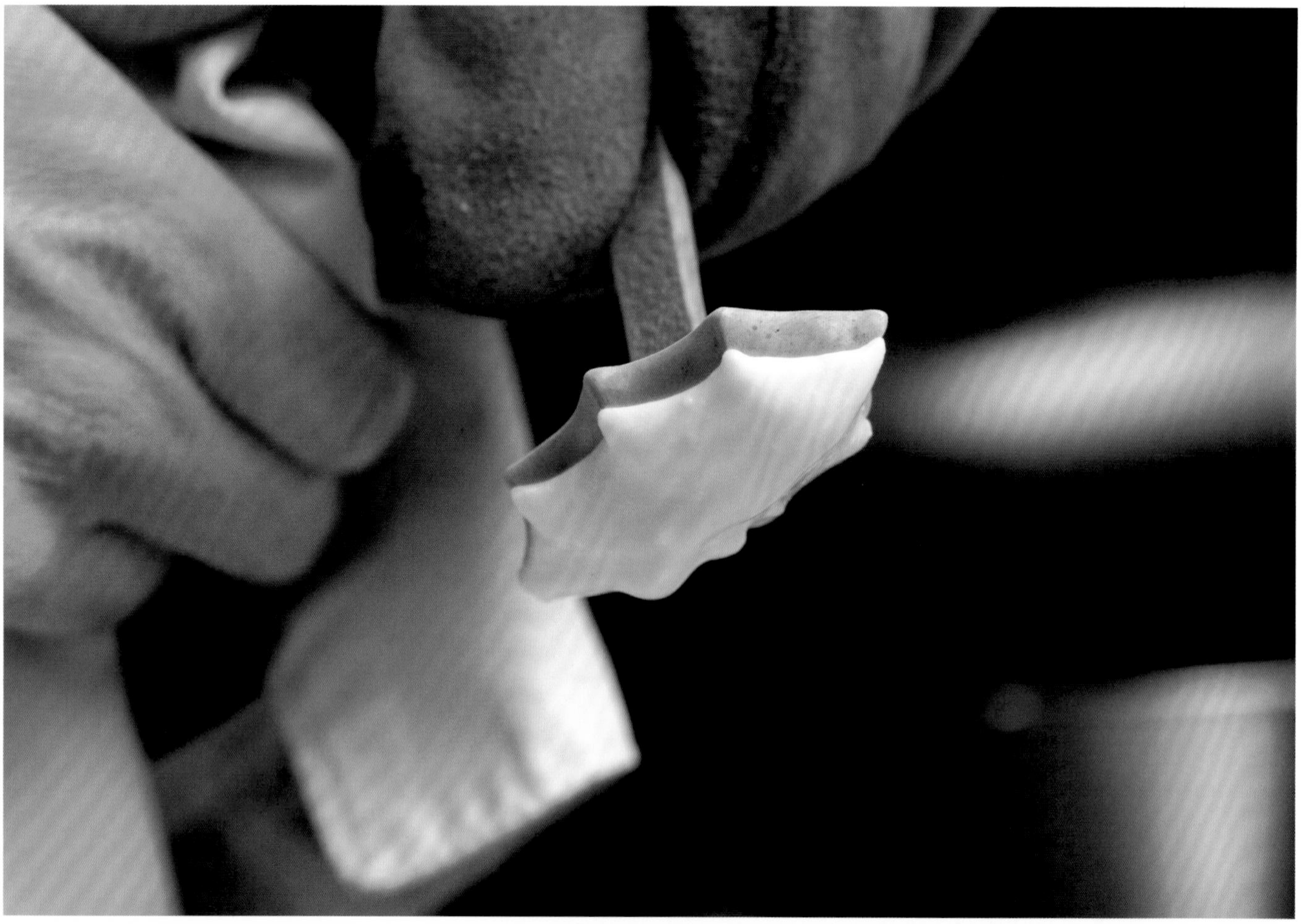

Mateu
El Bulli

Preparing the order sheets

Fifteen tables need fifteen sets of order sheets. The order sheet lists all the dishes that each guest will eat, and any additional dietary information.

At the beginning of each week Ferran selects the fifty or so dishes from which the menus for that week will be compiled. Every day, Albert Raurich and Eduard Xatruch create the order sheets for the day using Ferran's weekly menu. The task takes about an hour and a half. Other than creative work, it is one of the few morning jobs for the kitchen team.

To make the order sheets they will take many considerations into account: not only the guests' individual preferences and requirements, but also other factors like the time of year, in terms of the availability of ingredients, the temperature, and the fact that some dishes can only be made in certain weather conditions, like the *Pineapple paper tramontana with Parmesan*. This dish cannot withstand humidity and can only be made when the *tramontana*, the dry wind from the north, blows in spring and autumn. There are other practical considerations too: the products used in some dishes are so scarce that only a limited quantity can be made.

Later on, Ferran will check the order sheets and make alterations where necessary. His phenomenal memory retains many details about the guests who have eaten at elBulli before, but there is also a database that keeps a record of every dish that a guest has been served, along with other dietary information.

13:35

A page from the reservations book

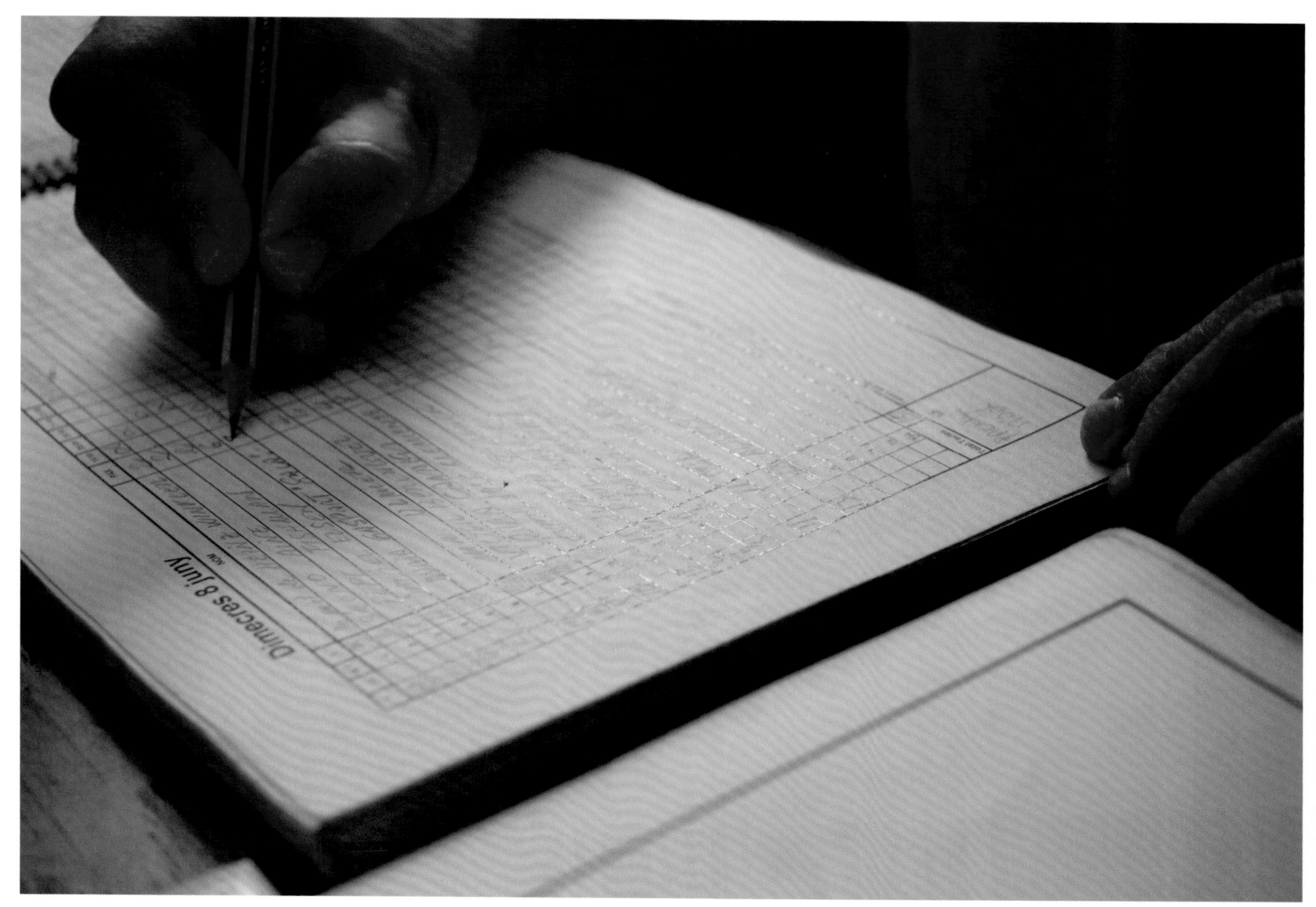

How does the reservation system work?

After many years of hard work, the question of reservations is now the only unsatisfactory aspect of elBulli. The disparity between the number of requests and the restaurant's capacity is huge, and continues to grow. Expanding elBulli might ease the problem, but it would undoubtedly have a negative effect on the restaurant. In fact, to ensure that guests receive the very best experience it would almost be preferable to have fewer diners each night.

Another possibility would be to open for lunch as well as dinner, and to stay open for ten months a year instead of six. This would increase the number of meals served each year from 8,000 to between 20,000 and 30,000. However, since millions of requests for reservations are received each year, the number of refusals would still be enormous, and the service would certainly suffer.

The decision to close in winter was first made for practical reasons, but over time it has resulted in a firmly established programme that has enabled creativity to become the reason for elBulli's existence. It takes six months to create a new collection of dishes for the next season, and anything that altered or compromised the creative operations would not be a solution. If the restaurant were open longer, the business interests that provide vital income for the restaurant would have to be neglected or even abandoned entirely. People have asked why the price of a meal at elBulli is not higher, but covering the costs of the lengthy development period for each dish has never been the aim. It is important that the restaurant does not become inaccessible due to its price, and this policy also means that the chefs have the freedom to focus on creativity, rather than financial considerations.

Only a small percentage of requests for reservations can be accommodated, and strict criteria are employed to allocate the tables. Juli and Ferran rarely use their influence, requesting tables only for specific business or social purposes. The person who really decides is Lluís García, the dining room manager. When the restaurant closes, reservation requests for the following year are accepted. These are divided into four categories, from which the tables are allocated equally: guests who are new to elBulli, those who have eaten at the restaurant before, people who live in Spain, and people from other countries. They are also divided according to whether a specific date has been requested, as in the case of a birthday or anniversary, or whether the date has been left open. Based on these criteria Lluís García begins the task (or jigsaw puzzle) of allocating tables for the season. It is not an easy one.

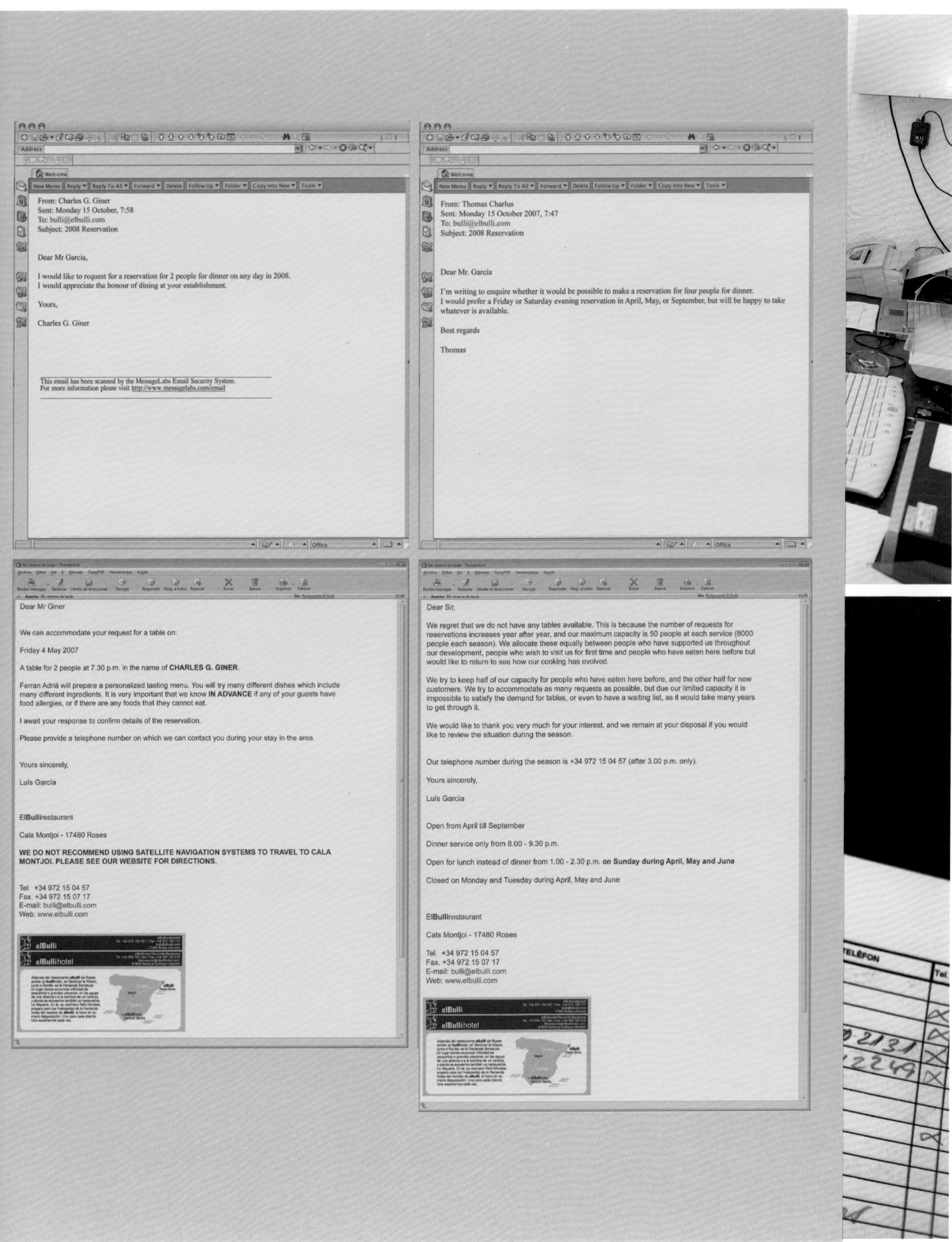

From: Charles G. Giner
Sent: Monday 15 October, 7:58
To: bulli@elbulli.com
Subject: 2008 Reservation

Dear Mr Garcia,

I would like to request for a reservation for 2 people for dinner on any day in 2008.
I would appreciate the honour of dining at your establishment.

Yours,

Charles G. Giner

This email has been scanned by the MessageLabs Email Security System.
For more information please visit http://www.messagelabs.com/email

From: Thomas Charlus
Sent: Monday 15 October 2007, 7:47
To: bulli@elbulli.com
Subject: 2008 Reservation

Dear Mr. Garcia

I'm writing to enquire whether it would be possible to make a reservation for four people for dinner.
I would prefer a Friday or Saturday evening reservation in April, May, or September, but will be happy to take whatever is available.

Best regards

Thomas

Dear Mr Giner

We can accommodate your request for a table on:

Friday 4 May 2007

A table for 2 people at 7.30 p.m. in the name of **CHARLES G. GINER**.

Ferran Adrià will prepare a personalized tasting menu. You will try many different dishes which include many different ingredients. It is very important that we know **IN ADVANCE** if any of your guests have food allergies, or if there are any foods that they cannot eat.

I await your response to confirm details of the reservation.

Please provide a telephone number on which we can contact you during your stay in the area.

Yours sincerely,

Luis Garcia

ElBullirestaurant

Cala Montjoi - 17480 Roses

WE DO NOT RECOMMEND USING SATELLITE NAVIGATION SYSTEMS TO TRAVEL TO CALA MONTJOI. PLEASE SEE OUR WEBSITE FOR DIRECTIONS.

Tel. +34 972 15 04 57
Fax. +34 972 15 07 17
E-mail: bulli@elbulli.com
Web: www.elbulli.com

elBulli
elBullihotel

Dear Sir,

We regret that we do not have any tables available. This is because the number of requests for reservations increases year after year, and our maximum capacity is 50 people at each service (8000 people each season). We allocate these equally between people who have supported us throughout our development, people who wish to visit us for first time and people who have eaten here before but would like to return to see how our cooking has evolved.

We try to keep half of our capacity for people who have eaten here before, and the other half for new customers. We try to accommodate as many requests as possible, but due our limited capacity it is impossible to satisfy the demand for tables, or even to have a waiting list, as it would take many years to get through it.

We would like to thank you very much for your interest, and we remain at your disposal if you would like to review the situation during the season.

Our telephone number during the season is +34 972 15 04 57 (after 3.00 p.m. only).

Yours sincerely,

Luis Garcia

Open from April till September

Dinner service only from 8.00 - 9.30 p.m.

Open for lunch instead of dinner from 1.00 - 2.30 p.m. **on Sunday during April, May and June**

Closed on Monday and Tuesday during April, May and June

ElBullirestaurant

Cala Montjoi - 17480 Roses

Tel. +34 972 15 04 57
Fax. +34 972 15 07 17
E-mail: bulli@elbulli.com
Web: www.elbulli.com

elBulli
elBullihotel

13:40

—

The reservations are checked

Lluís García, the dining room manager, arrives and sits down at the computer with Juli. Until the evening service begins, both of them will answer emails, faxes and telephone calls related to reservation requests and arrangements for the evening's service. By the end of the year they will have replied to thousands of requests.

Lunch time

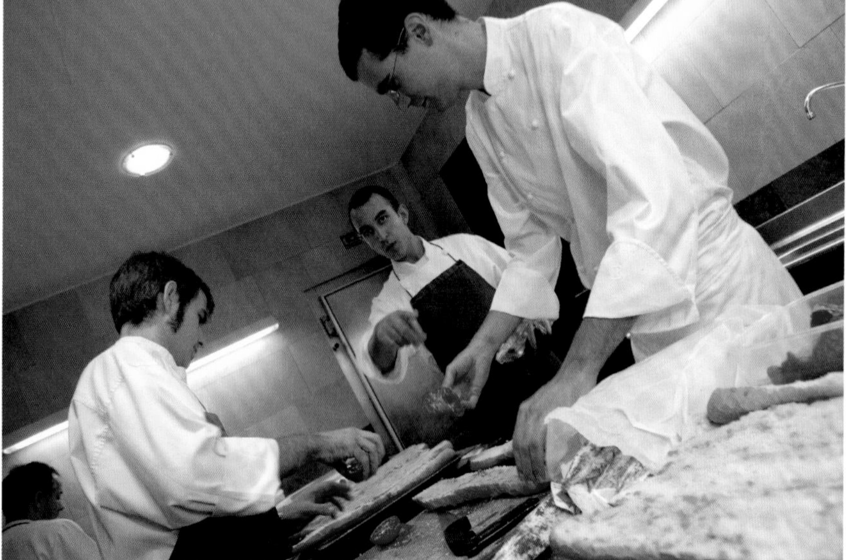

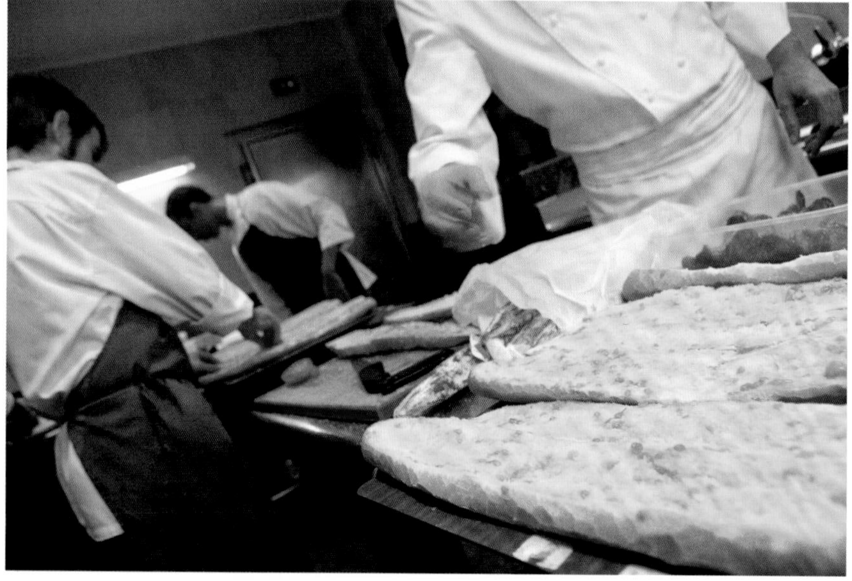

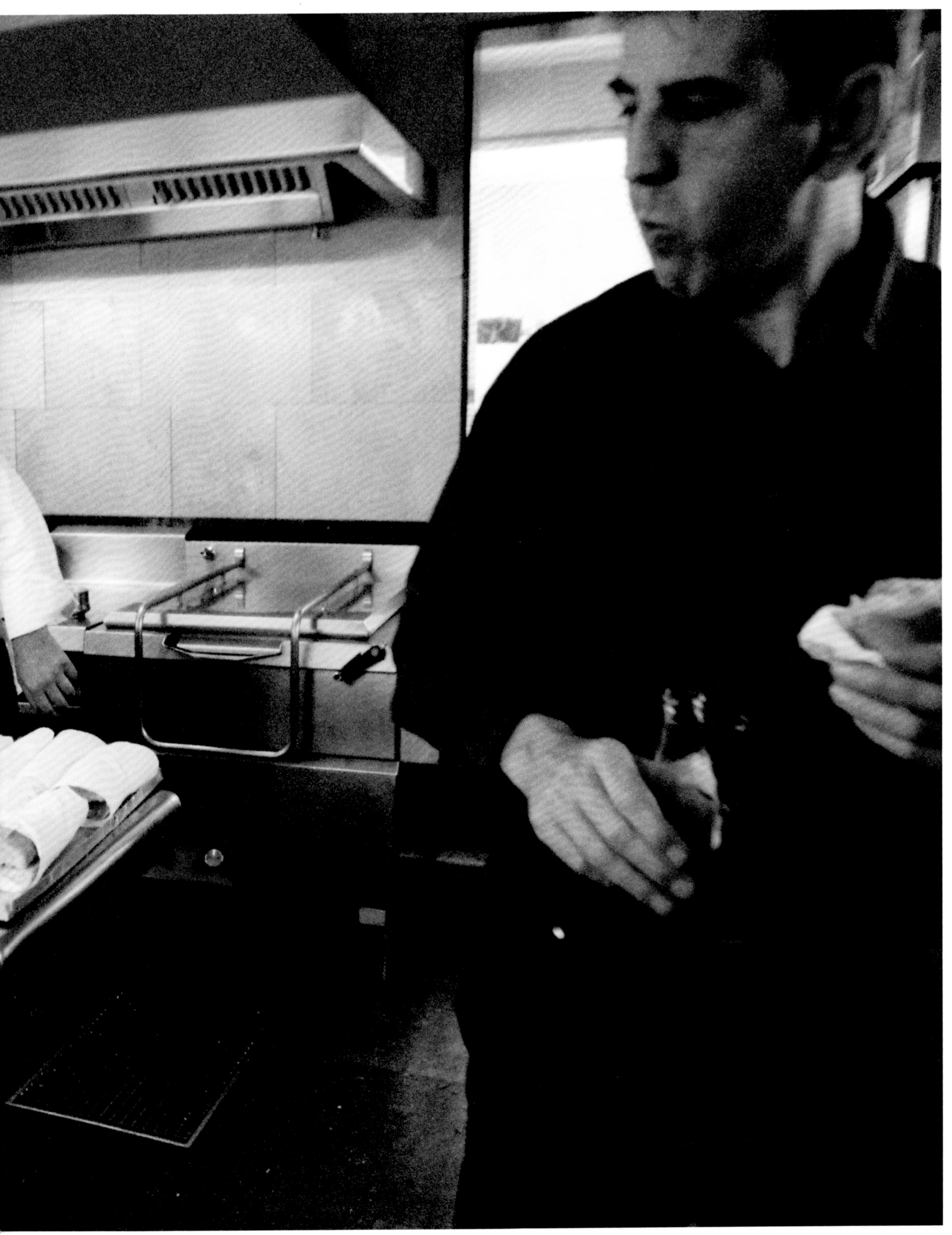

The rest o team arriv

They have a twel During the six m (in apartments pr the chefs arrange for transport to a

There are thirty t which point has l of which thirteen are stagers.

The stagers are c applicants who c year, and up to fi represented in th a passion to live some of them do whole six month have joined for t been here before different countri benefit from thei of their native cu

Ferran Adrià

Albert Adrià

Juli Soler

KITCHEN

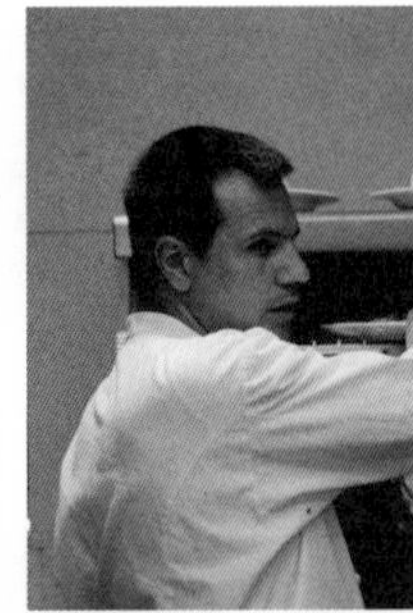

Oriol Castro
(*head chef*)

Albert Raurich
(*head chef*)

Eduard Xatruch
(*head chef*)

SWEET WORLD

Mateu Casañas
(*head chef*)

Loretta Fanella
(*chef de partie*)

SAVOURY WORLD

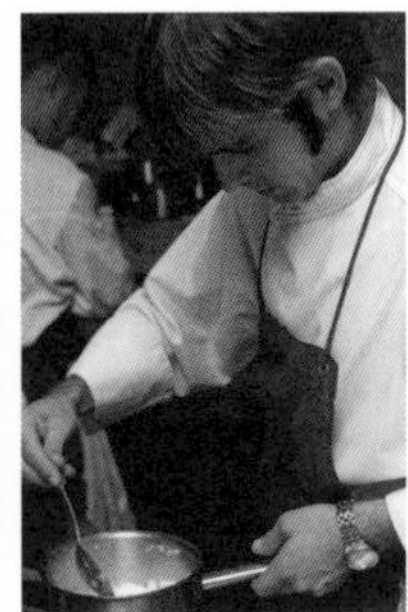

Marc Puig-Pey
(*chef de partie*)

Xavier Franquet
(*chef de partie*)

Jaume Biarnés
(*chef de partie*)

Jon Iñaki Monterroso, Luca Mecchieri
(*chefs de partie*)

Mauro Buffo
(*chef de partie*)

DINING ROOM

Lucas Payà
(*sommelier*)

Ferran Centelles
(*sommelier*)

Paco de la Horna
(*assistant sommelier*)

David López
(*head waiter*)

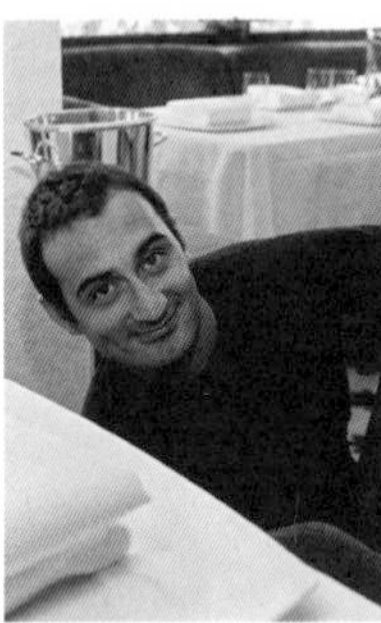
Félix Maena
(*head waiter*)

Anna Grau
(*waiter*)

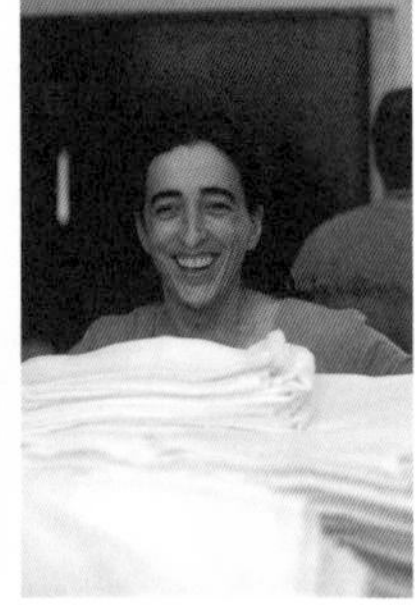
Aintzane Endemaño
(*waiter*)

Christian Farriols
(*waiter*)

Marga Fuentes
(*waiter*)

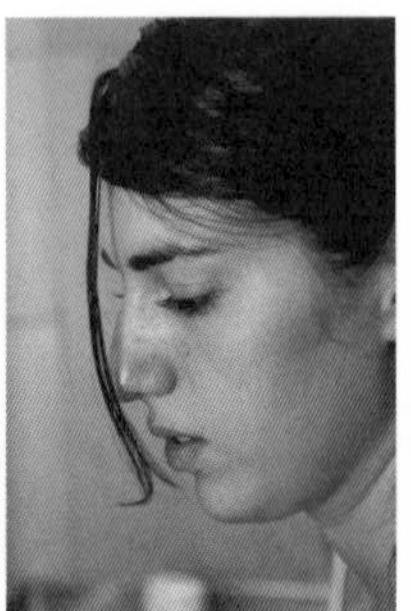
Berta López
(*waiter*)

Jordi Pon
(*waiter*)

Sonia de Castro
(*waiter*)

Sandra Armengol
(*stager*)

César Augusto
(*stager*)

Rodrigo Andrade
(*stager*)

Montse Gil (*waiter*), Núria Febrer (*assistant sommelier*), Xavier Gualde (*waiter*), Miguel Rodríguez (*head waiter*), Raúl Igual (*assistant sommelier*), Mariana Gabaldón (*head waiter*)

OTHER AREAS

Francisco Fernández (*pot wash*)

Fernando Martín (*pot wash*)

Ana Fernández (*pot wash*)

Vicente Barroso (*pot wash*)

Jose Mari López (*logistics manager*)

14:40

—

The afternoon meeting

At the daily kitchen meeting the creative team introduces the new dishes and discusses any improvements that can be made to service or *mise en place*.

Despite the different languages there is rarely any confusion, and in the end there is always complete understanding. Or nearly always.

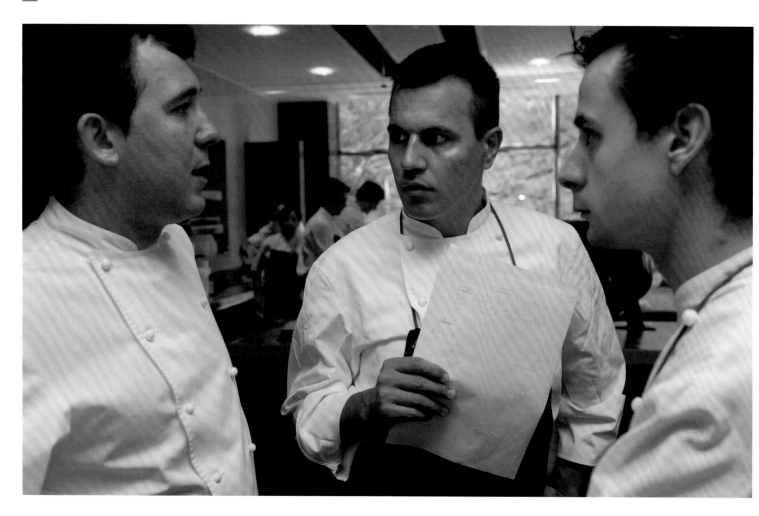

After the meeting

Oriol, Albert and Eduard work out the timing for the *mise en place* and check that all the preparation for the evening ahead is organized. The head chefs look at the order sheets and make a note of how many portions of each snack, tapas-dish or avant-dessert are required. In a small kitchen adjacent to the main one, the head chef of the sweet world checks that he has everything he needs for service.

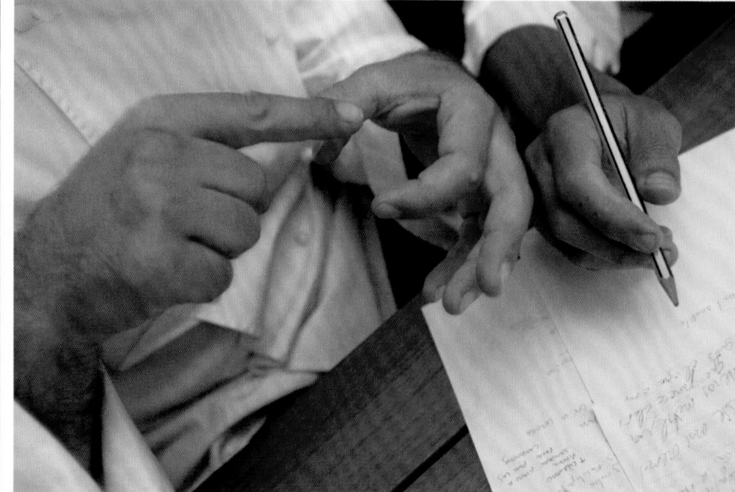

Mateu

The organization sheets

These are some of the sheets that are used to organize the kitchen. Every chef refers to them and they are essential for ensuring that things run smoothly, listing everything that the kitchen needs to produce.

HOJA SEMANAL 2008 FECHA: 6 al 11 de MAYO

MENU SEMANAL	ALTERNATIVAS SEMANA	PLATOS NUEVOS A INCORPORAR
COCKTEL		
1 SAKE / LULO / [illegible]		
2 OLIVAS		
SNAKS SECOS		
3 [illegible]		
4 TOMATE		
5 BOMBON	FRUTA LYO	
6 [illegible] / GOMINOLA SHISO	HOJA MANGO	
7 [illegible]		
8		
SNAKS FRESCOS		
1 HOJA MENTA + GG [illegible]		
2 [illegible] + MANTEQUILLA GG		
3 MOSHI + FRESA [illegible]		
4 CARBONARA	BIZCOCHO SÉSAMO	
5 ESPÁRRAGO MIJO		
6 NAVAJA / HORCHATA	H. ORO / BRIOCHE MOZZARELLA	
7 CANAPÉ [illegible]	PAPEL FLORES / MENTA [illegible]	
8 [illegible]		
TAPIPLATOS		
1 MANDARINA		
2 [illegible]		
3 MENESTRAS / HABA / LICHI	ANCHOA YOGUR	
4 [illegible] / RAVIOLI AJO		
5 THE SOUP / SOPA TUÉTANO		
6 GUISANTE		
7 [illegible]	ACELGAS	
8 GNOCCHIS		
9 ABALONE / [illegible]	ESPARDEÑA	
10 CANAPÉ / TRIPA BACALAO	ANGUILA TUÉTANO	
11 MANO COCHINILLO / CASTAÑUELA	[illegible]	
AVANT POSTRE		
1 BRIE TRUFADO / TRUFITAS		
2 MIEL PISTACHO / POMELO		
POSTRES	**PRODUCTO A INTRODUCIR/TRABAJAR**	**OTROS**
1		
MORPHINGS		
1		
2		
3		
4		
5		
		elBullirestaurant

Weekly menu

Drawn up by Ferran, this lists all the dishes that will be served in any given week. The selection of dishes will depend upon the time of year, the weather conditions and the availability of ingredients. Newly developed dishes from the creative sessions will be added to the weekly menu, and some dishes are listed with alternatives in case they are not suitable for any of the guests.

19.30 2

1 lulada
2 yuzu / sake / Kyoto
3 cereza kirsch
4 aceitunas verdes sféricas-I
5 nori-Trias
6 frutas LYO
7 gominola de shiso
8 pipas de mandarina
9 hojas de mango y flor de tagete
10 orquidea de pasión
11 "averantos"
12 galleta de tomate
13 bombones de piñones y chocolate
14 creps de Pekin
15 hoja de menta y coco
16 coral de remolacha
17 papel de flores
18 bizcocho de sésamo negro y miso
19 brazo de gitano
20 fresa a la parrilla
21 moshi de gorgonzola
22 "munster"
23 nata-LYO
24 horchata / trufa
25 leche de búfala
26 navaja / Laurencia
27 judión con panceta Joselito
28 flor de mandarina/aceite de calabaza con pipas de mandarina
29 almendras gelé con cocktail de almendruco "Umeboshi"
30 Umeboshi
31 lulo
32 canapé de perrechicos
33 ravioli de ajo negro
34 la piñonada
35 cous-cous de nabo con erizos
36 maíz-nato
37 lichi
38 nenúfares
39 the soup 2008
40 canapé de caza
41 rabo de cochinillo
42 sopa de tuétano
43 espárragos con miso
44 guisantes 2008
45 ñoquis de polenta con café y yuba al azafrán
46 ortiguilla de mar 2008
47 negrito 2008
48 crustaceos-anguila
49 espardeñas-espardeñas
50 abalone
51 tripa de bacalao
52 jugo de liebre con gelé-cru manzana al casís
53 castañuelas
54 miel ciprés con mato de mozzarella y cremoso arándanos
55 cítrico desgranado
56 caramelo de miel
57 "trufitas"

elBullimenús

PAISAJE.

After
mayo.
Aubar.

Order sheet
Prepared each day by the head chefs to Ferran's specifications, the order sheet indicates which dishes will be served to each guest.

C. FRIO

5/06/08

HOJA DE COMPRA PARTDA: ~~CARNES~~

RESPONSABLE: ~~X.QUERA~~

SEMANA del al del 2008

PLATO	PRODUCTO	MARTES		MIERCOLES		JUEVES		VIERNES		SABADO		DOMINGO	
		STOCK	PEDIDO	STOCK	PEDIDO	STOCK	PEDIDO	STOCK	PEDIDO	STOCK	PEDIDO	STOCK	PEDIDO
		Cereza	h.menta	Papel	Mosto	leche	flor	lulo	nenufar	Soup	miel	cítrico	Yerba
	Vongerchen		5	5	5	5	5		5	1		5	
	Hanson		4	4	4		4		4			4	
	Nicole		7		2		2	2		2		2	
	Miguel		7		7	7	7		7			7	
	Villagran		2	2	2	2	2	1		2		2	
	Ramedhu		6		6	6	6		6		6		
	USA		8		8	8	8		8			8	
	Sanz		4		4		4	4	4		4		
	Palermo		4		4		4			4	4		
	Rshaft	4	4			4	4	4		4	4		
	Avramov	2	2				2		2	2	2	2	2
	Hand	2	2				2		2	2	2	2	2
	F. Adm												1
		8	50	11	42	34	50	11	34	17	22	28	41

List of products from the cold section
This shows the products from the cold section and helps the chefs keep track of the many different tasks involved in the *mise en place*.

HOJA DIARIA MISE-EN-PLACE — **DIA:** 19 Abril.

	Hora	Cuarto Frío	Entrantes I	Entrantes II	Pescados	Carnes	Trabajos Peq	Trabajos en grupo
	13:30-14:30	Racionar Naranja Aire limón Algas Mazapán	Gominolas Sféricos Crocant - Masa crocant	Marcar polenta [illegible] Infusión caldo pollo 500 grs. Aire coco	Marcar liebre fría	Posada test Desc. pasta Cortar pan	Pipas. Mandarina. Sféric. avellana Hidratar avellana	Desvainar guisantes Desgranar guisantes Ajo negro [illegible]
	14:30-15:30	Mezcla gorgonzola Dados gorgonzola Gorgonzola / Gelée Toque Moshi	- Crema [illegible] - Caldo [illegible] - Sifón - Vinagreta [illegible]	Yuba Untar [illegible] pavina Racionar pomelo. Cortar pavina.	Gelée mantequilla GL Bolsa [illegible]	Mezcla [illegible] Escaldar [illegible] Mayo sésamo	Callar [illegible] Esencia mandarina.	Desmigar y [illegible] buey Pelar coco Pelar [illegible].
	15:30-16:00	Esencia Mandarina Toques Calabaza Cosquillos Hojuelas menta	ESP GRU - Aire [illegible] - Mahonesa	Biberón yema huevo 12 huevos. Ligar infusión Seleccionar [illegible]	Racionar [illegible] Cocer ruibarbo U. membrillo 250 gr.	Ligar [illegible] Semillas [illegible] Oli. bots	Limpiar [illegible] Limpiar abalon Esfera PK	Shots [illegible]. Esferificar [illegible] Pomelo Miró Polvorón [illegible].
	16:00-16:30	Toques [illegible] Licuar kobs Racionar kobs Gelée kobs	- [illegible] - Cous cous - Gelat. [illegible] Naranja	Seleccionar [illegible] Rellenar [illegible] Seleccionar hoja ostra. Rayar [illegible].	Triturar pan Ligar caldo jamón 300 gr. Ligar [illegible] [illegible] 300 gr.	Racionar [illegible] [illegible] Guisantes Aromat. [illegible]	[illegible] Cocer [illegible] Limpiar [illegible] Pancita [illegible]	[illegible] Deshojar estragón y [illegible] [illegible]
	16:30-17:00	Toques [illegible] Malto [illegible] Pipetas Mandarina	- Aire [illegible] - [illegible] - Cortar [illegible]	Racionar [illegible]. Esferificar quesos. Racionar erizo.	[illegible] leche + cdo. 200 gr. Racionar [illegible]	Ligar [illegible] Ligar menta Bibi. Soja	Sféricos PR [illegible] azúcar Esferificar quesos.	Shots [illegible] [illegible] Pepinos [illegible]
	17:00-17:30	Toques [illegible] Yogurt [illegible] Fizz y chupitos	- Cocer [illegible] - Cortar [illegible] - Mantequilla [illegible] - [illegible]	Montar nata.	H2O anchoa Caldo ostra + [illegible] 200 gr. Cortar ostra	Cocer [illegible] [illegible] [illegible] Guardar [illegible]/Sésamo.	Racionar [illegible] Seleccionar [illegible] Confitar panceta.	[illegible] [illegible] Limpiar [illegible].
	17:30-18:25	Chupitos flores Cortar papel flores	- Cortar [illegible] - Porcionar [illegible] - Caldo [illegible] - Crema [illegible]		Freír pan [illegible] ostra Espuma ostra	Toques Mango Miso	Repelar [illegible]. Cortar ostra. Flor guisantes Cortar [illegible]	Pelar y [illegible] Agua [illegible]. Desvainar habas. [illegible]
	18:30-19:00	CENA	CENA	CENA	CENA	CENA	CENA	Menú Patata [illegible] [illegible] salsa verde.
	19:00-19:30	Rollos coco		Cogollos albahaca Racionar pipas.		Cortar [illegible] [illegible]	Cogollos albahaca. Agua manzana.	Pimiento Vainilla [illegible]. [illegible]
	19:30-20:00						Bogavante. Patata	
	20:00-21:00							
	21:00-22:00							
	22:00-23:00							
	23:00-23:30							

Daily sheet of *mise en place*
This lists all the dishes that the kitchen needs to produce for one day's service, and it allows them to keep track of how many portions they need to make of each recipe.

5/6-08

PRODUCTO	Cantidad	Días	PRODUCTO	Cantidad	Días
Almejas			Morralets		
Anchoas			Navajas	20 NAVAJAS.	
Berberechos			Ostra	1 SERVICIO	
Bogavante			Percebe		
Buey de mar desmigado			Pulpitos		
Buey de mar			Rape		
Caballa			Salmonetes		
Cañeillas			Sardina		
Caviar	6 LATAS.		Sepia		
Cigalas			Sepiones		
Chipirones			Vieiras		
Erizos			Zamburiñas		
Escupiñas			NEGRITO	35 PAX	
Espardenyes	4 KG.	1 DÍA	AVALON	50 PAX.	
Gambas			ORTIGUILLA	30 PAX.	
Huevas			MEDUSA	6 UNIDADES	
Jurel					
Langosta					
Langostinos					
Mejillones					

List of stock in the fish fridges
This shows what types of fish and seafood are in the fridge, how many portions of each one there are and how long they have been stored, so that the chefs can assess the contents at a glance.

MISE EN PLACE PASTELERIA		FECHA: 6/6/08	
PASE	**MISE EN PLACE**	**HORNO**	**VARIOS**
Vaciar LULO	Montar donuts.		Pano x galleta / Chocolates.
Probar espuma yuzu	Escudillar bombón.		Bizkuits –
Piel limón confitada.	Pasar after		~~Donut [illegible]~~
Gelatina café	Probar mermelada melocotón.		Streusel piñones (Andoni)
Terminar Ambar.	Polvo helado chocolate		
Hojas Menta.	Bañar after.		
Mantequilla sésamo (PROBAR)	Bañar bombones.	Recoger donuts	Piel limón confitado.
Doblar HABAS CACAO	Bañar trufitas.	Recoger galleta grosella.	Huevo Jeff. Miel piñón?
Doblar orquídea / PINO / Pan especias	Helados planos		Hacer choco x jueves.
Pintar after / HADA / Piedra / Hoja.	Estirar after.		
Reponer caja chocolate.	Base sablé	Algas 120/180	Familia Jeff / Carol.
	Montar olivas	Estirar pan especias	Descongelar 40.
Gelé miel Pino. (JOTA)	Racionar SAKE.	Cocer sablé canela / POMPA / CACAO.	
Sacar olivas	Baños chocolate a punto.	Estirar croquant líquido cacao	
Hacer espuma yogur (PROBAR)	Hacer grosella polvo.	Hacer CRUTOMAT 150	– Probar 2 donuts.
Hacer espuma yuzu (PROBAR)	Cortar after.		
Jarabe vainilla. Almacenar [illegible]	Hacer sférico. sauco.	Cocer streusel almendra 160	~~– Saquitos de pan especias.~~
Hacer cóctel LULO	Desmoldar trufita.		
Mantequilla albahaca	Puré piel lima.	Hacer galleta parma 180	– Pasión crispy puré x orquídea
Gelé mascabado	Cocer y hacer sésamo / yogur.	Hacer crêpes	~~Hierba [illegible] jengibre.~~
Panas x paisaje	Hacer [illegible] donuts.	Pañuelos CRUMIEL	
Yogur mango / Paisaje / Pino	Alginato x 3.	HORNO 210°C.	~~– Receta mango x A.A.~~
Bizcocho chocolate / Nata	Montar merengue Pino		~~Pino x A.A.~~
Baño sauco		Cocer [illegible]	
Cuarto Petit	19:00 Deshidratar PINO	Cocer crêpes.	
Toffee a punto (café?)	Hacer sférico sauco.		
Agua cacao	Montar brazos.	Descongelar mango.	
Praliné piñones. +SAL.	Montar mango	Caramelizar pan especias x 20	
	Puré grosella.		
Fever Tree / Madreselva.	Polvo merengue regaliz		
A punto pompas.	Hacer olivas.	Estirar croquant cacahuete / Pistacho	
Preparar brazos.	Sacar donuts.		
17:30 Reponer LULOS	Polvo	Bizcocho chocolate (1 receta)	
Descongelar pasteles	Hacer Base Sauco.		
Desmoldar AMBAR	Polvo frambuesa 40.		
Probar sifones.	Hacer Pescaíto.	Cortar Algas.	
Bizcocho chocolate a punto.	Descongelar helado viento / PINO	" Brick / Cortezas.	
Cremoso frambuesa	Descongelar helado trufa	" Piñones.	
Montar mango	" pulpa cacao		
Cremoso [illegible]	Cortar vasos.		
A punto Pampas			
	Mousse choco x 40.		
	Hacer choco air.		

Daily sweet world preparation sheet
This lists everything that the sweet world needs to produce, including cocktails, snacks and morphings, as well as desserts.

14:55

—

Cooking begins

Once the *mise en place* for service is organized, the work in the kitchen begins. Although the techniques of classical cuisine form the foundations of all the cooking at elBulli, many new processes have been developed. As well as using heat, the chefs might 'cook' in another sense by transforming an ingredient through extreme cold using liquid nitrogen.

'A creative person tries to do what they don't know how to do.'

Other new techniques include a method of caramelization using caramel made with Isomalt, a natural sweetener. Using this technique, a capsule is created. The exterior is a very fine film of caramel with pumpkin seed oil inside. The result is a magical, crunchy creation with a liquid centre.

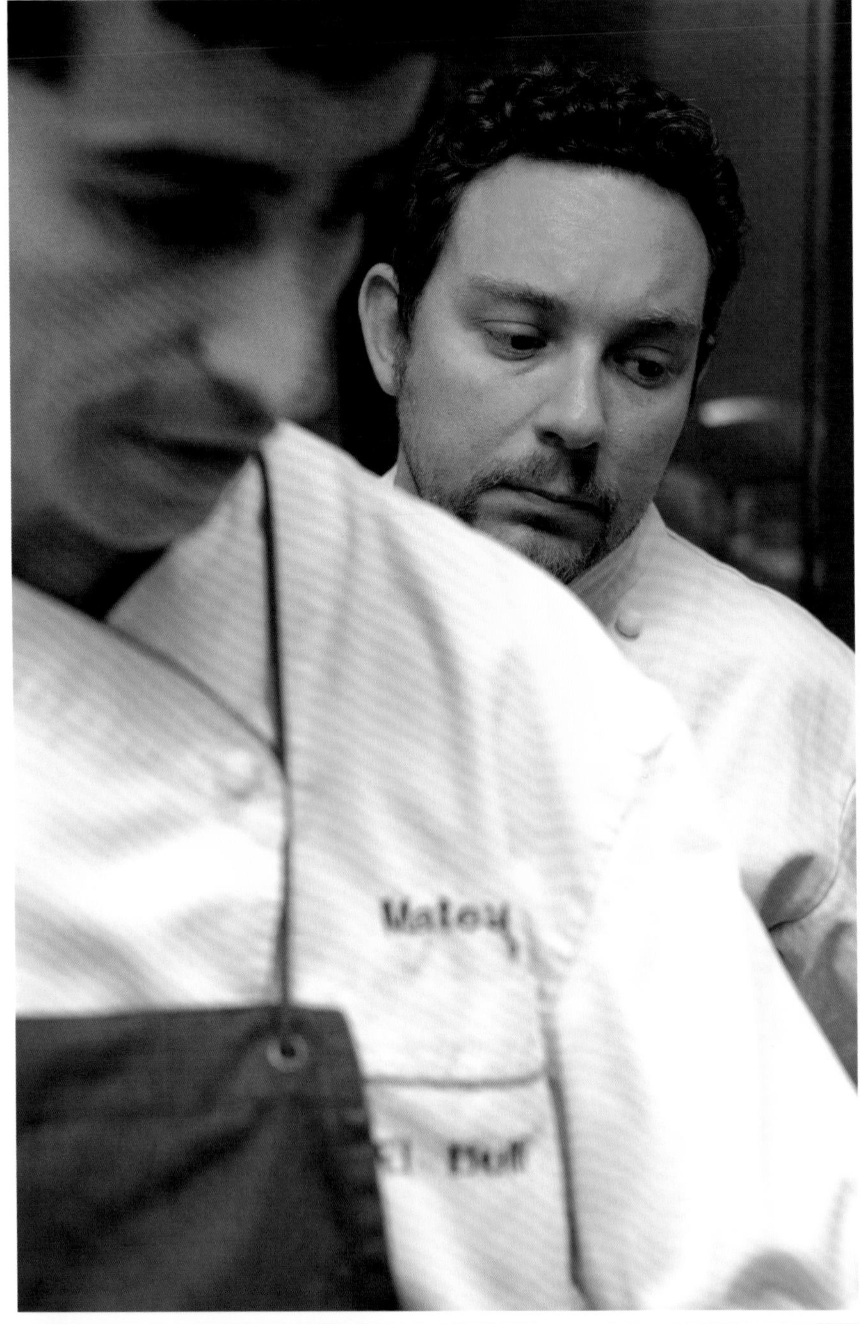

The sweet world meeting

There are separate meetings for the sweet and savoury worlds so that problems can be considered in depth. As well as talking about the previous night's service, the sweet world chefs might discuss improvements or refinements that can be made to the new dishes, so that they can be produced more easily for the larger numbers required by the restaurant.

The sweet world represents a high percentage of the menu at elBulli, and has its own characteristics and its own way of working.

A moment for reflection

Ferran does not do the *mise en place* himself. He oversees what is happening in the kitchen, but until the evening service begins he will carry on doing creative work with Oriol. At around three o'clock he makes time to stop and recap on what has been achieved so far.

'How things taste is one of the most difficult things to put into words.'

Creative methods 1

CREATIVE METHODS I
- Traditional and local cuisines
- Influences from other cuisines
- Technique-concept search
- Techniques and concepts applied to food

CREATIVE METHODS II
- Association
- Inspiration
- Adaptation
- Deconstruction
- Minimalism
- Changes to the structure of the menu
- The search for new ingredients

CREATIVE METHODS III
- The senses as a starting point
- The sixth sense
- Symbiosis of the sweet and savoury worlds
- Commercial food in high-end cuisine
- New ways of serving food
- Changing the structure of dishes

Creativity is what keeps elBulli open. This is not only because it is central to the passion and commitment of every member of the team, but also because the creativity of the food is what makes people want to eat here. The restaurant is like a workshop where new dishes, concepts and techniques are developed and shared with the guests. Without an audience, the creations would have no meaning. The guests' enjoyment of the food is difficult to quantify because every person has their own views about cooking and the types of food they enjoy. Creativity, on the other hand, can be measured: it is possible to document a technique and to establish whether it is new. But to be truly creative, a dish must be interesting as well as new. The aim at elBulli is to create dishes and techniques that engage guests' sensory, emotional and intellectual faculties to the full, to surprise them and to encourage them to experience food in new and unexpected ways.

Like many other chefs, Ferran's goal when he joined elBulli was to gain three Michelin stars. He never dreamed of the new concepts and techniques that the creative team would go on to develop, and he has far surpassed all hopes and expectations of the creative levels he could achieve as a chef. As a result there is a real sense of freedom and lack of pressure in the Barcelona workshop, for anything achieved during the creative sessions is a welcome addition to the success that elBulli has already enjoyed. The dishes, techniques and concepts that come out of the creative sessions are not secrets. Each one has been documented and published, and the hope is that the discoveries made at elBulli can help restaurant cuisine as a whole to evolve and develop. The real challenge for the team is to go on creating new dishes every year.

The creative methods are the synthesis of twenty years of exploration in the kitchen, and they were often identified as creative methods only several years after they were developed, through in-depth study and analysis of the evolution of elBulli's food. The creative model is constantly shifting, and it can be difficult to recognize the significance of a method when it is first being used. A more general study of the creative methods used in the fields of music, art and fashion, such as mental visualization, lateral thinking, free association and brainstorming, shows that many of the same methods can be applied to creativity in cuisine. In the same way, some of the creative methods detailed here could be shared with other artistic disciplines. Some of the terminology used is also employed in those disciplines: 'deconstruction', for example, was a term first suggested by an architect friend as a description of one of the ways in which elBulli re-imagined classic and traditional dishes. 'Decomposition' and 'reconversion' were first considered and rejected (for obvious reasons), and 'deconstruction' was eventually settled on. The term has specific meanings in architecture, literary theory and other fields, of course, but it is not used at elBulli to draw parallels or to imply a sharing of particular theoretical tenets: it is simply the most accurate label.

When chefs have acquired the technical mastery to be able to perfect the dishes of classic cuisine, some of the creative methods listed here might help them start to experiment with those dishes, and to create new ones. Each method has been more or less prominent at different stages of elBulli's history, and each one could contain the seeds of new methods.

Traditional and local cuisines

When Ferran became head chef in 1984, elBulli's food was strongly influenced by nouvelle cuisine, a new cooking style that had emerged in France during the 1970s and advocated shorter cooking times and a lighter cooking style. One of the lesser-known ways in which the leading exponents of nouvelle cuisine challenged the rules of classic French cuisine was by seeking influences from traditional and local dishes, ingredients and cooking techniques. Although the term is no longer widely used, the legacy of nouvelle cuisine can be seen in the presence of 'local food' like gazpacho or aioli on the menus of fine dining restaurants, and many ingredients previously considered unsophisticated, such as olive oil, now have an important place in high-end food.

Local cuisine as a source of inspiration was an important factor in elBulli's early evolution from 1987, and although this creative method had its roots in nouvelle cuisine, it also helped elBulli forge an independent style. The dishes from that time made great use of local ingredients that had rarely been seen in fine dining restaurants, such as sea dates and razor clams from the Cap de Creus. However, in the more radical expressions of this method, traditional cooking techniques like char-grilling vegetables or using escabeches were applied to prestigious ingredients, and traditional concepts like the Catalan *mar y montaña* (literally 'sea and mountain', or surf and turf) were translated into refined dishes such as *Bone marrow and caviar* in 1992. This creative method informed elBulli's early explorations of the traditional food of Catalunya, of the rest of Spain, of Italy and finally of the whole of the Mediterranean.

Influences from other cuisines

The exchange of ingredients and cooking techniques between countries has a history as long as travel and exploration. Even classic French cuisine, traditionally seen as quite conservative, made use of foods and dishes native to other parts of the world. These influences did not usually involve much development or analysis of the foreign techniques, but were assimilated straight into the cooking styles of their adoptive country. However, once local food traditions had started to influence nouvelle cuisine they also started to cross national borders: pasta, for instance, was first seen in high-end Italian restaurants, and then started to appear in France and Spain.

Now that international ingredients have become more readily available, influences from other countries are a common sight on fine dining restaurant menus. The fusion cuisine that has become popular over the last few years combines ingredients, classic dishes and cooking techniques from several parts of the world in one dish, and in its worst form can lead to the banal inventiveness of a dish such as, say, 'Galician octopus sashimi with Thai-style guacamole'. The coherence of the finished fusion dish will depend on the skill and judgement of the chef. In fact, as a creative method it is most successful when it is used within the context of a chef's own individual style of cooking, where it can result in articulate and innovative dishes.

The creative method of absorbing influences from other countries is complex and can operate in many different ways, as it does in other artistic fields. Ferran and Albert's travels to South America in the early 1990s, for instance, opened their eyes to the range and possibilities of fruit. They discovered that, unlike many ingredients, fruit can fit into more than one of the basic taste groups (it can be sweet, sour and bitter all at once). This led to many new ways of using it, such as the Cuban-influenced *Banana salad with mojito water ice and mint jelly*, and the new understanding deepened the connections between the sweet and savoury worlds. When Ferran travelled to Japan in 2003 he was profoundly influenced by *kaiseki* cuisine, a style of formal dining with many courses that are finely balanced in taste, texture, cooking technique and presentation. In fact, the Japanese emphasis on the spirituality, ritual and sequence of eating, which values the experience of the whole meal and the flow of courses over individual dishes, had a deeper influence on the food of elBulli than the use of Japanese ingredients like seaweeds and miso, with which Ferran had already experimented in dishes such as *Warm sashimi of lobster and wasabi*.

TECHNIQUE-CONCEPT SEARCH

To define the terms, a technique is any process or combination of processes by which a product may be cooked or otherwise transformed. In the culinary sense, a concept is the idea or basic premise of a dish, which can be elaborated in different ways to create different recipes. It is a way of presenting ingredients in a particular, recognizable form. An example of a concept could be a carpaccio (the concept being thinly sliced raw beef), a salad (fresh leaves or vegetables dressed with a vinaigrette) or an omelette (lightly beaten eggs cooked and folded rapidly in a frying pan or skillet).

The search for new cooking techniques and concepts is the highest level of creativity, and it is the most important of all the creative methods. Developing techniques is the focus of the winter creative sessions at the elBulli workshop in Barcelona. Techniques and concepts will outlive trends and styles; foams and puff pastry may fall in and out of fashion, but the techniques used to develop them will endure and can be revisited. Restaurants need new techniques and concepts in order to evolve, and the work involved in developing them advances the field of high-end cuisine more than any other type of creative culinary endeavour.

The history of the technique-concept search at elBulli includes major discoveries alongside more minor developments. Some of the principal discoveries that have been central to elBulli's development are the creation of the frozen savoury world in 1994, the new non-pasta raviolis of the same year, or the liquid croquants of 1996; the major new techniques include spherification (by which tiny, intensely flavoured spheres of fruit or vegetable extracts can be created) and a new form of caramelization (by which any product can be coated with a very thin layer of brittle caramel). However, some of the most famous elBulli inventions, such as the foams, hot jellies and airs, are actually new techniques and concepts combined. The more minor offshoots and refinements to previous techniques can be just as important, even though they might be less noticeable. Sweet soups, for example, were refined in 1996 with the use of freshly squeezed orange juice to create *Orange soup with mango and ginger ravioli*. In some ways this was a small modification, but the simplicity of the dish greatly influenced elBulli's use of pure products and flavours.

Sometimes it takes a while to understand the significance of a new technique. The first dish to use the hot jelly technique was *Roquefort sorbet with hot apple and lemon jelly* in 1998, but on the first occasion it was served the guest did not notice anything unusual about the dish, even though it would certainly have been the first time that person had tasted a warm jelly. Gelatine, which had been almost universally used to make jellies up until that point, melts and loses its holding properties as soon as it is heated. The new seaweed-derived gelling agents that Ferran had encountered on trips to China and Japan had led to the creation at elBulli of jellies that could be served hot without melting, and this dish was the first to include one, but even the creative team did not realize the importance of the technique when the dish was being developed. Finally, however, when it comes to the experience of eating at elBulli, it is the dishes that matter, not the techniques. A guest does not need to appreciate a new technique in order to enjoy the dish, although it may add to the pleasure for an experienced restaurant-goer.

TECHNIQUES AND CONCEPTS APPLIED TO FOOD

This extension of the technique-concept search is such a prolific source of inspiration for the team at elBulli that it has now been classified as a creative method in its own right. The application of different techniques to specific food products has also led to the creation of many new concepts. Applying a new technique to an ingredient that has never been treated in that way before can produce very interesting results. A concept as simple as carpaccio must have come about in this way, when the technique of slicing very thinly was first applied to beef fillet.

The classic French cooking techniques for seafood are poaching or steaming. There is also a long Spanish tradition of other methods, such as deep-frying, grilling and barbecuing, which were assimilated into high-end Spanish cuisine during the 1980s and are now fully established cooking styles in their own right, resulting in many new seafood dishes. At elBulli, the reassessment of cooking methods for seafood led to the discovery that the old techniques, both French and Spanish, involved cooking them for too long, resulting in a loss of the natural flavour. To get closer to the natural 'gene' of the product, the creative team experimented with grilling the heads of crustaceans and then extracting their essence to obtain a sauce that accurately resembled their original flavour. The *Mollusc platter* is a deceptively simple dish consisting of several native Spanish shellfish immersed for a matter of seconds in boiling water, just long enough to open their shells, and then served encased in a light layer of jelly made from their own cooking liquor. The dish, although complex, is a presentation of seafood in its most natural form.

The sweet world gets back to work

There are countless techniques and methods of preparation in the sweet world, such as preparing baths of gelatine for fruit, making fresh passion fruit juice, tempering chocolate and preparing tarts with kataifi, a type of pastry in long, thin strands.

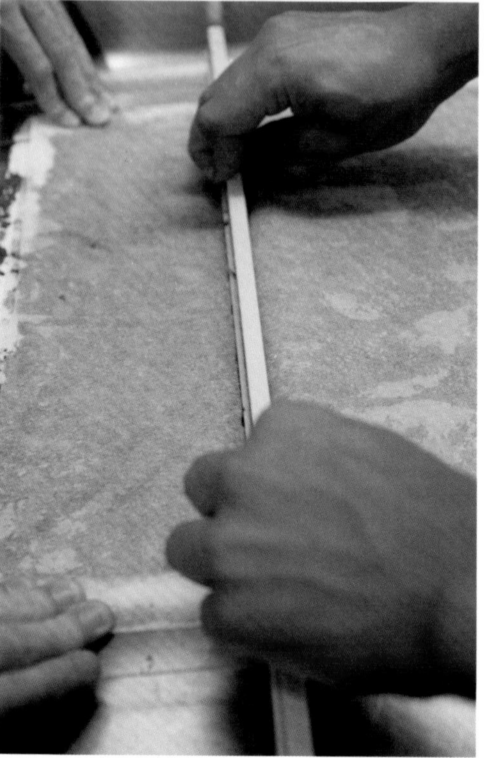

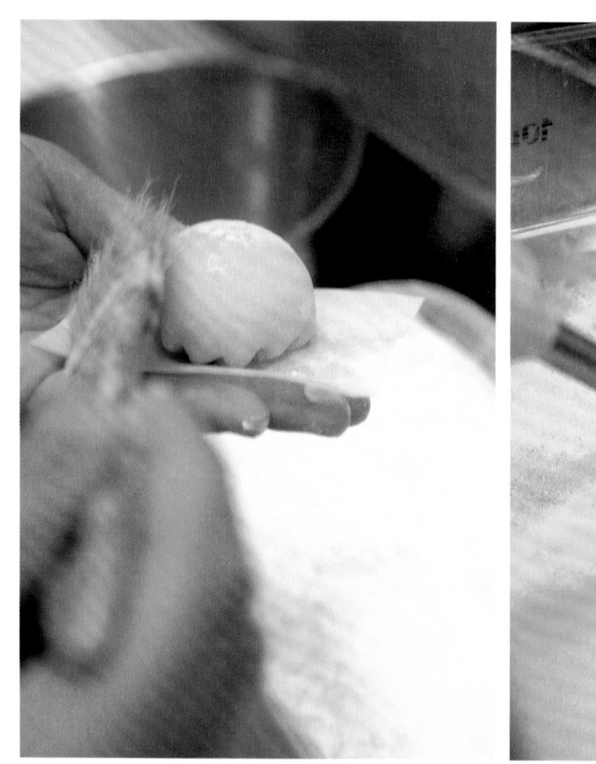

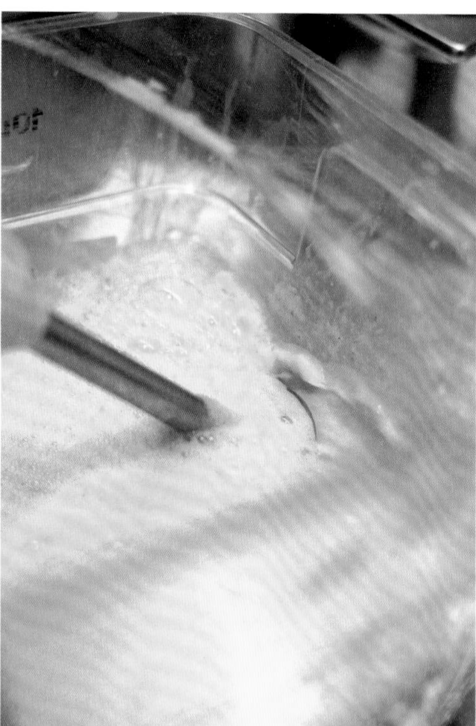

Here, the chefs make *mochis* (Japanese filled rice cakes), create airs, which are the light textures that form on the surface of a liquid when it is frothed, and roll out balls of brioche dough that will later be steamed.

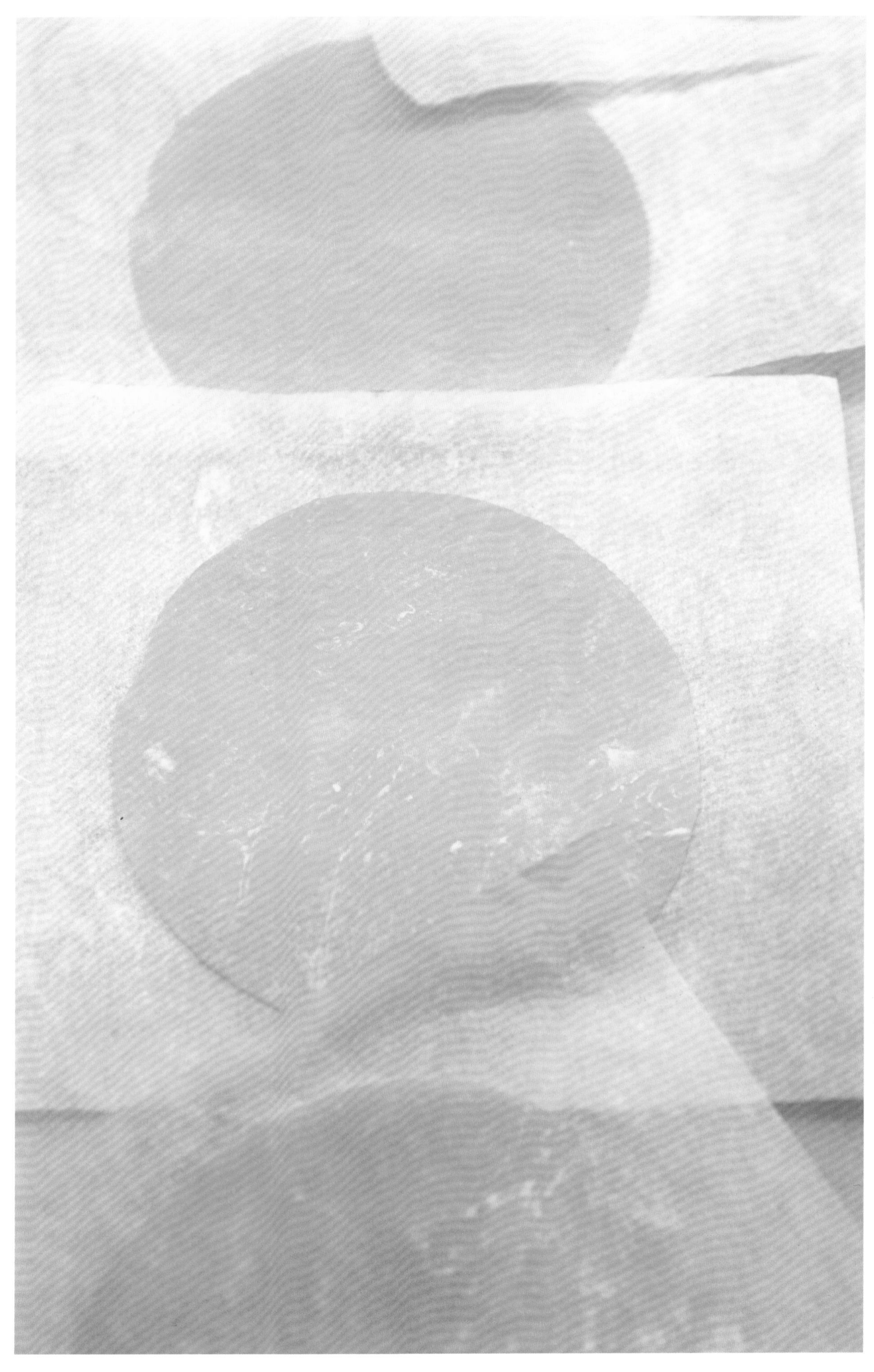

The front of house team

A restaurant cannot be defined by the style of its food alone: it would be nothing without the staff who serve the guests and liaise with the chefs. The waiters are true professionals, steeped in the spirit of elBulli. Every meal is a bit like a theatrical performance in which the waiters are actors playing the central characters, and they must know their lines perfectly. This does not mean that their conduct should be artificial or routine, but that their serving style is designed to create maximum enjoyment for the diner. To achieve this the waiters must use all their senses, stay alert at all times and be sensitive to the needs of every guest.

The front of house and kitchen teams are fully integrated and share the same understanding of gastronomy and of life. This attitude is characterized by generosity and cordiality, so that every guest feels like an old friend making a welcome return. The philosophy has always been to question accepted beliefs about how a restaurant should be managed, and not to follow conventions just because they are habits. Some traditional elements of service in fine dining restaurants create a distance between the chefs and the guests, but at elBulli the service is down-to-earth and natural, so that guests feel relaxed, happy and comfortable.

A guest's experience at elBulli is about more than just eating a meal: it is about the journey, the setting, the service, the flow of dishes and the conversation. It could not be recreated anywhere else. At the end of dinner, Ferran would prefer to hear that guests have enjoyed themselves than that the food was good.

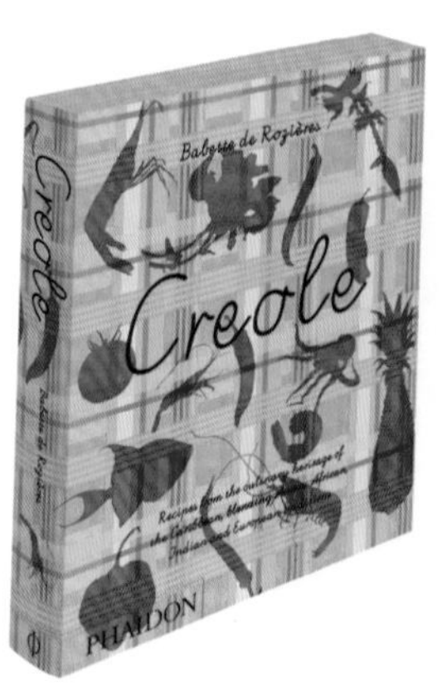
Creole
PHAIDON

Pork & Sons
PHAIDON

TERRINE
PHAIDON

The dining rooms are prepared

There are three main spaces where guests can eat at elBulli: the *comedor,* which is a typical Spanish dining room with a bar; the *salón*, which has space for a large table, French windows to the garden and a mezzanine level with a sofa; and the terrace outside.

All three dining areas have to be perfect. Glasses are cleaned, the table linen and all the table settings are checked. The team also cleans the windows and floors, and pays particular attention to the plants on the terrace.

15:50

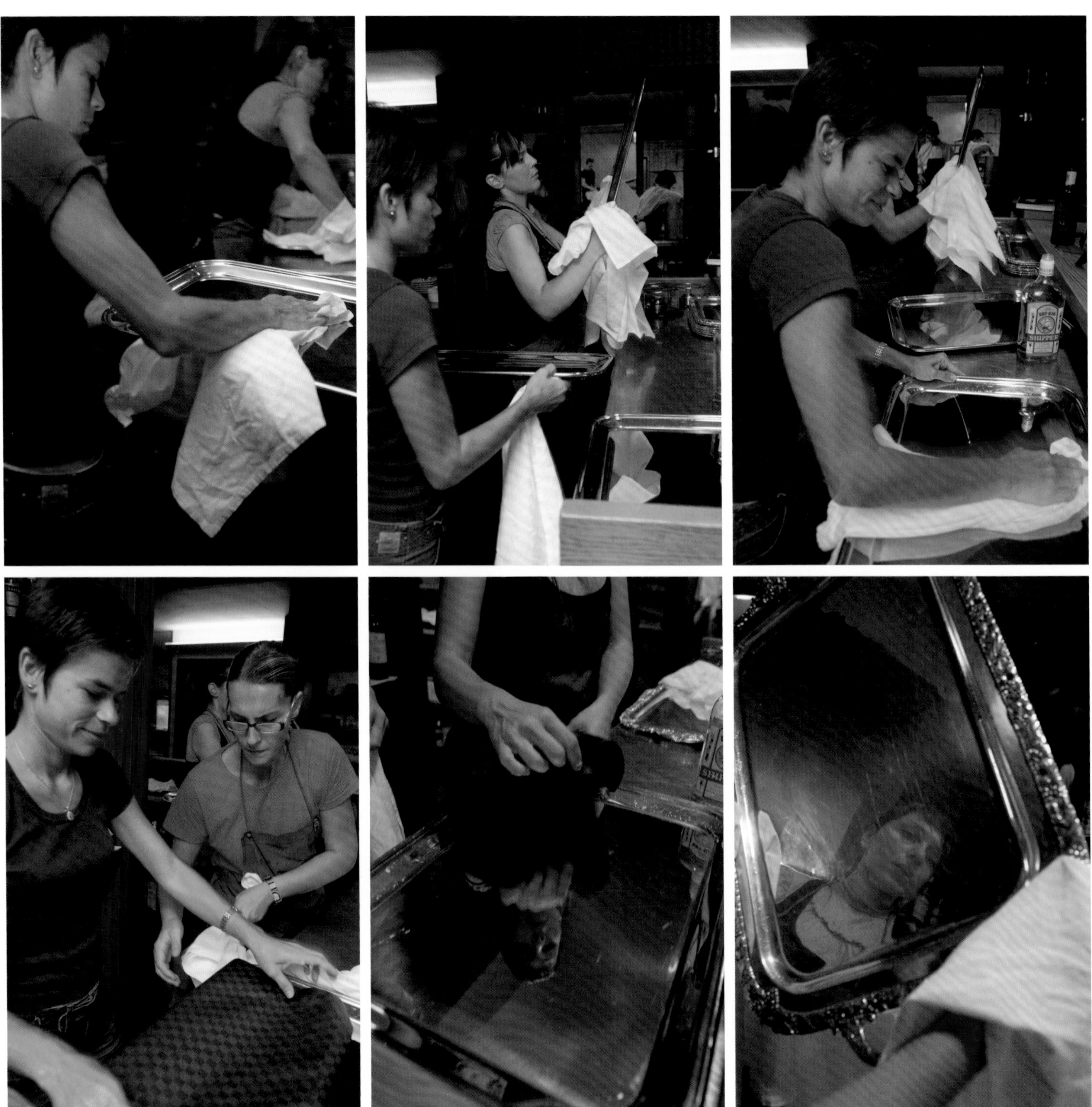

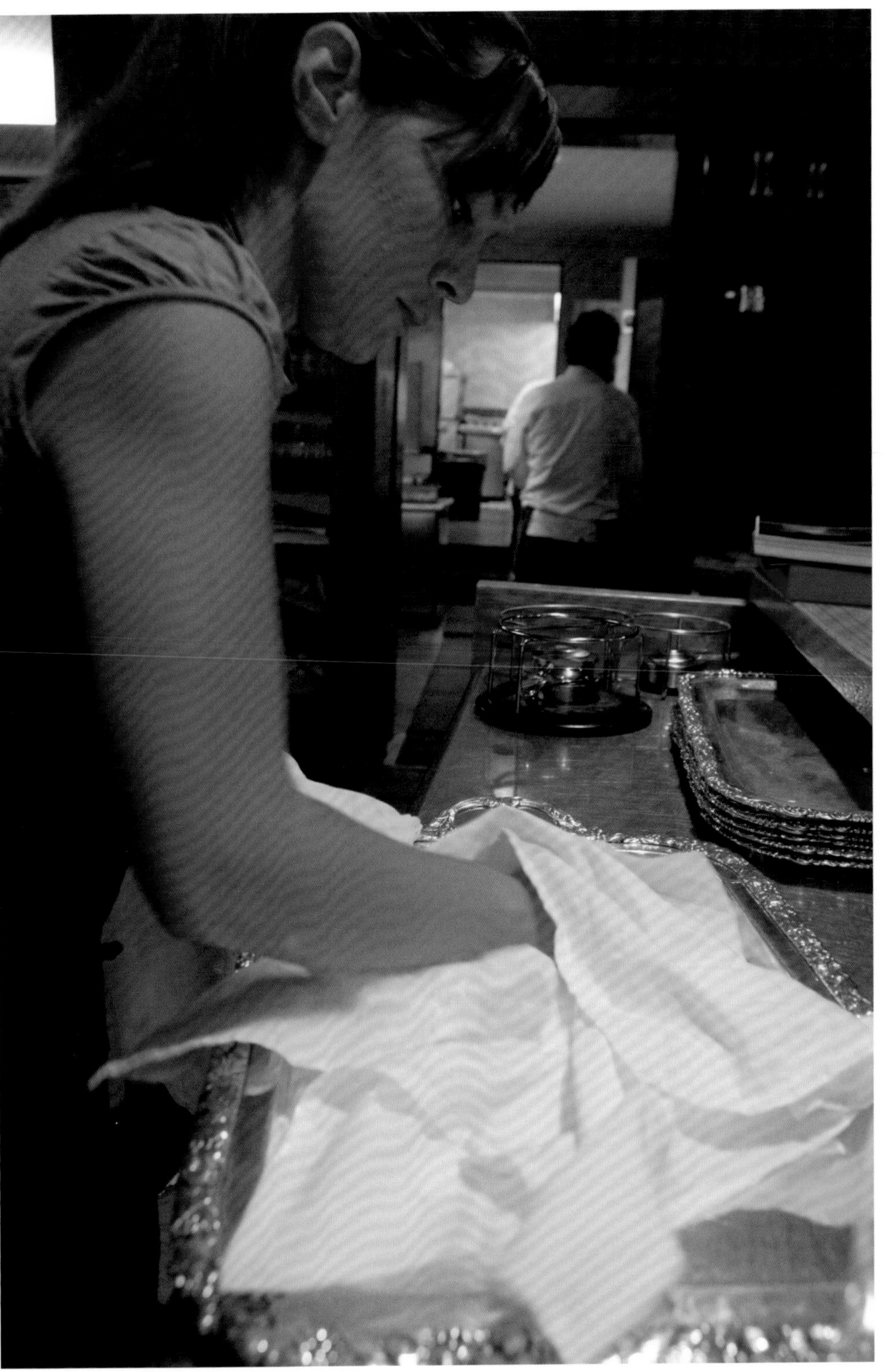

Spoons, knives, forks

In the last few years new types of cutlery have been introduced, which are used alongside the more traditional kind. For example, in 2001 a cross between a pipette and a skewer was created that enabled guests to squeeze a sauce into their mouths at the same time as eating from the skewer, which meant they experienced the dish in a different way. As early as 1997, tableware for the 'follies' (petits fours) was commissioned, and each folly was served on its own custom-made dish inspired by Japanese origami shapes. However, conventional silver cutlery is still very important and requires special attention. At elBulli it is treated with the greatest care and is always impeccable.

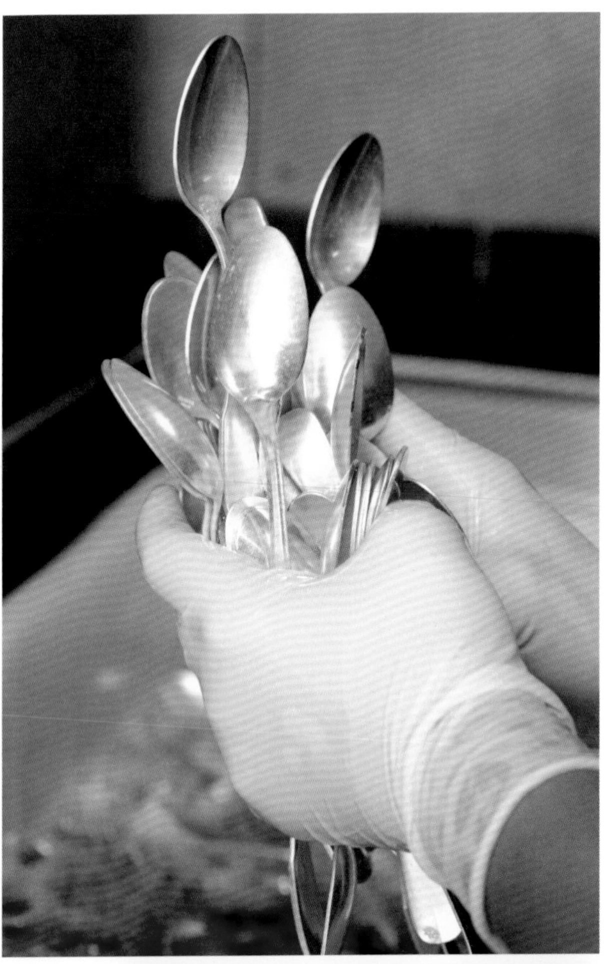

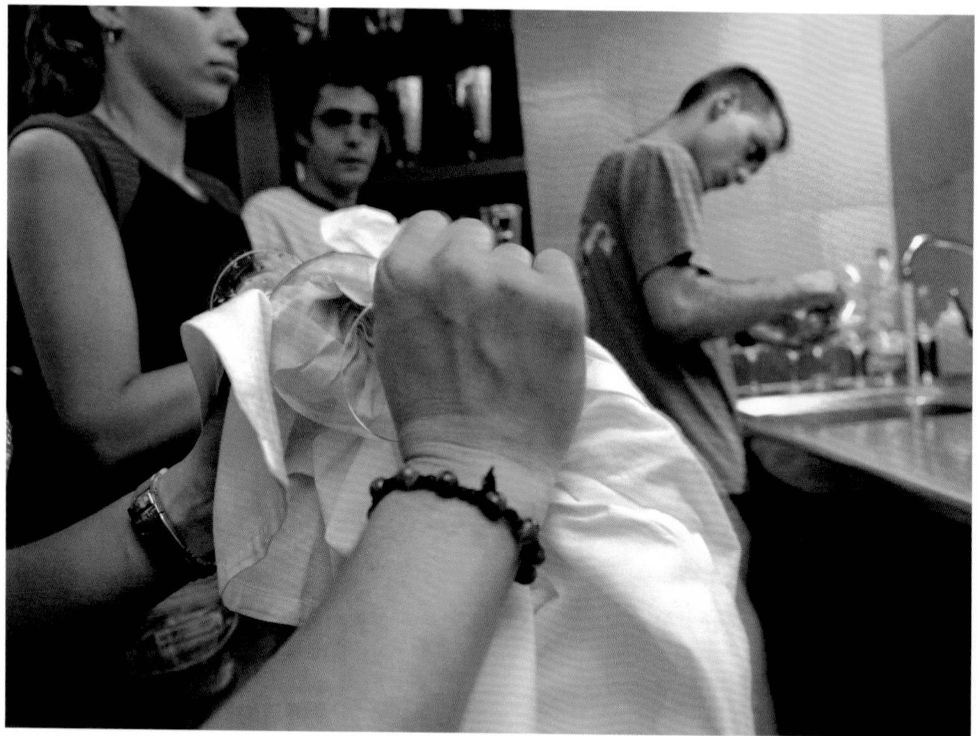

The sommeliers

The sommeliers check that the bottles are at the correct temperature in the wine coolers, monitor stock levels and make sure that all the wines from the previous night have been correctly invoiced. Every day the sommeliers' assistants wash and dry hundreds of glasses by hand with the utmost care.

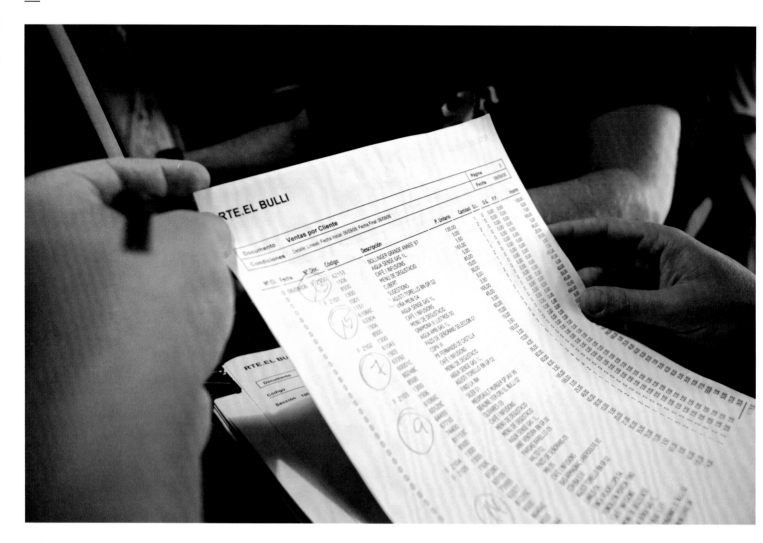

Checking the inventory

Sommeliers Lucas Payá and Ferran Centelles update the stock list with the previous day's sales. There are 1,666 wines in the elBulli cellar. Of these, 981 are red, 324 are white, 161 are sweet, 166 are sparkling and 34 are fortified. Sixteen countries are represented and there are 325 different DOCs. The cellar also stocks vintages ranging from 1952 to 2007.

The wines are purchased from specialist suppliers and regular tastings are held by Juli and the sommeliers to select the best. There are many rare fine wines as well as more unusual examples from less well-known producers.

16:10

vi

Chus checks the cigar stocks

There is a selection of Havana cigars available: Balboa Robusto, Partagás Serie D No.4, Partagás Serie P No.2, Partagás D No.3 Edición Limitada, Hoyo de Monterrey Epicure No.2, Cohiba SXI, Cohiba Robusto, Montecristo Robusto Edición Limitada, Montecristo 'A', Trinidad Robusto Extra, Punch Punch-Punch, Partagás 8-9-8, Montecristo Edmundo, Romeo y Julieta Exhibición No.4, Vegas Robaina Único, Davidoff Robusto 100, Ramón Allones Gigantes, Arturo Fuentes Opus X, Romeo y Julieta Petit Piramides Edición Limitada, Romeo y Julieta Hermoso No.2.

More produce arrives

There are some products that only certain suppliers can provide, such as the mussels and sea urchins from Cap de Creus, which local fisherman Rafael Linares brings, or the special seaweed that doesn't even have a name, sent from Galicia by Antonio Muiños.

These can arrive at any time during the morning or afternoon.

16:35

16:40

—

New techniques mean learning new skills, starting from scratch and forging new paths

A new technique could be anything from turning a savoury foam into Parmesan marshmallows, to making a cylinder out of olive oil caramel.

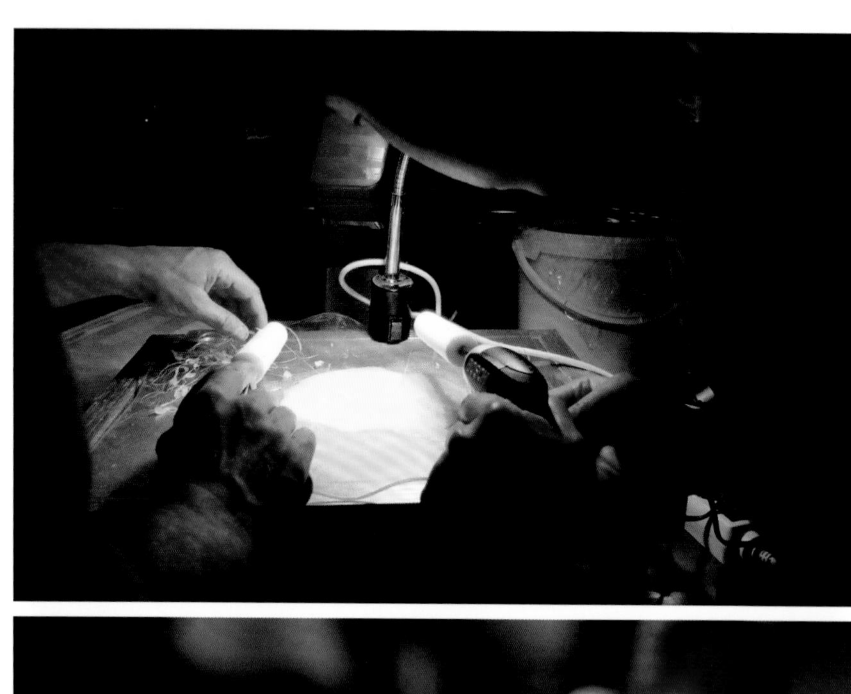

The olive oil cylinder is made from a special caramel made from olive oil and different sweeteners. Under a heat lamp, a fine thread of the caramel is wound rapidly around a cylindrical mould that has been fitted over a drill, and sets like a tightly coiled spring. The spring is then gently removed from the mould and served to the guest in a shiny black box that looks like a jewellery box. The guest puts the olive oil spring onto their finger like a ring, and places it in their mouth. The texture is crisp at first, and then the coil dissolves swiftly into pure extra virgin olive oil.

16:50

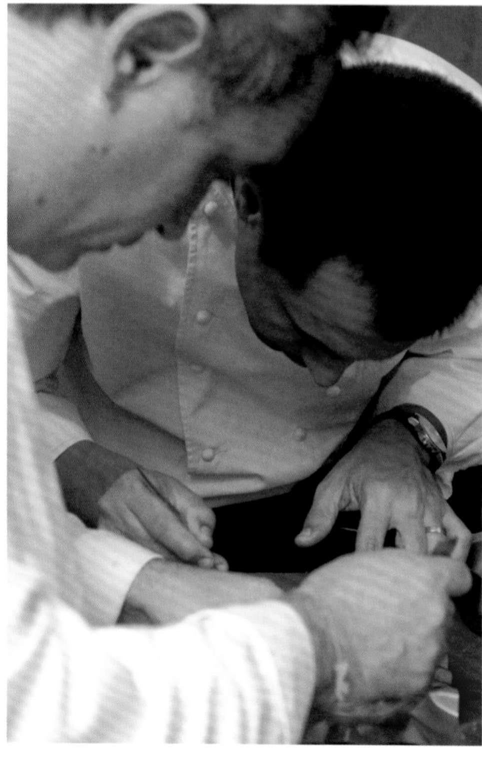

16:55

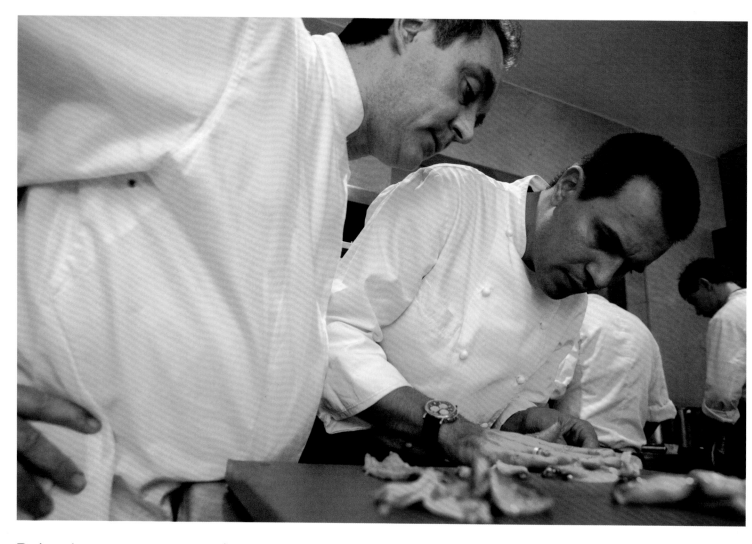

Being innovative is much harder today than it was ten years ago

After many years of creative development it becomes harder to push the boundaries, and now there are many more chefs striving to invent new techniques. That is why Ferran, Oriol and Albert continue their creative session until 19:30. They dedicate nine hours a day to creating. Here they are working with new ingredients: some giant clams that arrived from Galicia along with the seaweed.

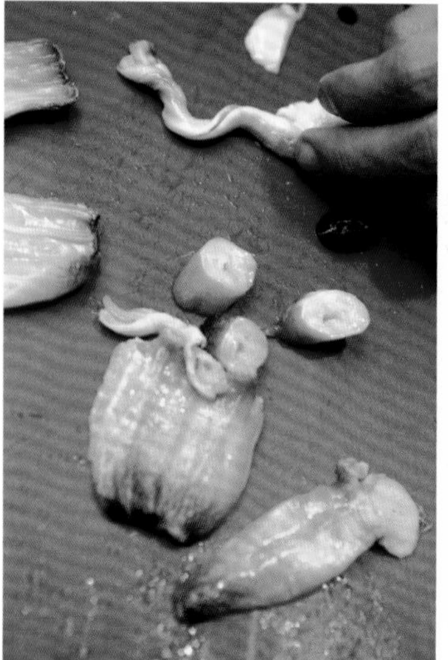

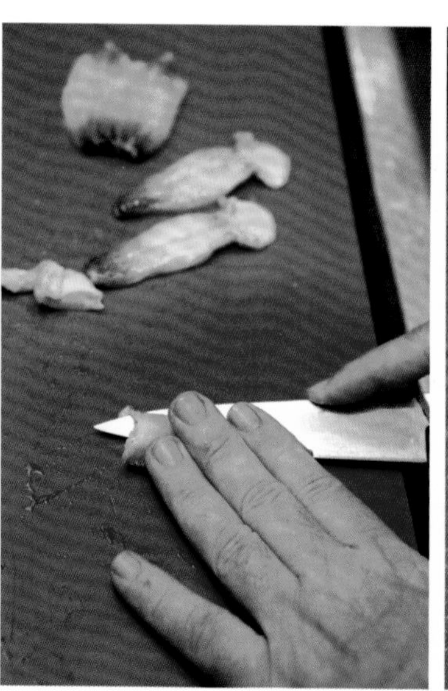

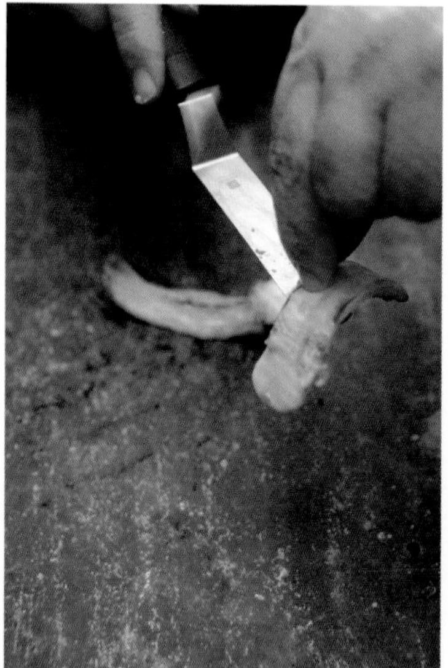

Shopping in Barcelona

Every Tuesday and Friday, Jose Mari shops in Barcelona for wine and exotic ingredients, and stops off at the stalls at the Boqueria market in the heart of town, where there are a number of trusted suppliers who know elBulli well. He also goes to elBullitaller (the creative workshop) and elBullicarmen, the office where publicity work and logistics are coordinated.

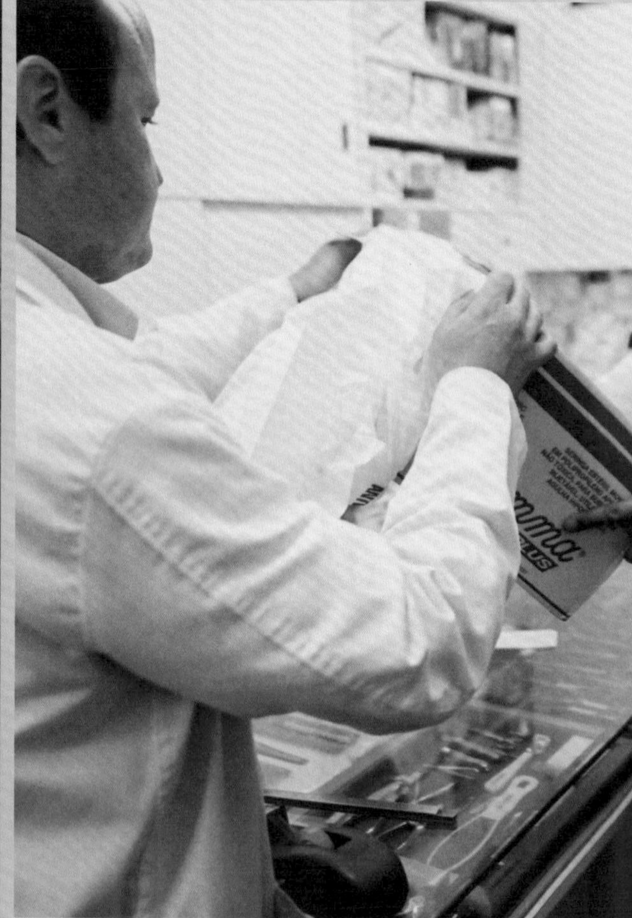

Visiting the workshop

On Tuesday and Friday, when Jose Mari drives down from Roses in the van to do his rounds in Barcelona, his first stop is elBullitaller. He delivers packages and collects anything that has arrived by air. He also picks up files and other documents for Ferran.

At the chemist

Here, Jose Mari stocks up on syringes for the spherical caviar, ascorbic acid (vitamin C), precision scales and latex gloves.

A trip to Asia

Extremo Oriente is a shop in the centre of Barcelona specializing in food from the Far East. They supply products such as soy sauce, miso, rice vinegar, fresh vegetables and spices.

Wine merchants

Jose Mari usually visits El Celler de Gelida or Vila Viniteca to buy the wines, liqueurs and other drinks needed for cooking. Specific orders are also placed if a wine on the list has run out. Most of the wines on the list are sourced from other specialist suppliers, who make recommendations based on the menu for the year. These are then tasted and analysed by Juli and the sommeliers before being listed.

Tokio-Ya

This shop sells Japanese products, so Jose Mari shops here only when he has been unable to find something in Extremo Oriente. He usually buys mentaiko, katsuobushi, dried seaweed, wasabi or miso here.

SUSHI
SOY SAUCE
SOY SAUCE

YAMADASHI
KOMBU
DRIED SEAWEED
NET WT. 8 OZ. (227 g)
SEAWEED
ONAL INC.

3人前

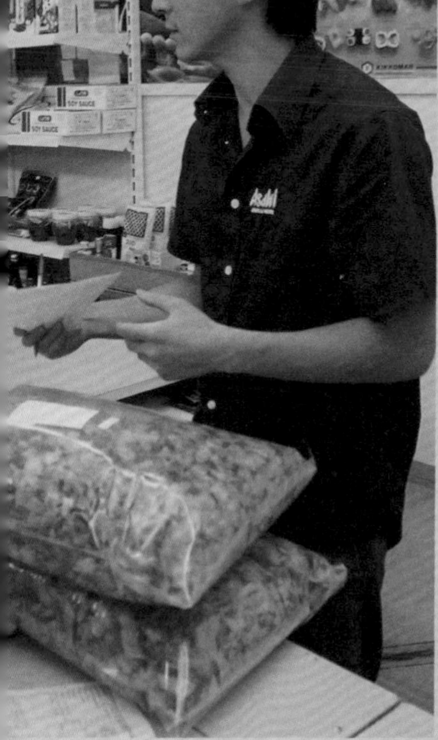

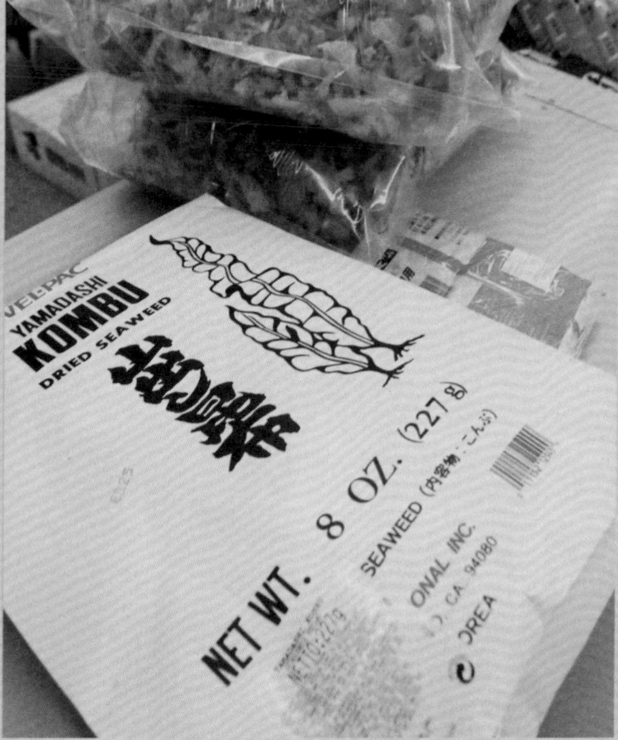

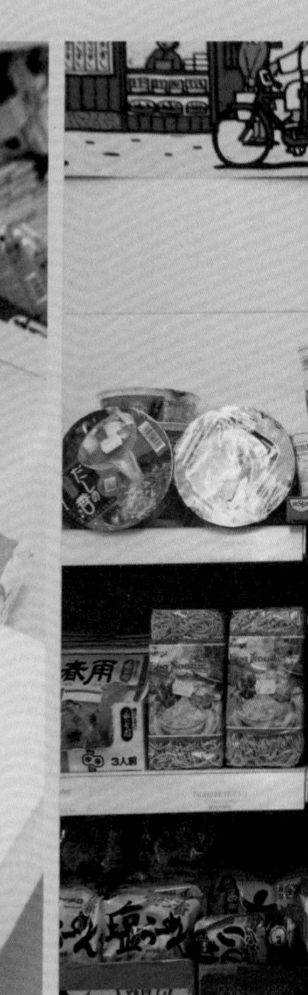

La Boqueria: the temple

Both elBullitaller and elBullicarmen are near the Boqueria market. There has been a market on this site for seven centuries, and the sheer range of food and the variety of the stalls make it an icon of gastronomy, a marvel for all the senses. Purchases made here include mushrooms and truffles from Petràs, fish from Genaro, meat from Casanovas and Capdevila, fruit and vegetables from Soley and pork products from Aroma Ibèric.

elBullicarmen

Just before returning to Roses, Jose Mari visits elBullicarmen. He usually leaves invoices for the accountants and collects layouts, photographs, editorial work and parcels for Juli.

Back in Roses

During the return journey to elBulli, Jose Mari sometimes stops in Granollers, a few miles from Barcelona, to collect caviar, at the usual supplier.

Checking the logistics

As well as working in the dining room, Pol and Christian are responsible for the generator, known affectionately as 'the old banger'. Although elBulli is connected to the central electricity network, the generator is maintained as a back-up, since the remote location of the restaurant means that there are sometimes problems with the power supply.

CENTRAL
CONDENSADOR

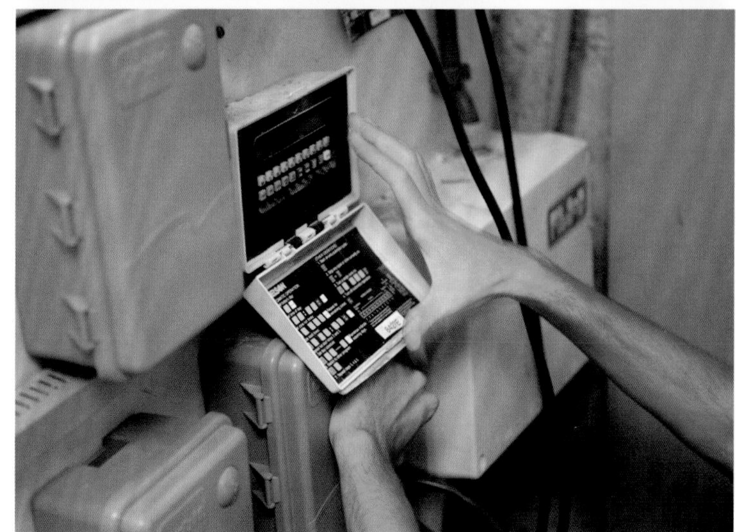

17:10

The restaurant is supplied by a well, and there is also a waste water treatment plant, both of which need to be checked daily.

17:15

At elBulli as much as possible is recycled and the environment is treated with respect, even though there is no urban infrastructure to help, because of the restaurant's remote rural location.

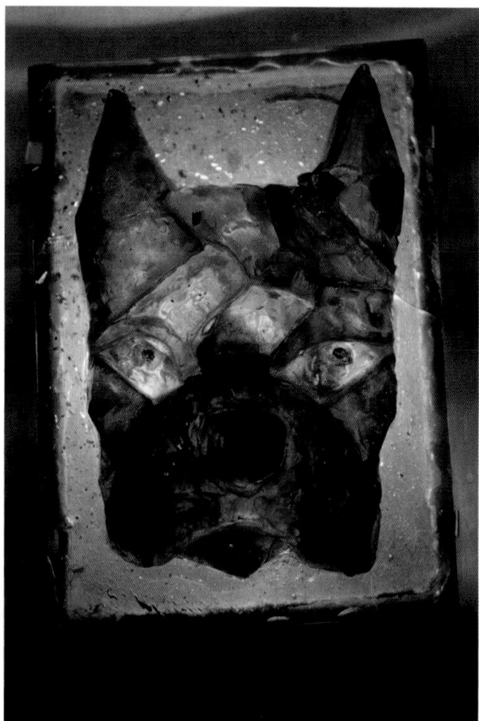

The restaurant was named 'El Bulli' by the original owners, Hans and Marketta Schilling, after their beloved French bulldogs, which are known locally as *bullis*.

A history of elBulli

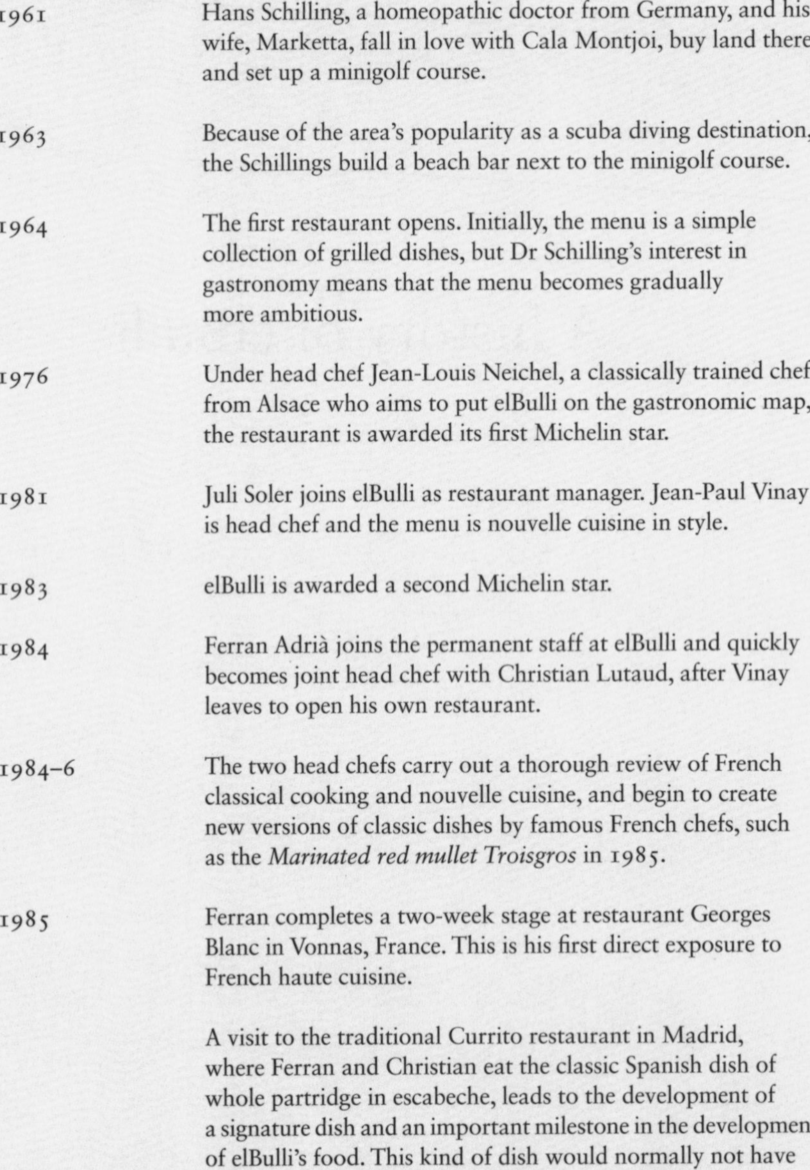

1961 Hans Schilling, a homeopathic doctor from Germany, and his wife, Marketta, fall in love with Cala Montjoi, buy land there and set up a minigolf course.

1963 Because of the area's popularity as a scuba diving destination, the Schillings build a beach bar next to the minigolf course.

1964 The first restaurant opens. Initially, the menu is a simple collection of grilled dishes, but Dr Schilling's interest in gastronomy means that the menu becomes gradually more ambitious.

1976 Under head chef Jean-Louis Neichel, a classically trained chef from Alsace who aims to put elBulli on the gastronomic map, the restaurant is awarded its first Michelin star.

1981 Juli Soler joins elBulli as restaurant manager. Jean-Paul Vinay is head chef and the menu is nouvelle cuisine in style.

1983 elBulli is awarded a second Michelin star.

1984 Ferran Adrià joins the permanent staff at elBulli and quickly becomes joint head chef with Christian Lutaud, after Vinay leaves to open his own restaurant.

1984–6 The two head chefs carry out a thorough review of French classical cooking and nouvelle cuisine, and begin to create new versions of classic dishes by famous French chefs, such as the *Marinated red mullet Troisgros* in 1985.

1985 Ferran completes a two-week stage at restaurant Georges Blanc in Vonnas, France. This is his first direct exposure to French haute cuisine.

A visit to the traditional Currito restaurant in Madrid, where Ferran and Christian eat the classic Spanish dish of whole partridge in escabeche, leads to the development of a signature dish and an important milestone in the development of elBulli's food. This kind of dish would normally not have appeared in a fine dining restaurant, but Ferran and Christian add their own interpretation of it to the menu at elBulli, replacing the whole partridge with a boned-out pigeon and refining the presentation.

Albert Adrià joins elBulli.

1986 Ferran completes a stage at the Maison Pic restaurant in Valence, France. That October, Christian Lutaud leaves and Ferran becomes sole head chef of elBulli.

1987–8 Ferran visits the Chantecler restaurant at the Negresco hotel in Nice, run by Jacques Maximin. During a talk for the Escoffier Foundation, Maximin gives a definition of creativity that inspires a radical new approach at elBulli: 'Creativity means not copying'. From then on, Ferran leaves the masters behind and begins to forge his own creative direction.

For the first time, elBulli closes for the winter from October to March. This allows a whole six months for creating new dishes, and, combined with inspiration from Jacques Maximin, marks the beginning of Ferran's plunge into creativity.

1990 elBulli regains its second Michelin star, which had been removed upon the departure of Jean-Paul Vinay.

Ferran Adrià and Juli Soler buy the restaurant from the Schillings.

Trips to the restaurants of leading French chefs Michel Bras and Pierre Gagnaire provide further inspiration for the direction of elBulli's food. Gagnaire teaches that anything is possible in cooking, and Bras emphasizes the discipline of cooking based on nature and the importance of the inherent purity of the flavour of each ingredient. Until this point, elBulli's food has been rooted in local cooking styles, but now this is combined with a more experimental, avant-garde style.

1991 In the second major departure from the traditional format of fine dining restaurants, the dessert trolley is no longer used.

1992 A series of conversations about art and creativity with the sculptor Xavier Medina Campeny result in the use of his workshop in Barcelona to create new dishes. This is Ferran's first experience of cooking purely as a creative process, without having to serve food to restaurant customers. During this period he does not attend every service at the restaurant and focuses instead on creative development.

1993 A new kitchen is built, designed to Ferran's exact specifications by the architect Dolors Andreu. It greatly expands the space available and facilitates the production of more ambitious dishes.

1994 The first dedicated team is set up to structure and organize the creative process, both during the winter when the restaurant is closed and at elBulli in the summer. The development of new cooking techniques and concepts, as well as new dishes, becomes the focus of creativity. From 1994, the team forges the creative identity that it is known for today.

The first classes for chefs and food enthusiasts are held at elBulli. Involving both theory and practical cooking, they lead to a more detailed analysis of elBulli's cooking styles.

1995 The elBulli catering company is created to take the restaurant's food to a wider public. It operates as a separate entity based in Barcelona.

The Gault Millau restaurant guide gives elBulli a score of nineteen out of twenty, placing it on the same level as the very best restaurants in France.

The kitchens of the Talaia restaurant in Barcelona are used as a creative workshop.

1996 Oriol Castro joins elBulli as a stager. A year later he joins Albert and Ferran as the third member of the creative team.

From 1996 on, the cheese trolley is no longer used. Avant-desserts are introduced to the menu as a bridge between the savoury and the sweet worlds.

Influential French chef Joël Robuchon gives an interview describing Ferran Adrià as the best chef in the world, providing the first international recognition of his talents.

1997 The first independent elBulli workshop is set up at the headquarters of elBulli catering.

elBulli is awarded its third Michelin star.

The first bespoke (custom-made) tableware for elBulli is commissioned from young Spanish designers. A different dish for each petit four is created, and these mark the first investigations into new serving techniques and receptacles.

1998 elBulli starts working with the Hacienda Benazuza in Seville, which becomes the first elBulli hotel.

Cocktails are made by the chefs with the same cooking techniques used for the dishes, and cocktails become part of the tasting menu.

In the first step towards the tasting menu concept that elBulli is to develop, bread and butter is no longer served. Ferran believes that, no matter how high the quality, bread and butter is something that can be eaten anywhere, and does not add anything new to the experience of eating at elBulli. It is replaced with snacks served when guests first arrive.

1999 Consultancy work for several different brands begins.

Ferran is heralded as the world's best chef on the front page of *El País Semanal*, the weekly magazine of Spain's national newspaper *El País*.

2000 elBullitaller, a new workshop on Calle Portaferissa, is set up, and the creative team works there throughout the winter on creating new dishes for the restaurant, as well as developing ideas for other projects.

The task of cataloguing every dish created at elBulli begins.

2001 The complexity of the menu leads to the decision to open for only one service per day, usually dinner. This allows creative sessions to continue during the day at elBulli in the season when the restaurant is open.

Work with industrial designers such as Luki Huber begins, leading to the development of new cooking processes, as well as new utensils for producing, serving and eating the food. This opens the door to a whole new level of creativity.

elBullicarmen, the office that manages all projects not directly related to creating new dishes for the restaurant, is set up above the Boqueria market in Barcelona.

2002 A retrospective is held, and for the season of 2002 there are no new dishes on the menu, only dishes from previous years. This allows a year of reflection and analysis to determine the future direction of elBulli. The menu is taken away and the tasting menu is established as the only option.

2003 Ferran appears on the cover of the *New York Times Magazine* in a feature entitled 'Spain is the new France'.

He visits Japan and learns about *kaiseki* cuisine, which has a huge influence on him.

A science department is created in elBullitaller. Headed by chemists Pere Castells and Íngrid Farré, it researches new scientific techniques and instruments, and studies the physical and chemical properties of food. Until then, any scientific processes behind elBulli's food had been developed purely through the chefs' own observations.

2004 A research centre devoted to the study of food and science is set up by the government of Catalunya and Manresa Bank, with Ferran Adrià as head of the Board of Trustees. The Alícia Foundation aims to make scientific advances in gastronomy and to provide education on good dietary habits.

Ferran appears on the cover of the *Le Monde* Sunday magazine in a feature that heralds elBulli's progressive Spanish cuisine as a true rival to French culinary dominance. He also features on the cover of *Time* magazine, in which he is named as one of the hundred most important people in the world.

In partnership with NH Hoteles, Ferran sets up Fast Good, a series of food outlets designed to offer quality fast food at reasonable prices.

2005 A Ferran Adrià Chair in gastronomic culture and food sciences is created at the Camilo José Cela University in Madrid.

2006 An international panel of experts for *Restaurant* magazine votes elBulli 'Best Restaurant in the World'. elBulli has already received this accolade in 2002.

Ferran wins the Lucky Strike Design Award from the Raymond Loewy Foundation. This prize, acknowledging the work of designers, is awarded to professionals who innovate in the field of design.

2007 elBulli participates in Documenta 12, the contemporary art exhibition in Kassel, Germany. The restaurant becomes a pavilion within the exhibition. Each day two randomly selected Documenta visitors travel to Spain to have dinner at elBulli, in order to start a dialogue between high cuisine and contemporary art. It is the first time that a restaurant has been invited to exhibit.

Ferran receives the Gold Medal for Merit in Fine Arts from the Spanish Ministry of Culture, and is awarded an honorary doctorate in chemistry by the University of Barcelona.

2008 elBulli is voted 'Best Restaurant in the World' for the third consecutive year.

2009 elBulli is voted 'Best Restaurant in the World' for the fifth time.

2010 In January, Ferran announces that the restaurant will be closing after the 2011 season. elBulli will open again in 2014 having evolved into the elBullifoundation, a culinary think tank and research centre.

2011 July 29th sees elBulli close its doors as a restaurant for the last time. For the final service, the team prepares a 49-course feast comprising the greatest dishes from Ferran's time as head chef.

Taking the rake for a walk

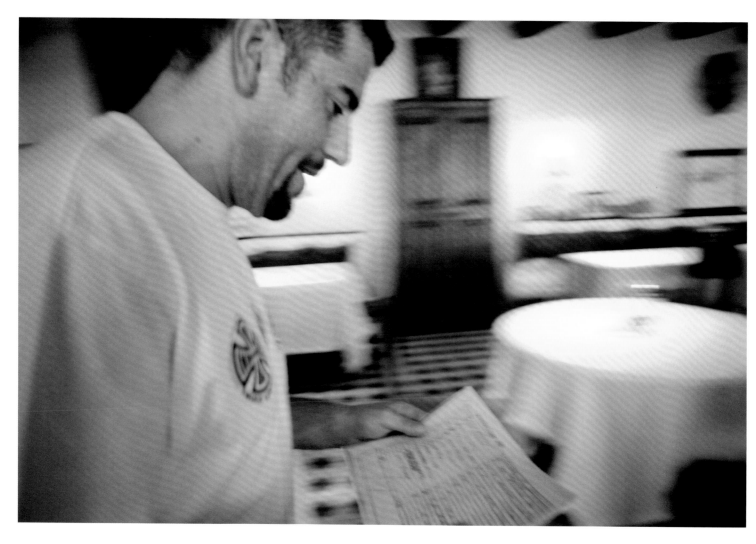

Last-minute changes

Lluís Biosca notes any amendments to the sheets for the final allocation of tables. Bad weather might mean that the terrace can't be used, or there might be a cancellation at short notice.

17:35

Two hours before service begins: the dining rooms are ready

The dining rooms have been like this for many years. The first time it was decided to change them there wasn't enough money, and the second time there were problems with the laws governing the nature reserve. But the way they look now is an essential part of the restaurant's heritage. One of the rooms is almost exactly as it was when elBulli first opened, and the second was refurbished in 1982.

The *mise en place* doesn't stop

Fresh beetroot is juiced and later the juice will be transformed into different textures such as a jelly or a crisp.

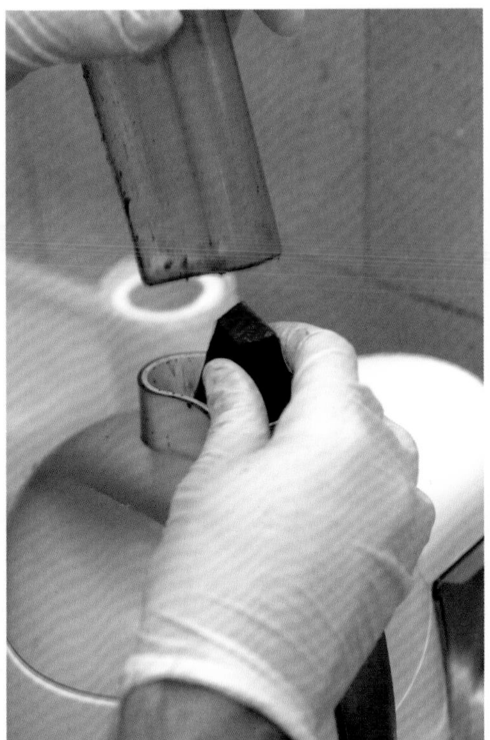

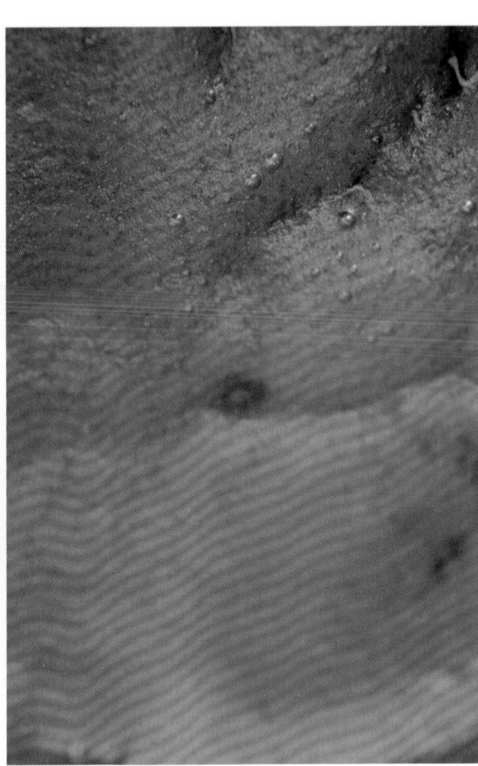

17:40

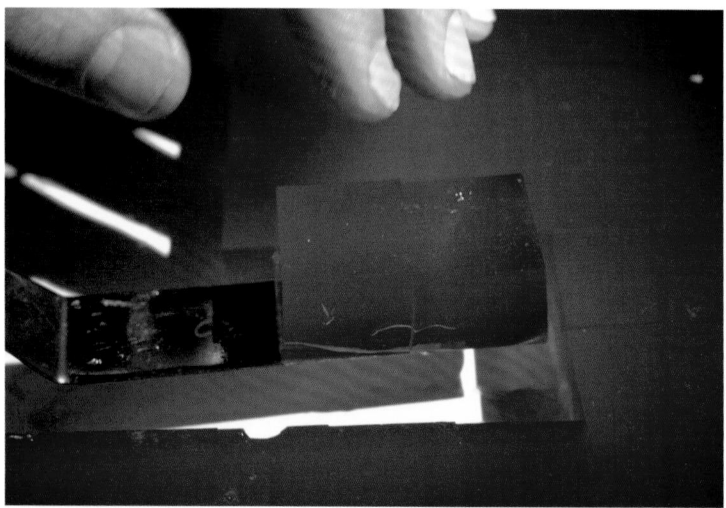

The hibiscus infusion for *Hibiscus paper with blackcurrant and eucalyptus* is dehydrated on a glass tray, and then carefully lifted off as a sheet of edible paper.

Beakers for the Pacojet, a machine used to make sorbets and frozen powders, are filled with powdered green pine cone infusion, and mangosteens are segmented in preparation for service.

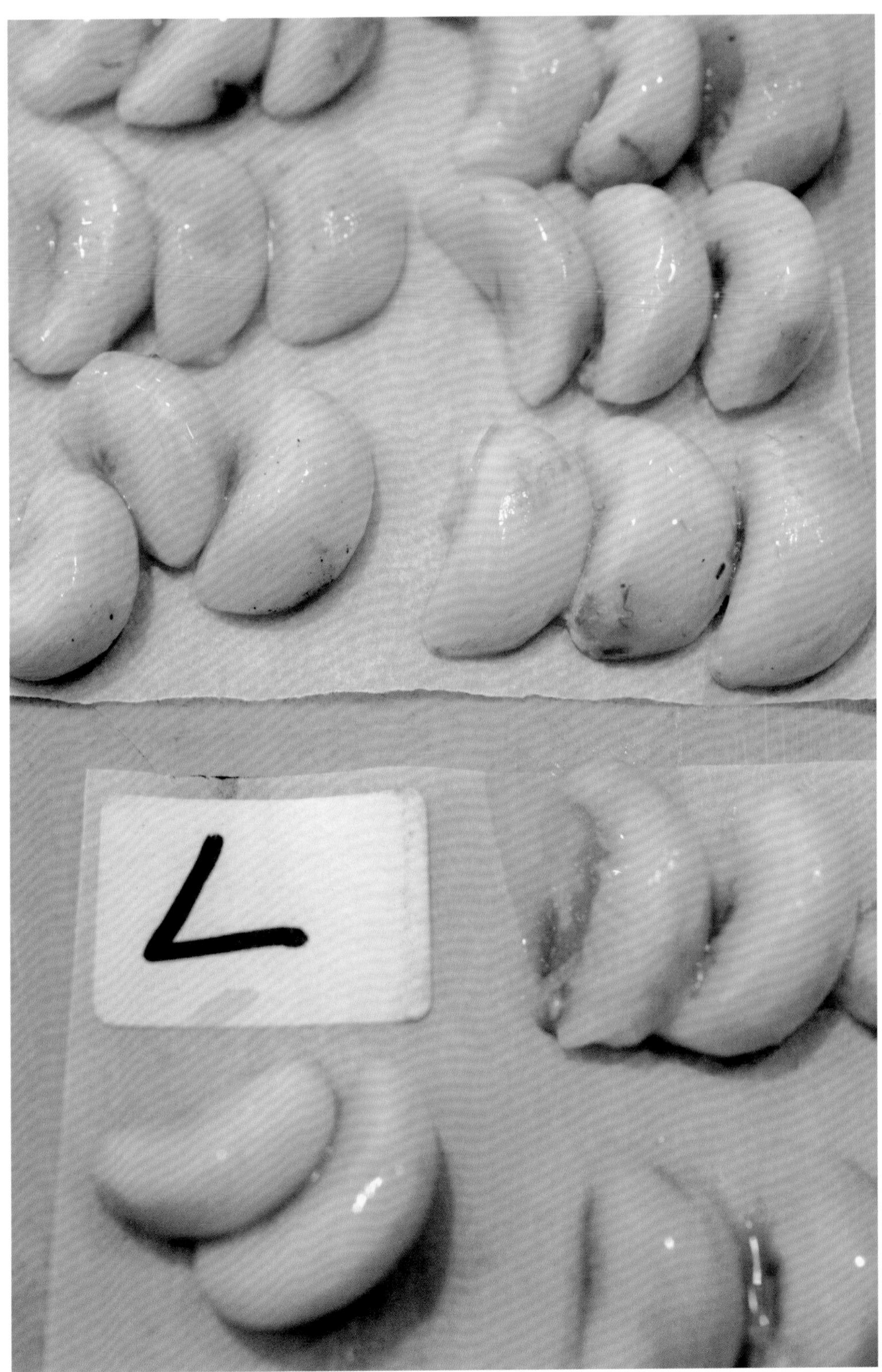

Pistachios are coated in their own praline paste and submerged in liquid nitrogen to create *Pistachios garrapi-nitro*. The name refers to the process of candying (*garrapiñar*) used for products such as sugared almonds, but at elBulli the crunchy exterior is created by rapidly freezing a layer of praline around the nuts with the aid of nitrogen.

Soya spaghettini are produced using a syringe. An ice cube is applied to the tip of the syringe to help the gelatine set as soon as the liquid comes out.

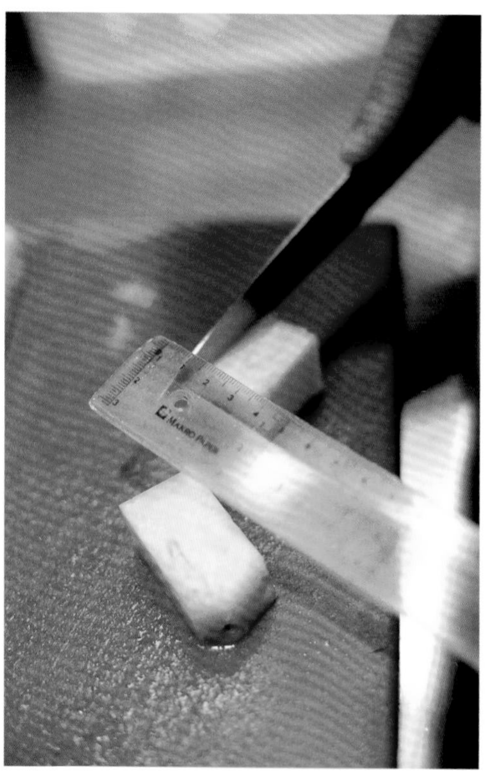

The chefs measure the pineapple batons for *Pineapple/fennel*, pick leaves of *ficoïde glaciale* (ice plant), make sugar film paper and prepare flowering cucumbers, artichokes and kumquats.

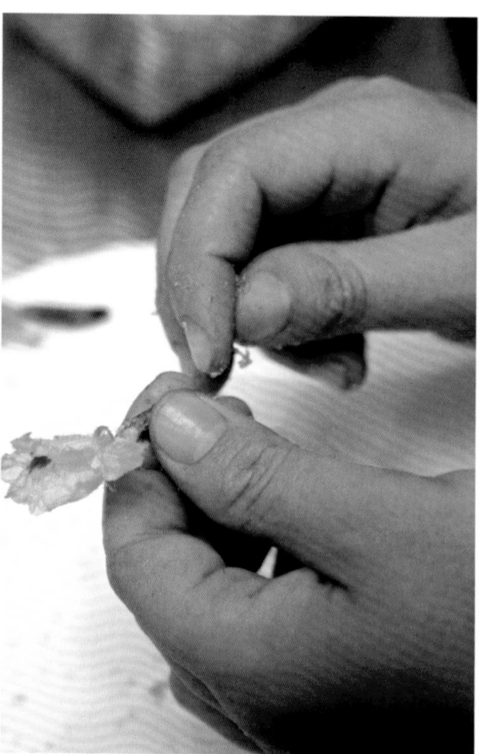

The head chefs' most important job

Once a recipe has been developed, if the execution is not perfect the dish will not turn out as expected, even when the very best ingredients available have been used. All the effort that has gone into making the dish will have been for nothing. The head chefs check the seasoning, the consistency of a sauce or a soup, the quality of an ingredient, the thickness of a slice, the size of a portion and how skilfully a technique has been applied.

Once service begins it is almost impossible to rectify mistakes.

Eduard Xatruch

CENTRO HOTELERO ALBERTO
Pablo

As well as the conscientious preparation of the numerous ingredients for all the dishes to be served that evening, during the early hours of the afternoon *mise en place* alternates with preparing food for the staff.

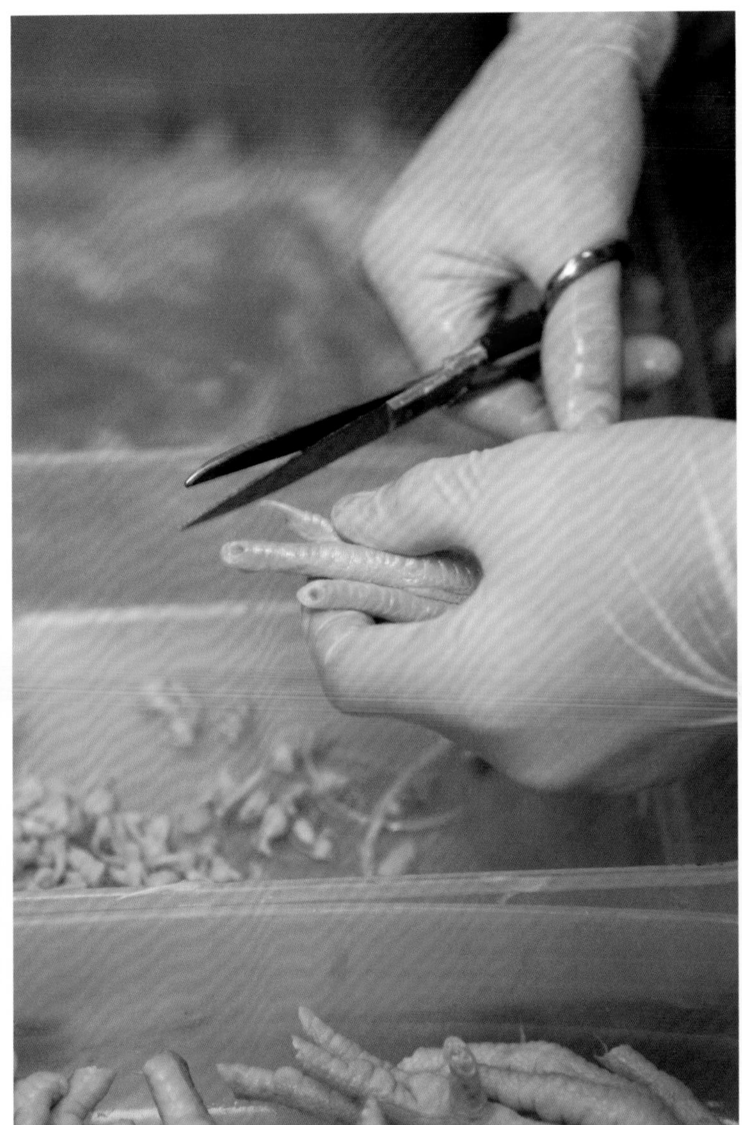

The staff family meal

Staff food is very important at elBulli. If the staff are not looked after, they cannot look after the guests. The menus for the staff meals are planned in detail at the start of the season. Every day the meal is prepared with care and attention by one of the chefs.

Who says elBulli doesn't serve traditional food?

A typical menu for the staff family meal.

Monday
Endives with dried fruit and nut vinaigrette
Pork cheek casserole

Tuesday
Macaroni carbonara
Roast artichokes with romesco sauce

Wednesday
Cream of courgettes with croutons
Curried chicken leg with apple

Thursday
Cauliflower au gratin
Pork escalopes with tomato salad

Friday
Green salad
Roast beef with mashed potatoes

Saturday
Potatoes with salsa verde and poached eggs
Grilled sardines

Sunday
Tomato and basil soup
Rabbit pilaff

17:55

After spending twelve hours a day together, the elBulli team becomes your family

18:20

—

A ten-minute break

Time for a coffee, but little else. It is not long until the show begins.

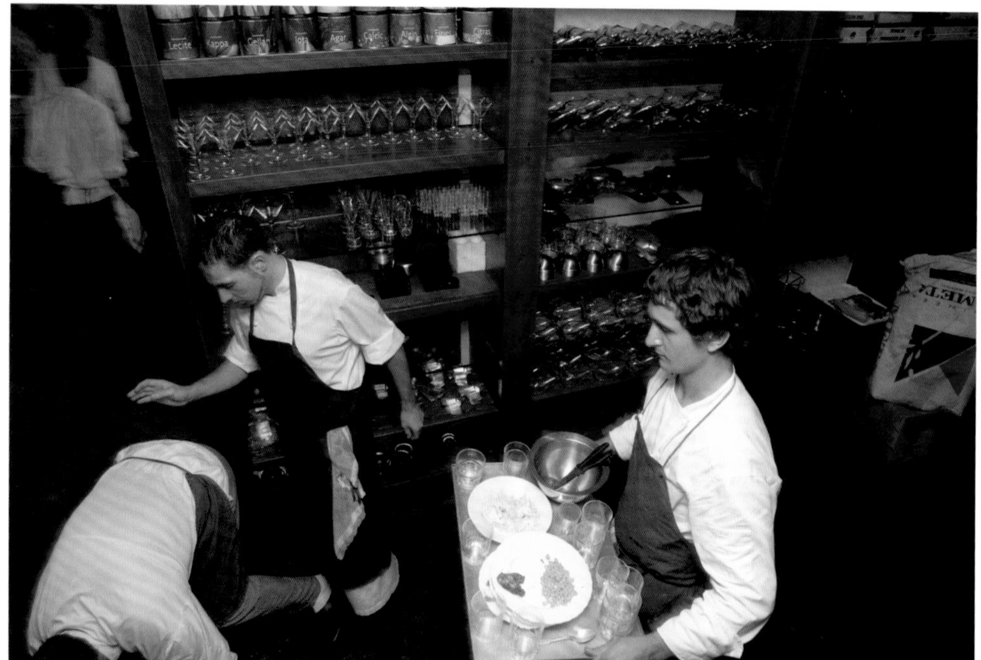

Cambio de tercio

This Spanish bullfighting expression, which literally means 'change of stage', refers to the moments of transition between the main stages of the fight, when the tension and anticipation of the next stage are palpable. There is a similar feeling when the kitchen is ready and the chefs change their aprons in preparation for service.

The plates are put out and the *mise en place* is moved to the small kitchen. Only the last-minute finishing touches will be done in the large kitchen.

The story of an order sheet

The journey made by an order sheet before, during and after service is the thread that runs throughout the day at elBulli. The order sheet is the guide to the menu for each table, the specifications for all the dishes which will be served to particular customers.

The story of an order sheet for any given day begins the night before, after service, when a check is made that all the ingredients are in stock. The following day's menu is then decided from the weekly menu Ferran has already created.

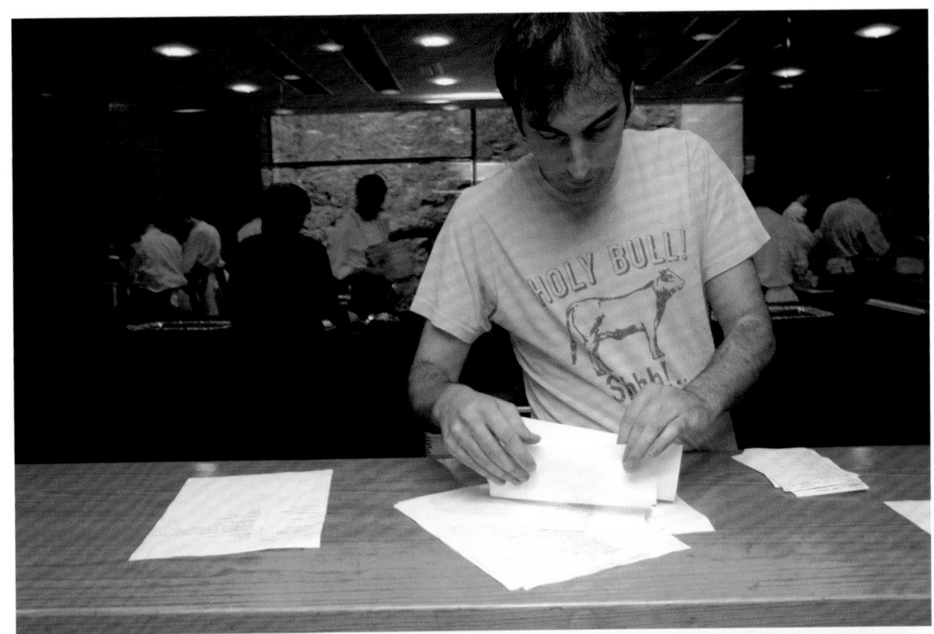
HOLY BULL!

HOLY BULL!

HOLY

Depending upon who is expected, Ferran makes a note of anything he needs to bear in mind to prepare the order sheets for the following day. A shopping list is made of any ingredients that are needed.

The next day, at 13:05, the head chefs have the menu finalized. At 15:30 the order sheets are collected and the definitive menus are prepared on the computer.

At 18:50 the head chefs go over the order sheets for the last time. Twenty minutes later they are printed out and a copy is given to each of the *chefs de partie* and the dining room managers.

At 19:45 the first guests arrive. From then until 23:30 the order sheets determine everything that happens in the kitchen and the dining room.

At the end of the meal, each guest receives a copy of their menu, and at 00:30 examples of the day's menu are filed for the kitchen's records.

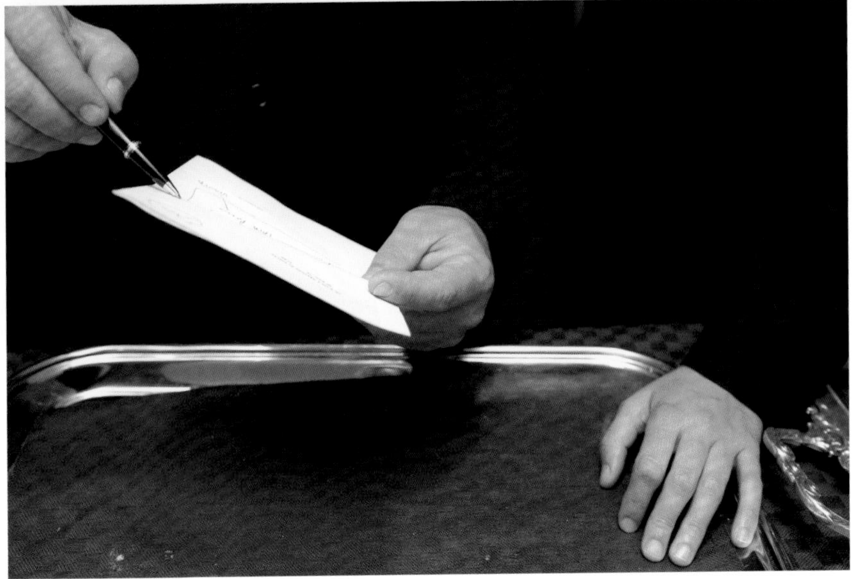

A final check of the order sheets

This is the last chance to check everything, right down to the tiniest specifications on the order sheets, or what has been prepared during the *mise en place*. There is no time for queries or doubts during service, and identifying any little problem at this point means peace of mind in the hours to come.

Creative methods II

ASSOCIATION

This straightforward creative method was one of the first to be used at elBulli. It consists of making lists or tables of ingredients, cooking methods, sauces and accompaniments as an aid to the chef who is trying to think of new ways of cooking an existing ingredient, or new ways of putting ingredients together. The lists of association are built up over time, and those at elBulli are the product of many years of creating dishes. They can provide a starting point to which chefs will add their own imagination and knowledge. The tables can generate limitless combinations of flavours, ingredients and techniques, and the chefs must use their common sense and mental palate to choose which paths to follow.

One of the earliest dishes to be created at elBulli using association was *Carpaccio of confit cep with a salad of potatoes, black truffle and lamb's lettuce with rabbit kidneys*. The starting point was a desire to find a new way of preparing fresh cep (porcini) mushrooms, and preserving was chosen from the list of possible cooking methods. From the list of procedures, carpaccio seemed like an interesting possibility. Next, the list of side dishes was consulted, and salad was chosen. The mental palate came into play when deciding on suitable ingredients for the salad, bearing in mind that they should combine successfully with a carpaccio. Lamb's lettuce, potato and black truffle were chosen, both for their flavours, which would enrich the carpaccio, and for their textures and colours. When looking at the list of cold sauces, the knowledge of what had already been selected governed the choice of black truffle juice and a pine nut vinaigrette. As a finishing touch, rabbit kidneys were chosen from the list of meat and offal products. In all of these decisions, the range of options presented by the tables represented a useful list of possibilities as an *aide-mémoire*, but it is always the chef's knowledge and experience that informs the selection.

INSPIRATION

Of all the creative methods, inspiration is the easiest to understand but the hardest to explain. It requires a reference from any field – art, fashion, music, gastronomy, architecture, nature – to form the starting point of a dish, which then emulates in some way the form or spirit of the original source of inspiration. The inspiration for the early dish *Raw and cooked beetroot salad with caviar*, for example, was the petals of a flower, and *Nest of green beans with lobster claws and veal sweetbreads* took its inspiration from a bird's nest, as the name suggests. Nature has continued to be an important source of inspiration throughout elBulli's development: much later, *Thaw* was inspired by a photograph of a landscape covered in snow with new grass shoots and flowers poking through. A frozen water dust that perfectly imitated snow was developed, and fresh herbs were added to resemble the new shoots.

Man-made creations can also provide inspiration. Over the years elBulli has paid homage to several artists, starting in 1987 with *Red mullet Gaudí*, in which the courgettes (zucchinis) and tomatoes on top of the fish resemble one of the Catalan master's mosaics. More recently the restaurant has devised *'Gran cru negra', tribute to Tàpies*, which is built around sesame paste formed into a large black cross, a motif characteristic of the works of the twentieth-century Catalan artist Antoni Tàpies.

ADAPTATION

In its most basic form, adaptation means taking a dish that already exists, which could be an icon of classic French cuisine or a traditional Spanish dish, and remaking it according to one's own tastes, style of cooking or aesthetic vision. Adaptation has become very popular in fine dining restaurants, particularly when it involves adapting traditional or local dishes by refining the presentation and upgrading the ingredients to create a new version of an old dish. elBulli's *Lobster gazpacho* is an example of this: the cold vegetable soup from Andalucía, which traditionally comes with chopped vegetables and croûtons to be added by the diner, was adapted so that the extra components became the main focus of the dish. The guest was presented with a dish of beautifully arranged herbs and vegetables, each prepared and cut in a different way, including tiny tomatoes stuffed with lobster. The soup itself was then poured at the table by the waiter, at which point the dish became recognizable as a gazpacho. In order to be fully effective as a creative method, adaptation depends on the guest's visually recognizing the original dish. It requires a degree of interpretation on the guest's part to appreciate fully the chef's intention. Adaptation need not be only of traditional or classic dishes, however. At elBulli many dishes have been adapted from the sweet to the savoury world, and vice versa, as in the case of the savoury *Aubergine (eggplant) soup with aubergine ravioli and balsamic caramel-flavoured yoghurt*, which also became *Aubergine (eggplant), yoghurt and honey ravioli* as a dessert the same year.

DECONSTRUCTION

As a creative method, deconstruction is an extension of adaptation, and it first came about in 1995. Both methods share the reference to an original dish as a starting point, and depend upon the guest's memory of the original dish for their success. With adaptation, although the dish undergoes a transformation in the hands of the creative chef, the final result retains some visible and recognizable features of the original dish. In the example above, the identity of the gazpacho, although not immediately apparent when the dish is first placed in front of the guest, becomes obvious when the soup is poured. The original concept of a gazpacho remains unaltered. In deconstruction, however, every part of the original dish, including its form, is modified, whether in appearance, form, texture or all of these. Although in its flavour the dish retains an essence of the original (indeed, the purpose of deconstruction can be to accentuate or point up the original flavour), in its appearance the new dish is unrecognizable. Deconstruction depends even more than adaptation on the guest's knowledge of the original dish, as without a reference point the dish is a construction based on nothing. In order to work, the game being played by the chef needs the participation of the guest.

Deconstruction also depends on the name given to a dish. An early example of deconstruction at elBulli is *Two ways of presenting chicken curry*, in which the elements of a chicken curry are transformed into curry ice cream, apple jelly, coconut soup and chicken juice, and the whole dish is presented in two different ways, both more reminiscent of a dessert than a main course. If the dish had been named *Curry ice cream with apple jelly and coconut soup* the gastronomic game would not have worked. As well as deconstructing a whole dish, one element of a classic dish, such as a hollandaise sauce, can be deconstructed. Or a single ingredient can be deconstructed into different textures, as in the many forms of the fruit in *Pineapple in textures*, although this is sometimes referred to as minimalism.

Two other methods are closely connected with deconstruction: reconstruction and 'inconstruction'. These refer to the creative methods used in the making of the dish, and the differences are not easily perceived in the finished product. Reconstruction takes a completed dish, whether traditional or brand new, looks at its elements and recombines them, without necessarily modifying them, to make a different dish. Inconstruction is based on ingredients rather than a dish: the original textures and forms of the ingredients are modified or transformed in some way, but the finished dish has no recognizable original dish reference point, as it does in deconstruction. Inconstruction was the method behind dishes such as *Carrot-LYO foam with hazelnut air-foam and Córdoba spices*.

MINIMALISM

Difficult to define within a culinary context, minimalism as a creative method at elBulli has come to mean the method by which maximum 'magic', or sensory appeal, can be created with minimum ingredients. Whether a dish is or is not minimalist is open to debate, as the concept is a subjective one. Here, the term is used to refer not to a modern, austere style of presentation, but to the practice of transforming as few ingredients as possible into an engaging and creative dish. It can be distinguished from simplicity by the fact that the products themselves, although few, may have been transformed by several processes. A recipe may be complex but still minimalist in its conception. Also, it does not necessarily follow that the dish is small – but it does mean that there will not be a large number of different ingredients on a plate.

Several types of minimalism feature in dishes at elBulli. First, there is a minimalism based on one bite, which expresses as much as possible within that single mouthful, for example the *Caramelized quail egg*. Most of the snacks at elBulli fall into this category, such as the *Spherical raviolo of coconut with traditional balsamic vinegar*. A larger dish can be minimalist too, however: *Frozen duck foie gras quinoa with consommé* is an example of a tapa that employs very few ingredients but presents them in very different textures and temperatures (an iced powder and hot liquid) to create the maximum sensory stimulation. 'Declension' is a grammatical term referring to the different suffixes that can be applied to a word stem to alter its meaning (for example show*s*, show*ing*, show*ed*). The term has been used at elBulli to describe a type of minimalism that focuses on a single ingredient presented in many different forms and textures. It can also be a category within deconstruction, in which the ingredient itself has been deconstructed. *Textured tomatoes* is a perfect illustration of culinary declension. It comprises tomato granita, essence, jelly and foam, as well as making use of a part of the tomato that is often overlooked but is in fact one of the most interesting: the seeds, complete with the jelly-like substance that holds them together, which are presented unadorned as part of the dish. A related variety of minimalism is what elBulli calls pluralism, in which foods from a single family, rather than a single ingredient, are presented together in a dish. This type of minimalism could also be described as 'monothematic', and might include dishes of grilled vegetables or seafood assortments, as in the *Mollusc platter* in which many crustaceans native to Spain are presented together, each one precisely cooked to accentuate its natural qualities.

CHANGES TO THE STRUCTURE OF THE MENU

Until fairly recently, menus in classic fine dining restaurants had remained unchanged for many years. They offered lists of starters (appetizers), main courses (entrées) and desserts from which guests chose what they wanted to eat. There would often be a cheese trolley from which the guest could make a selection, and petits fours might be served with coffee. The emergence of nouvelle cuisine in the 1970s brought with it the tasting menu, or *menu dégustation*, which allowed head chefs to showcase their talents and encapsulate their signature styles in a longer, fixed menu of smaller dishes from which the guest did not choose, and which was generally served to the whole table. Tasting menus now feature alongside the à la carte menu at most fine dining restaurants, and they reveal a lot about the culinary philosophy of a restaurant.

At elBulli the menu is even more emblematic of the creative team's food philosophy than it is at most restaurants. Unlike the practice in most other Michelin-starred restaurants, no menu is offered to guests to choose from, and in fact the guests do not receive a menu of any kind until after they have eaten, as a memento of their meal. The menu served to each guest is decided in advance and personalized by Ferran, taking into account the guest's food preferences. Rather than being imposed arbitrarily upon diners, this approach to the menu has evolved naturally: in 1997, sixty per cent of guests were already opting for the fixed tasting menu, and by 2001 this had risen to ninety-nine per cent. By the time guests have secured a reservation – and frequently they have to travel long distances, too – they generally want to try as many dishes as possible. The full culinary philosophy of elBulli can be conveyed only over the course of many dishes, a carefully considered sequence of cocktails, snacks, tapas-dishes, avant-desserts, desserts and morphings.

The structure of a menu should be planned in the same way that the narrative of a film or short story might be structured. The menu should set out a coherent culinary philosophy, and through it chefs should show a belief in their own convictions. Portion sizes, the order and timing of dishes and the preferences of the guest should all be considered, and the menu should have several themes running through it rather than repeating the same ones.

The tasting menu at elBulli has evolved over the years. In 1983 the meal began with an aperitif, which was followed by four savoury dishes, then the cheese trolley, the dessert trolley and finally petits fours. Between 1991 and 1995 the menu evolved further as tapas were introduced and the dessert trolley was replaced with plated desserts. Once desserts were

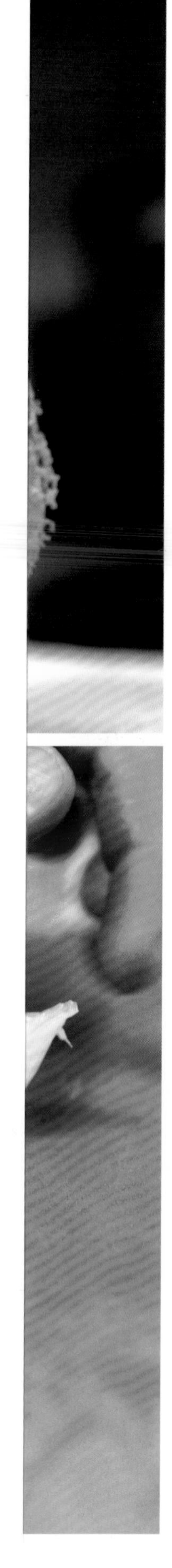

removed from the trolley, they could achieve the same level of creativity and drama as the savoury courses. The tasting menu in 1995 consisted of an aperitif, three tapas, five small main course dishes, the cheese trolley, two desserts and petits fours. In further departures from a conventional tasting menu format, avant-desserts were added in 1996, fresh and dry snacks in 1997 and cocktails made by the chefs were included from 1998. 'Follies' were invented in 1998 to be served at the end of the meal as a development of petits fours. Morphings were originally served before the desserts, but eventually replaced follies in 2003. As their name suggests, morphings are a fluid, ever-changing concept, intended as a light-hearted way to end the meal. The cheese trolley was removed in 1997, and tapas and dishes were amalgamated into tapas-dishes in 2003. Currently, a typical menu will include one cocktail, five dry snacks, four fresh snacks, fifteen tapas-dishes, one avant-dessert, two desserts and several morphings.

Although the evolution of the tasting menu has been gradual, comparing the menus from 1983 and 2008 reveals how radical the changes have been, and the extent to which elBulli has questioned traditional notions of 'eating out', and what should be served to a guest. Constructing the menu in this way allows the meal to be choreographed as a whole experience. As a creative method, an analysis of the menu's structure can help a chef to understand, refine and place in context the sensory experiences created by each dish.

THE SEARCH FOR NEW INGREDIENTS

Although it has always been an important part of dish development at elBulli, the search for new ingredients has only recently been elevated to the status of creative method. This is because if they are inspired by the ingredient's 'gene' (or unique set of characteristics), dishes that are developed using new ingredients will often break new ground in terms of concept or composition, and may require new techniques. Synergy of several creative methods will often be involved, and a dish inspired by a new ingredient could be just as innovative as a dish created using a new technique. In fact, in the last few years one of the chefs at elBulli has spent the whole year sourcing new products at markets and trade fairs, contacting suppliers and constantly investigating possibilities for new ingredients, including from non-culinary contexts. Charcoal as a food was one such interesting discovery – it first came to the attention of the creative team as a traditional cure for colds when mixed with milk. Experimentation in the creative workshop led to the discovery that it worked better when the burnt-out embers were blended with oil, and charcoal oil led to the creation of dishes such as *Charcoal-oil flavoured lambs' brains.*

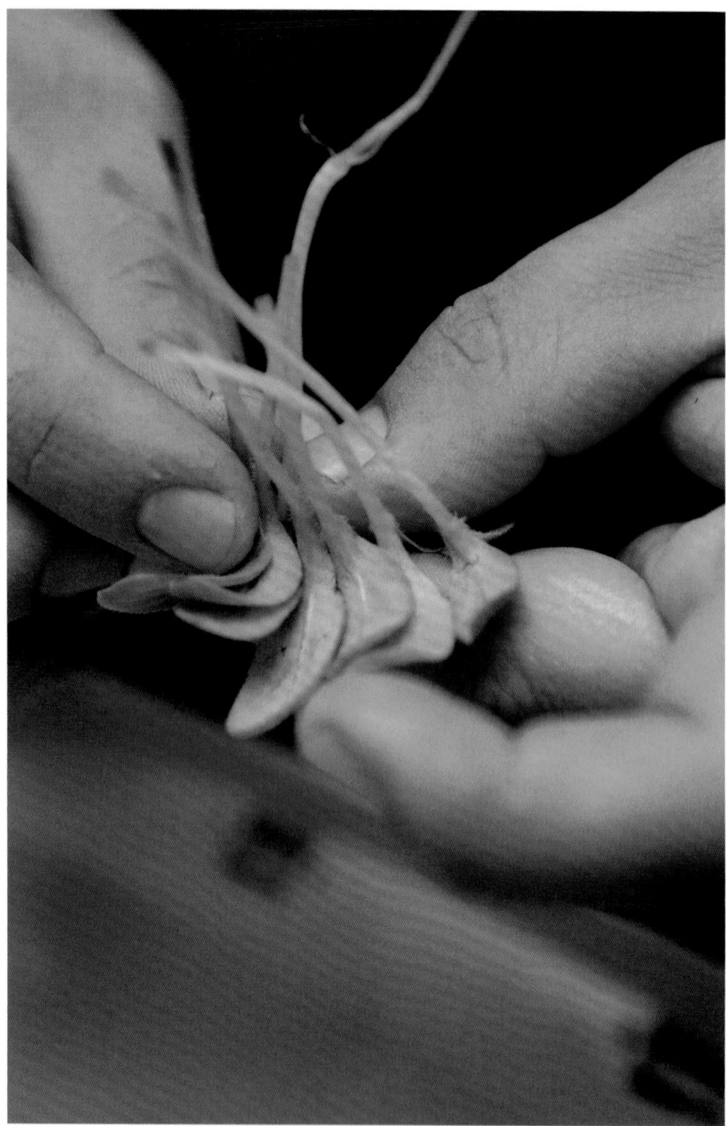

Checking every last little detail

Fresh herbs are an important ingredient at elBulli, and their distinctive flavours, textures and aromas are often incorporated into dishes. Although herbs can be an essential part of the presentation of a dish, they are not included for their appearance alone.

19:00

—

The car park is opened

Guests who arrive early park their cars and can stroll around the garden before dinner. It is planted with native plants and aromatic herbs in a style typical of the area. It was designed to feel pure, natural and part of the surrounding landscape.

The meeting between front of house and the kitchen

At the meeting between the waiters and Ferran, Oriol or Albert Raurich, issues relating to the guests for the evening are dealt with. Who is coming to dinner? Are there any regulars? Any allergies or dislikes are highlighted to the waiters, and anything to bear in mind from yesterday's service is also mentioned.

New dishes or changes to recipes are explained, and guests' reactions to a particular snack and their feedback on the new dishes are discussed. The way a dish is described to the guest is very important, and this is a crucial part of the meeting. If a guest is given a new dish concept, they need to be told how best to approach it in order to experience it at its best, in the same way that someone who has never eaten a fondue or sashimi before needs to have it explained to them. The guest's perception of the dish is strongly affected by how it is presented to them.

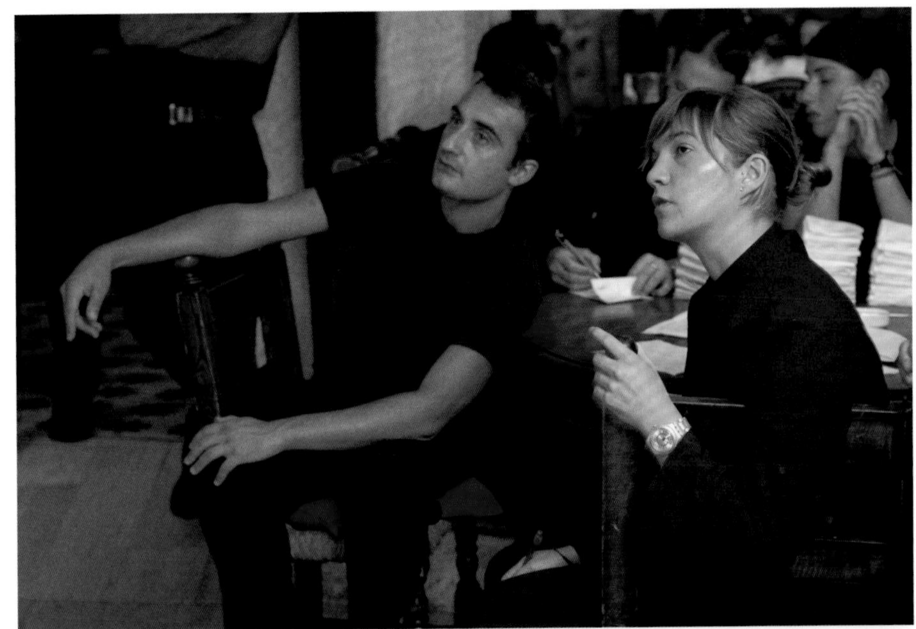

19:15

—

Fifteen minutes to go

The head waiters, dining room managers and chefs are ready and the final order sheets are in place. Everything is ready to begin.

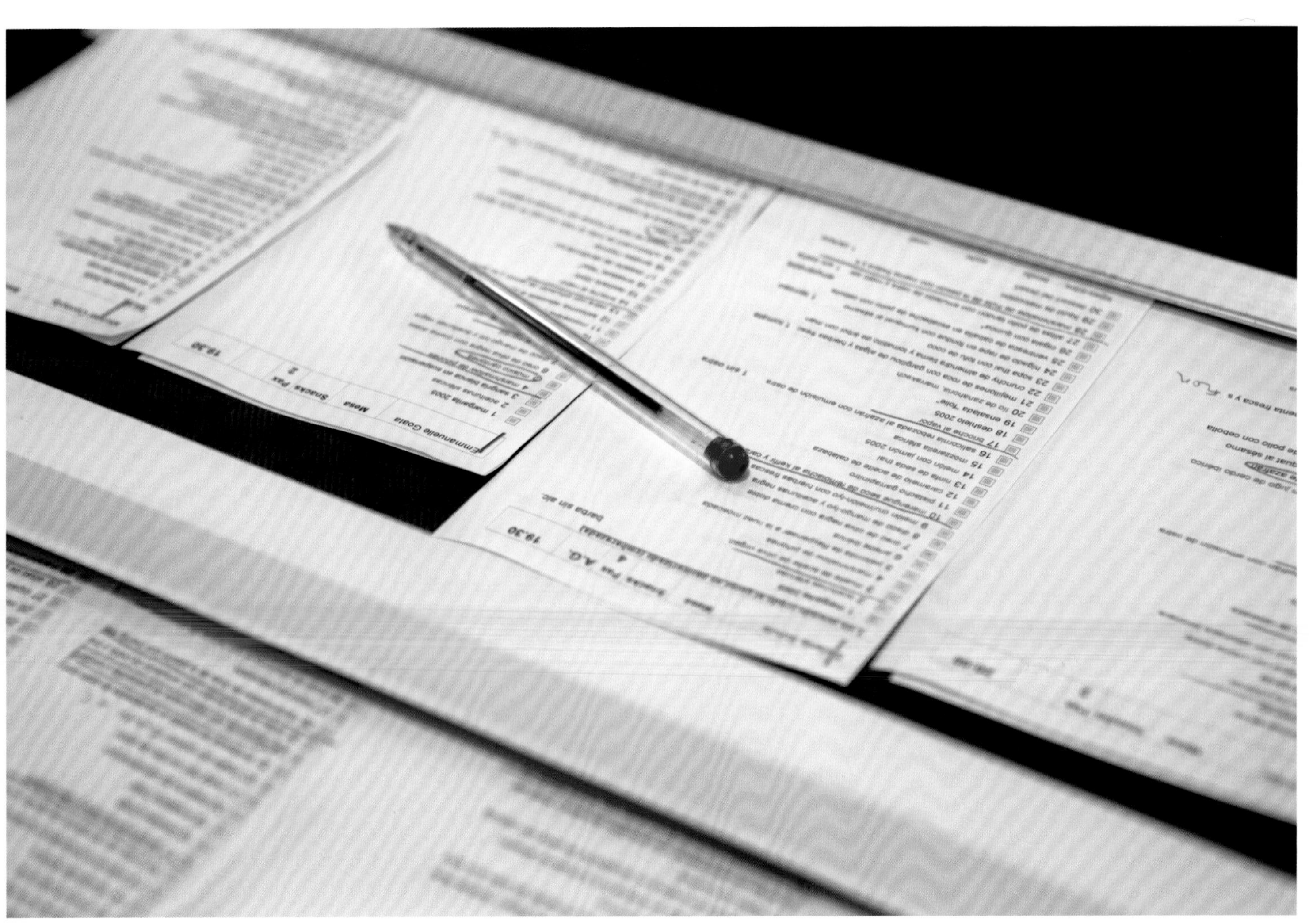

19:25

—

The final check

19:30

—

The doors are opened

19:35

—

On the way to elBulli, the excitement of not knowing what you will find is part of the experience.

19:45

—

The scene is set

The first guests arrive

Act one starts with a cocktail

On arriving, the guests are taken into the kitchen to be greeted by Ferran.

Once at their table, they are served a welcome cocktail created by the chefs followed by sherry, cava, champagne, or whatever they prefer to drink with the first snacks.

They choose their wine from the list. They might choose to start drinking it immediately or with the next snacks.

'You have to find a balance between what you want to do, what is possible and what the guest would like.'

A guest eating *Caipirinha-nitro*, a version of the classic Caipirinha cocktail, which has been transformed into a very fine-textured sorbet.

Served extremely cold, it dissolves instantly into liquid on the tongue, which will not detect any ice crystals.

The effect of the alcohol and fresh mint is simultaneously refreshing and soothing.

Chefs make cocktails

Originally, cocktails were made according to the classic rules. But since 1998 the chefs have made them using the same culinary techniques and concepts they use for the snacks, tapas-dishes and desserts. For example, the *Margarita* consists of a Margarita frappé with a salt air served in a cube of ice. The waiter grates Himalayan salt crystals over the top of the air, and the cocktail is eaten with a tapas spoon.

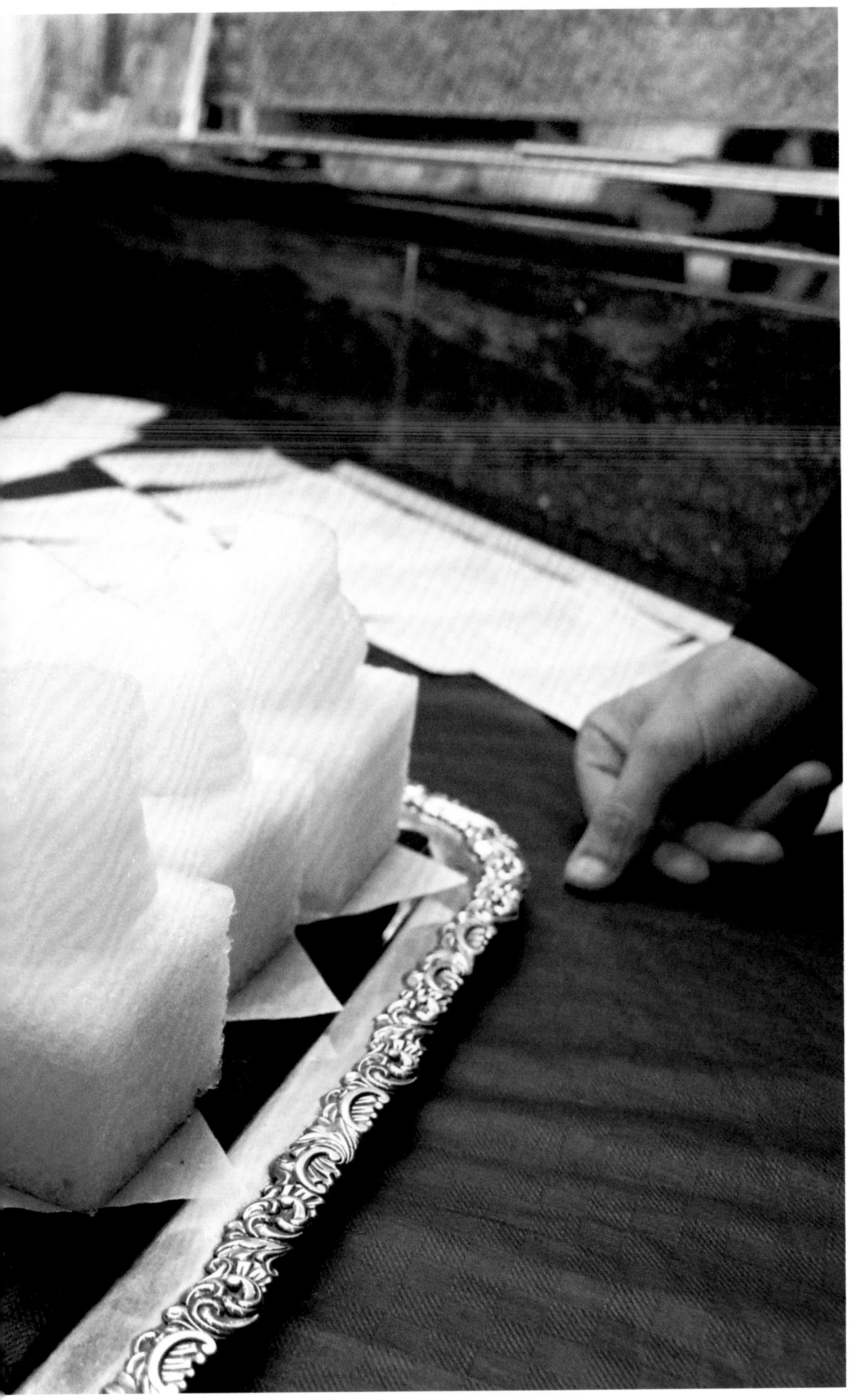

Margarita
(Margarita)

Serves 10

100% syrup

» 75 g (⅓ cup) water
» 75 g (⅓ cup) sugar

—

1. Mix the water and sugar and bring to the boil.
2. Refrigerate.

Margarita frappé

» 160 g (⅔ cup) lemon juice
» 150 g (⅔ cup) water
» 100 g (⅓ cup) 100% syrup, previously prepared
» 120 g (½ cup) tequila
» 30 g (2 tbsp) Cointreau

—

1. Mix all the ingredients together and place in a container to a depth of 2 cm (¾ in).
2. Freeze the mixture.
3. Once frozen, crush with a spoon until a granular, frappé-like texture is achieved.

Ice moulds

» 2 kg (4½ lb) ice cubes
» 1 x 8 cm (3½ in) square perspex mould, 6 cm (2½ in) deep
» 1 x 5 cm (2 in) cylinder, 5 cm (2 in) long

—

1. Crush the ice and press it into the perspex mould to a height of 4 cm (1¾ in).
2. Place the cylinder in the middle and fill in the space around it with crushed ice.
3. Remove the cylinder.
4. Repeat this process to make 10 ice moulds with a cylindrical gap in the middle.

—

Alternatively, the ice mould can be made by simply filling a silicone mould with water and letting it freeze.

Salt air mixture

» 2.5 kg (10½ cups) water
» 345 g (1¾ cups) salt
» 9 g (2 tsp) Lecite

—

Mix all the ingredients in a bowl and process with a hand-held blender.

EXTRAS

» 1 x 3 cm (1¼ in) Himalayan salt crystal
» Microplane grater

FINISHING AND PRESENTATION

1. Put 50 g (2 oz) Margarita frappé into the ice mould.
2. Work the hand-held mixer over the surface of the salt air mixture until it emulsifies and the air forms.
3. Leave the air to stabilize for one minute to achieve a more compact texture. Then, put 2 dessertspoons of salt air over the Margarita frappé.
4. The waiter should grate a little Himalayan crystal salt over the air in front of the diner with the Microplane grater.

—

This dish, like the *Margarita spray* and *Frozen Margarita* from 2003, is an adaptation of the classic Margarita cocktail.

—

Cutlery:
Tapas spoon, 14 cm (5½ in) long and 3 cm (1¼ in) wide at its widest point.

How to eat:
From bottom to top, taking frappé and air at the same time.

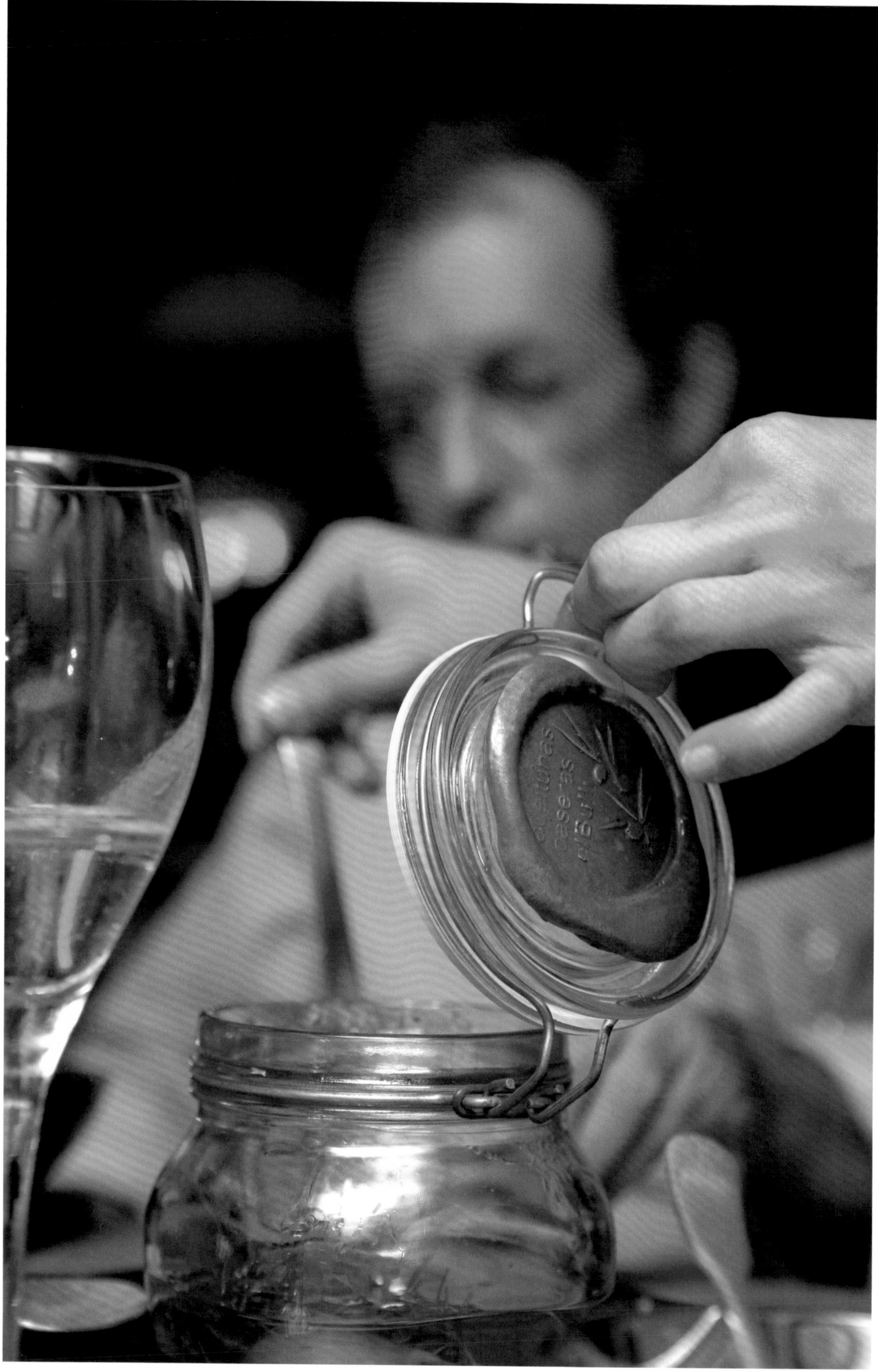
Caseras

The menu at elBulli

The menu has an uninterrupted flow, but it can be divided into four separate acts, each with its own character.

ACT ONE

To welcome guests, cocktails, and snacks are served, usually on the terrace, when the weather allows it.

- Margarita
- Spherical-I green olives
- Pine nut marshmallow
- 3Ds with ras-el-hanout and lemon basil shoots
- Cantonese *músico*
- Mango and black olive discs
- Five pepper melon-CRU/melon-LYO with fresh herbs and green almonds
- Pumpkin oil sweet
- Thai nymph
- Melon with ham
- Spherical-I mozzarella
- Samphire tempura with saffron and oyster cream
- Steamed brioche with rose-scented mozzarella

ACT TWO

This is the most substantial part of the menu and consists of the savoury tapas-dishes; in other words, the dishes that are eaten with cutlery.

- Thaw
- Carrot-LYO foam with hazelnut foam-air and Córdoba spices
- 'Folie' salad
- Rock mussels with seaweed and fresh herbs
- Baby snails in court bouillon with crab escabeche and amaranth with fennel
- Earthy
- Monkfish liver fondue with ponzu and white sesame-flavoured kumquat
- Belly of mackerel in a chicken escabeche with onions and vinegar caviar
- Langoustine with quinoa[3]
- Tandoori chicken wings with borage shoots, oyster cream and frothy *máto* cheese

ACT THREE

Guests now immerse themselves in the sweet world, beginning with the avant-desserts and going on to the desserts.

- Peach liquid
- Coulant/soufflé of granadilla with toffee and cardamom
- Chocolate air-LYO with crispy raspberry sorbet and eucalyptus water ice

ACT FOUR

The final act, during which morphings are served, often takes place back on the terrace, and has no time limit. It lasts as long as the after-dinner conversation, the coffee, liqueurs and cigars.

- Passion fruit tree
- Fruit-LYO in chocolate
- Yoghurt and raspberry *mochi*
- Pineapple/fennel

- Coffee and liqueurs

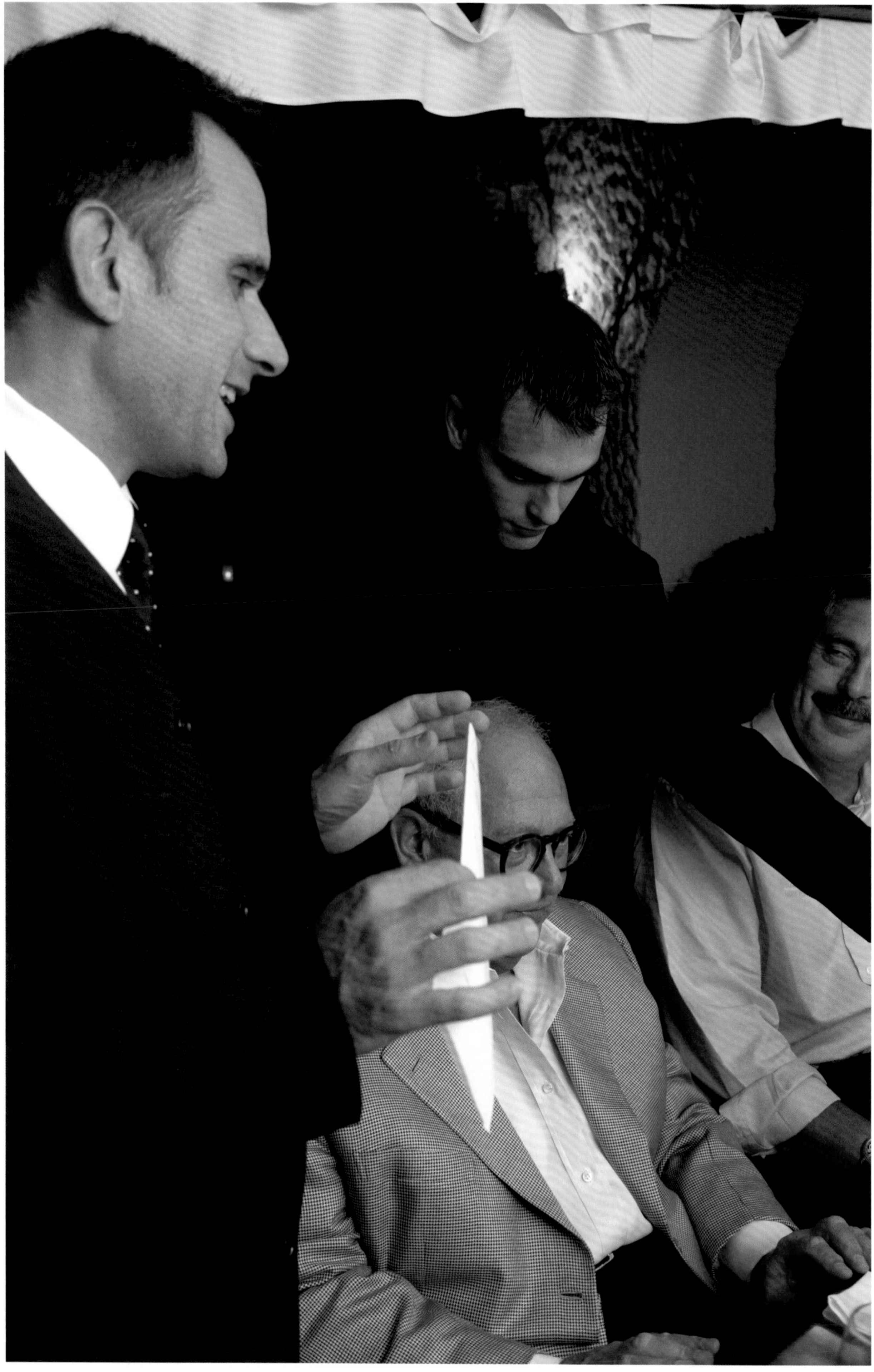

'Ferran has prepared a personalized menu for you'

This is how the dining room managers begin when they introduce the menu at each table. They then check that any information about allergies or foods guests do not like has been received. They also mention any unusual ingredients that may not be to everyone's taste so that guests can decide whether they will have the dish or swap it for another.

If guests are diabetic, or allergic to gluten, dairy products, nuts, seafood or any other ingredient, this may mean that they cannot eat up to twenty per cent of the dishes on the menu. For these guests an equally extensive menu is prepared so that they can enjoy elBulli as much as anyone else. But it is difficult for the kitchen if this information is not received in advance, so full dietary information is always requested beforehand.

Guests have not been given a menu to choose from since 2002.

Juli welcomes the guests

He has been greeting guests as they arrive at the restaurant for twenty-eight years, and he is at the heart of the elBulli experience.

'Don't talk about the restaurant, talk about your experience in the restaurant.'

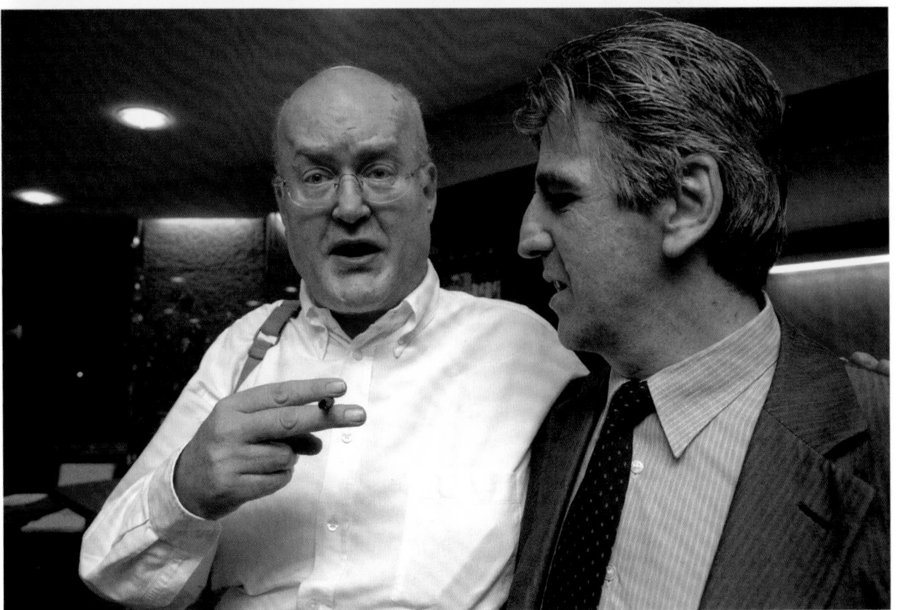

20:20

—

Act one will last for about forty-five minutes

Although the average meal will last for three to four hours, the timing of the thirty courses is swift and precise. A delay of two minutes per course would mean that dinner takes an hour longer to serve. But however demanding the rhythm of the spectacle may be, the waiters never lose sight of the needs of the guests.

'The menu is like a film with different sequences.'

Snacks ready to be served: *Malt flour air-baguette with caramelized cinnamon 'sweet'; Black olive Oreo cookie with double cream; Parmesan marshmallow.*

Aceitunas verdes sféricas-I
(Spherical-I green olives)

Serves 10

Algin solution

- 7.5 g (1½ tsp) Algin
- 1.5 kg (6⅓ cups) water

—

1. Mix the water and Algin with a hand-held blender until the mixture is lump-free.
2. Leave it to stand in the refrigerator for 48 hours until the air bubbles disappear and the Algin is completely rehydrated.

Green olive juice

- 500 g (1 lb 2 oz) green Verdial olives

—

1. Stone (pit) the olives.
2. Blend the olives in a liquidizer.
3. Strain the purée through a Superbag, pressing the mixture through.
4. Refrigerate the juice.

—

Verdial is a variety of green olive from southern Spain, often served as part of tapas.

Spherical-I green olive base

- 200 g (¾ cup) green olive juice, previously prepared
- 0.75 g Xantana
- 1.25 g Calcic

—

1. Add Calcic to the juice and leave for one minute to hydrate well.
2. Mix with a whisk and sprinkle the Xantana over the surface.
3. Mix with a hand-held blender at medium speed.
4. Refrigerate for 24 hours.

Aromatized olive oil

- 500 g (2 cups) extra virgin olive oil
- 4 cloves of garlic
- zest of 4 lemons
- zest of 4 oranges
- 4 sprigs of fresh thyme
- 4 sprigs of fresh rosemary
- 12 black peppercorns

—

1. Lightly crush the garlic cloves and fry them in 100 g (⅓ cup) of olive oil without allowing them to brown.
2. Add the remaining oil and wait for it to heat up before adding the rest of the ingredients. Allow to cool.
3. Store the oil in an airtight container in a cool, dry place.

Spherical-I green olives

- Spherical-1 green olive base, previously prepared
- Algin solution, previously prepared
- Aromatized olive oil, previously prepared

—

1. Fill a 5 ml measuring spoon with the spherical-1 green olive mixture.
2. Drop the contents of the spoon into the Algin solution to form spherical olives. Make two olives per person. Do not allow the olives to touch one another, as they may stick.
3. Leave the olives in the Algin mixture for 2½ minutes.
4. Remove the olives from the Algin solution using a slotted spoon and dip them in cold water to rinse them.
5. Carefully strain the olives and place them in the aromatized oil without letting them touch one another.
6. Refrigerate for 12 hours.

EXTRAS

- 2 glass olive jars

FINISHING AND PRESENTATION

1. Put one piece of lemon zest, one piece of orange zest, one sprig of thyme, one sprig of rosemary and 4 black peppercorns into each jar.
2. Divide the 20 spherical olives between the 2 jars.
3. Cover with the aromatized oil.
4. Serve each jar on a slate accompanied by one slotted spoon per jar and as many medicine spoons as there are guests.

—

Cutlery:
Medicine spoon.

How to eat:
In a single mouthful.

Marshmallow de piñones
(Pine nut marshmallows)

Serves 10

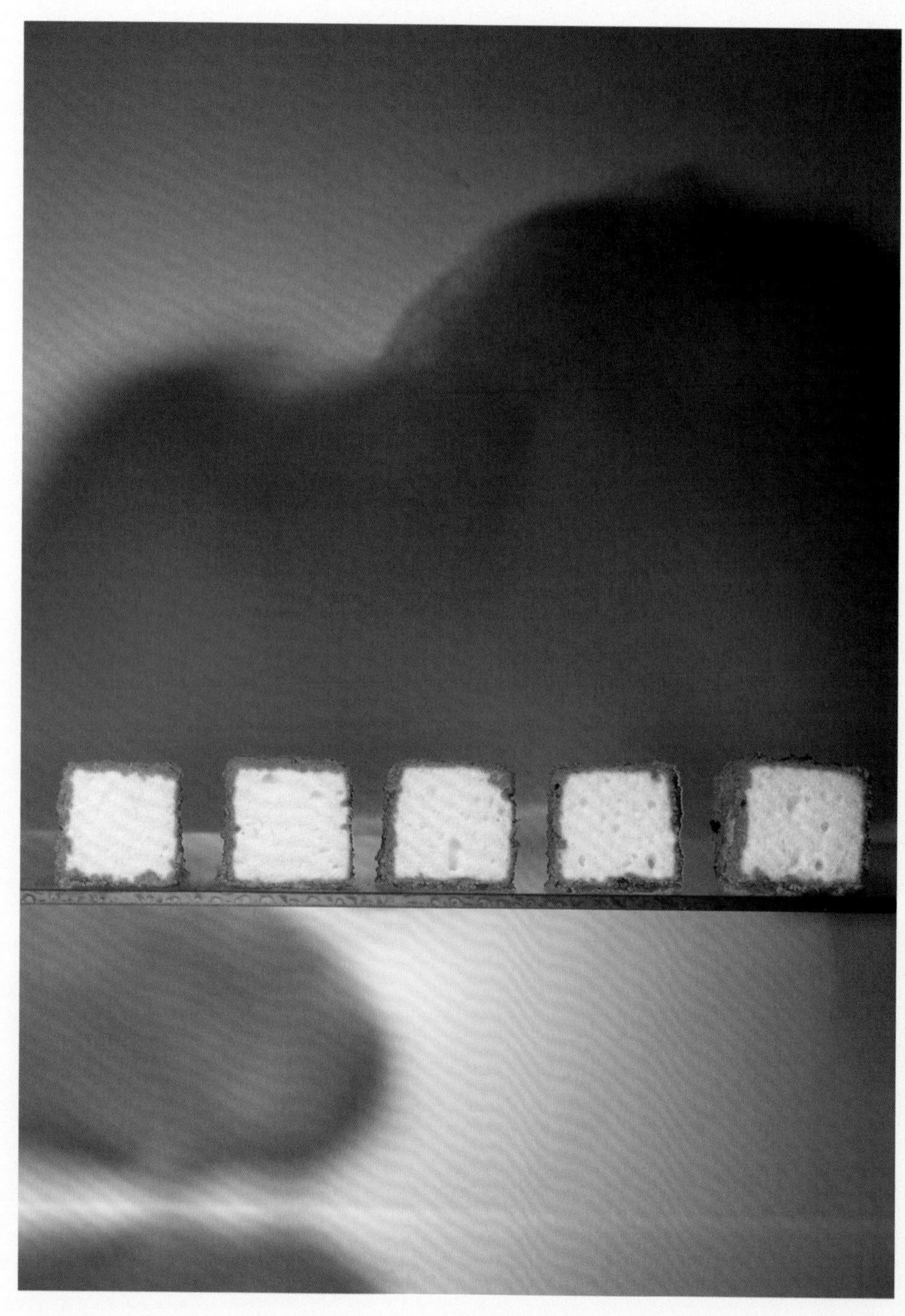

Pine nut marshmallows

- 500 g (2 cups) milk
- 9 x 2 g gelatine leaves, rehydrated in cold water
- 40 g (2⅔ tbsp) virgin pine nut oil
- 75 g (⅔ cup) toasted pine nut powder
- salt

—

1. Place 400 g (1¾ cups) milk in the freezer until it cools to 3°C/37°F.
2. Meanwhile, mix the gelatine with the remaining milk in a pan.
3. Dissolve the gelatine at 40°C/105°F and pour into a mixing bowl.
4. Start to whip the mixture. After 30 seconds, add all the cooled milk in one go.
5. Continue to whip for 3 minutes. Add the pine nut oil.
6. Keep whipping for another 30 seconds and spread out over a transparent sheet to a thickness of 2.5 cm (1 in).
7. Refrigerate for 2 hours.
8. Cut into 2.5 cm (1 in) cubes.
9. Refrigerate in an airtight container.
10. Immediately before serving, lightly salt the cubes and coat 4 sides with toasted pine nut powder, leaving 2 uncoated sides.

FINISHING AND PRESENTATION

1. Serve 2 pieces per person on a blue glass tray.

—

Cutlery:
None.

How to eat:
In a single mouthful.

3D al ras-el-hanout con germinado de albahaca limonera (3Ds with ras-el-hanout and lemon basil shoots)

Serves 10

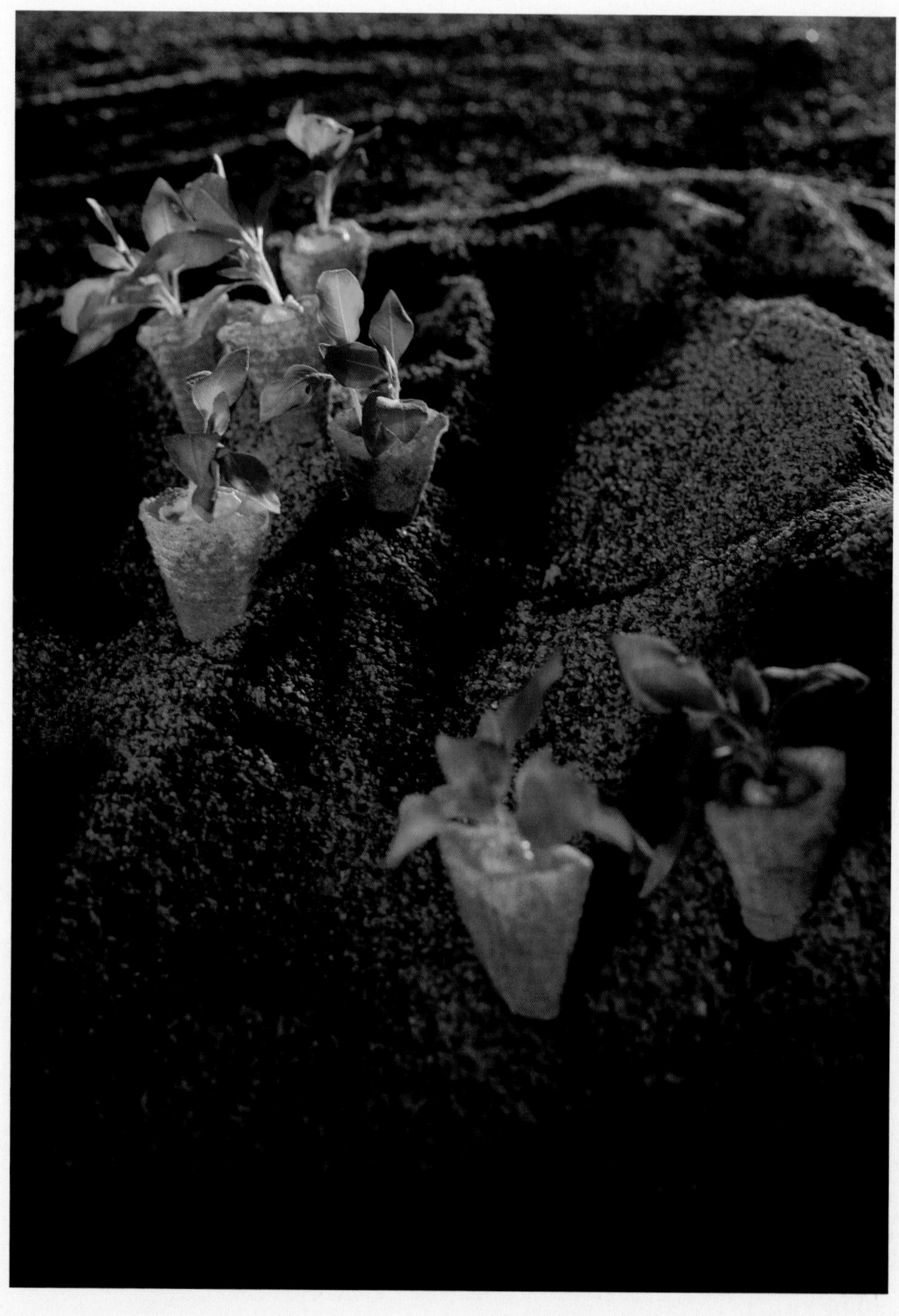

Fried 3Ds

- 20 raw 3Ds
- 500 g (2 cups) olive oil
- 10 g (2 tsp) Fatéma Hal's ras-el-hanout
- salt

—

1. Heat the oil to 180°C/350°F.
2. Deep-fry the 3Ds until they puff up and turn a light golden colour.
3. Take them out with a slotted spoon and drain the excess oil on a paper towel.
4. Season with salt and ras-el-hanout.

—

3Ds are a brand of cone-shaped potato crisp (chip).

Fry the 3Ds immediately before finishing and presentation, and only fill those with a well-defined opening.

Ras-el-hanout is a Moroccan spice blend that includes cumin, coriander, turmeric, ginger and cardamom, amongst others. Fatéma Hal is a Moroccan food writer.

EXTRAS

- 10 g (2 tsp) Fatéma Hal's ras-el-hanout

Filling

- 100 g (½ cup) thick double (heavy) cream
- 60 lemon basil shoots

—

1. Put the cream into a piping bag and keep refrigerated.
2. Trim the lemon basil shoots to a length of 3 cm (1¼ in).

FINISHING AND PRESENTATION

1. Fill each 3D with cream.
2. Place 3 lemon basil shoots in each cream-filled 3D.
3. Finish by sprinkling a little of the ras-el-hanout over the 3Ds. Take care not to stain the lemon basil shoots.

—

Cutlery:
None.

How to eat:
Eat each 3D separately and in a single mouthful.

—

elBulli's collaboration with snack manufacturer Lays has made the use of 3Ds possible.

Músico Cantonés
(Cantonese *músico*)

Serves 10

Honey confit walnuts

- » 20 x 2 cm (¾ in) walnut halves, shelled
- » 300 g (1⅓ cups) water
- » 225 g (1¼ cups) sugar
- » 450 g (2 cups) rosemary honey

—

1. Divide the water, honey and sugar equally between the 3 pans, so that each pan contains a third of the water, a third of the sugar and a third of the rosemary honey.
2. Place the walnuts into one of the pans and slowly bring to the boil, skimming off the froth. Remove the nuts and put them in next pan.
3. Repeat the same operation, place the nuts in the final pan, and repeat again.
4. Keep the walnuts covered with the cooking liquid in a container and refrigerate for 24 hours.

Honey confit green pistachios

- » 300 g (1⅓ cups) water
- » 225 g (1¼ cups) sugar
- » 450 g (2 cups) rosemary honey
- » 60 green pistachios, shelled

—

1. Divide the water, honey and sugar equally between the 3 pans, so that each pan contains a third of the water, a third of the sugar and a third of the rosemary honey.
2. Place the pistachios into one of the pans and slowly bring to the boil, skimming off the froth. Remove the nuts and put them in next pan.
3. Repeat the same operation, place the nuts in the final pan, and repeat again.
4. Keep the pistachios covered with the cooking liquid in a container and refrigerate for 24 hours.

Honey confit wild pine nuts

- » 300 g (1⅓ cups) water
- » 225 g (1¼ cups) sugar
- » 450 g (2 cups) rosemary honey
- » 80 wild pine nuts

—

1. Divide the water, honey and sugar equally between the 3 pans, so that each pan contains a third of the water, a third of the sugar and a third of the rosemary honey.
2. Place the pine nuts into one of the pans and slowly bring to the boil, skimming off the froth. Remove the nuts and put them in next pan.
3. Repeat the same operation, place the nuts in the final pan, and repeat again.
4. Keep the pine nuts covered with the cooking liquid in a container and refrigerate for 24 hours.

Spice powder

- » 12 g (¾ tbsp) Szechuan pepper
- » 12 g (¾ tbsp) star anise
- » 16 g (1 tbsp) coriander seeds

—

1. Grind the spices to a fine powder.
2. Store in an airtight container in a cool, dry place.

EXTRAS

- » 1 kg (4 cups) sunflower oil
- » salt

FINISHING AND PRESENTATION

1. Drain the 3 types of nut from the syrup and fry them separately in sunflower oil at 165°C/330°F until caramelized.
2. Remove from the oil and dust lightly with the salt and spices. Allow to cool on a tray lined with parchment paper so that the sugar crystallizes and a crunchy coating develops.
3. Arrange the nuts on a black slate.

—

Músico is a traditional Catalan snack of dried fruit and nuts served at the end of a meal. The name originates from the fact that travelling musicians would take a handful at the end of a meal to snack on after the performance.

—

Cutlery:
None.

How to eat:
Eat one at a time and alternate the nut variety.

Disco de mango y aceituna negra (Mango and black olive discs)

Serves 10

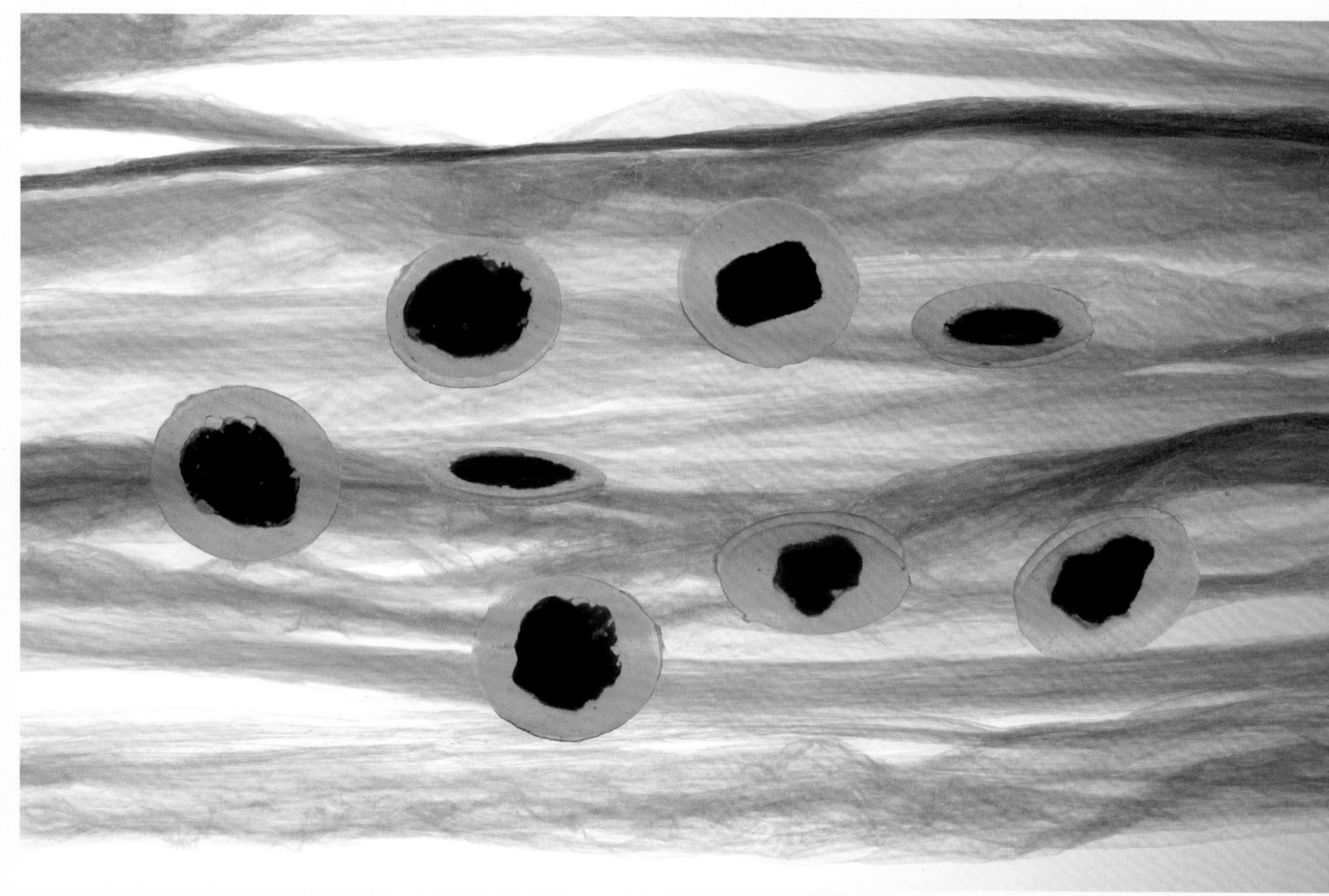

Mango crisp base

- » 150 g (⅔ cup) Garnier mango purée
- » 25 g (1⅔ tbsp) Isomalt
- » 5 g (1 tsp) glucose
- » 45 g (3 tbsp) icing (confectioner's) sugar

—

1. Blend the mango purée, Isomalt, glucose and half the icing (confectioner's) sugar in a Thermomix at 80°C/175°F for 5 minutes.

2. Strain the mixture and add the rest of the sugar, stirring with a whisk.

3. Store in an airtight container.

Black olive water and oil

- » 400 g (14 oz) black Aragón olives

—

1. Stone (pit) the olives and purée them in a liquidizer.

2. Squeeze the purée through a Superbag to obtain as much liquid as possible.

3. Pour the liquid into a measuring cup and store in a cool, dry place.

4. After 12 hours, the fat will have risen to the top. Separate the fat from the liquid.

5. Refrigerate both parts.

Dehydrated mango crisp discs

- » 150 g (⅔ cup) mango crisp base, previously prepared
- » 1 transparent sheet the same size as the dehydrator disc with 20 x 2.5 cm (1 in) diameter circles cut out
- » 1 Silpat the same diameter as the dehydrator disc

—

1. Place the transparent sheet over the Silpat and spread the mango crisp mixture evenly over the circular holes to a depth of 1 mm.

2. Dry out in a dehydrator for 48 hours at 55°C/130°F.

3. Once completely dried, store the mango discs in an airtight container in a cool, dry place.

Black olive emulsion

- » 50 g (¼ cup) black olive water, previously prepared
- » ½ x 2 g gelatine leaf, rehydrated in cold water
- » 0.5 g Sucro
- » 50 g (2 oz) black olive fat, previously prepared
- » 0.5 g Glice

—

1. Dissolve the gelatine with a third of the black olive water over a medium heat, then add the remaining water.

2. Add the Sucro and process with a hand-held blender.

3. At the same time, dissolve the Glice with the black olive fat at around 50°C/120°F.

4. Gradually add the fat to the black olive water while processing with the hand-held blender.

5. Refrigerate for 2 hours.

6. Once it has set, make 10 x 0.2 g portions.

FINISHING AND PRESENTATION

1. Fold 3 small sushi rolling mats, tucking the sides under to create a long platform.

2. Arrange the mats on a slate.

3. Place 10 mango discs on the mats and put 0.2 g of olive emulsion on top of each disc.

4. Place another mango disc on top of each one.

—

Cutlery:
None.

How to eat:
In a single mouthful.

Melón-CRU/melón-LYO a las cinco pimientas con hierbas frescas y almendras tiernas (Five pepper melon-CRU/ melon-LYO with fresh herbs and green almonds)

Serves 10

30% syrup base

- » 500 g (2 cups) water
- » 150 g (¾ cup) sugar

—

1. Combine the water and sugar and bring to the boil.
2. Refrigerate.

Freeze-dried cantaloupe melon cubes

- » ½ cantaloupe melon

—

1. Remove the seeds from the melon with a spoon.
2. Slice the melon lengthways into 6 segments.
3. Remove the skin from each segment with a small, sharp knife.
4. Cut the ends off each slice and cut 10 x 2 cm (¾ in) cubes.
5. Place the cubes in the freeze-dryer.
6. Once the freeze-drying process is complete, store in an airtight container in a cool, dry place.

Cantaloupe melon cubes

- » ½ very ripe cantaloupe melon

—

1. Follow instructions 1–4 above.
2. Refrigerate in an airtight container.

***Piel de sapo* melon pieces**

- » ½ *piel de sapo* (toad skin) melon

—

1. Follow instructions 1–3 for the freeze-dried cantaloupe melon cubes.
2. Remove the ends from each slice and cut 3 x 2 cm (¾ in) cubes.
3. Cut 3 x 2.5 cm (1 in) equilateral triangles.
4. Cut 4 diamonds with 2.5 cm (1 in) sides.
5. Refrigerate.

Mint and basil melon-CRU

- » 10 cantaloupe melon cubes, previously prepared
- » 10 *piel de sapo* melon pieces, previously prepared
- » 10 fresh mint leaves
- » 10 fresh basil leaves
- » 500 g (2 cups) 30% syrup, previously prepared

—

1. Place all the ingredients in a vacuum-pack bag.
2. Vacuum seal. The syrup will soak into the fruit and herbs.
3. Chill in the freezer but do not allow to freeze.

Peeled green almonds

- » 20 green almonds

—

Peel the green almonds and store them in an airtight container in the refrigerator.

Silver flowerpots with ice

- » 5 silver flowerpots
- » 2 kg (4½ lb) ice cubes

—

1. Crush the ice.
2. Fill the 5 flowerpots with crushed ice and store in the freezer.

EXTRAS

- » Five types of peppercorn in a pepper grinder

FINISHING AND PRESENTATION

1. Open the vacuum-sealed bag and drain the contents.
2. On each flowerpot arrange 2 pieces of cantaloupe melon-CRU, 2 pieces of *piel de sapo* melon-CRU, 2 fresh basil leaves, 2 fresh mint leaves and 4 green almonds.
3. Just before serving, grind the five pepper mixture over each piece of melon.
4. Place each flowerpot on a slate with 2 sets of silver tweezers.
5. Place 2 pieces of freeze-dried cantaloupe melon on each flowerpot and serve.

—

Cutlery:
Silver tweezers.

How to eat:
Eat a different cube with every mouthful.

Caramelo de aceite de calabaza (Pumpkin oil sweet)

Serves 10

Pumpkin oil sweet

- 200 g (1 cup) Isomalt
- 75 g (1/4 cup) Familie Engl pumpkin seed oil

—

1. Melt the Isomalt in a pan over a medium heat until the temperature reaches 120°C/250°F.
2. Place 4 g (1 tsp) of pumpkin oil in a 18 g (3/4 oz) hemispherical measuring spoon.
3. Dip the sharp edge of a 2.5 cm (1 in) metal pastry cutter in the melted Isomalt caramel and remove it slowly so that a fine film forms across the base of the cutter.
4. Quickly pour the pumpkin seed oil from the spoon through the still-hot film on the cutter. In this way, the oil will be coated in a thin layer of caramel.
5. With scissors, cut the sugar thread that forms on top of the sweet to a length of 4 cm (1½ in).
6. Repeat the operation to make 10 sweets.
7. Keep the pumpkin oil sweets in an airtight container in a cool, dry place.

—

It is important to maintain the Isomalt caramel at 120°C/250°F and not to let it take on any colour, in order to give the sweets a fine, even coating.

EXTRAS

- 1 5x5 cm (2x2 in) sheet of gold leaf
- salt

FINISHING AND PRESENTATION

1. Put a pinch of salt on each sweet and apply a piece of gold leaf with a fine brush.
2. Serve on a black slate with holes.

—

Cutlery:
None.

How to eat:
Pick up a sweet carefully with your fingers and place in your mouth. Without chewing it, let the sugar melt and the pumpkin seed oil flow out.

Ninfa Thai
(Thai nymph)

Serves 10

Cucumber batons

» 1 x 300 g (11 oz) cucumber

—

1. Peel and halve the cucumber lengthways.

2. Remove the seeds with a spoon.

3. Cut the cucumber into 10 batons each measuring 5 x 1 x 1 cm (2 x ½ x ½ in).

4. Refrigerate.

Thai filling

» 20 g (¾ oz) coriander (cilantro) shoots
» 4 g red curry paste
» 10 toasted peanuts, shelled
» 50 fresh coriander (cilantro) leaves
» 20 x 1 cm (½ in) fresh basil leaves
» 4 g Madras curry powder
» 6 g (1¼ tsp) toasted white sesame seeds
» 5 g (1 tsp) tamarind paste

—

1. Clean the coriander shoots and remove any seeds.

2. Lay out the coriander shoots on parchment paper and form 10 small 2 x 5 cm (2 in) rectangular piles.

3. Place a spot of red curry paste on each of the peanut halves and place 2 on top of each coriander shoot pile.

4. Arrange 5 coriander leaves and 2 basil leaves on top of each shoot pile.

5. Dust each pile with Madras curry powder and the toasted white sesame seeds.

6. Keep at room temperature so that they do not become moist.

7. Put the tamarind paste in a piping bag.

EXTRAS

» 50 g (¼ cup) sugar
» 10 g (2 tsp) coconut milk powder

FINISHING AND PRESENTATION

1. Put 8 g (1½ tsp) of sugar into a candyfloss (cotton candy) machine collect the floss to make 10 cm (4 in) strips.

2. Place the candyfloss strips on a tray lined with parchment paper.

3. Sprinkle the coconut milk powder over the candyfloss strips and place a coriander shoot salad on each one, leaving a 6 cm (2½ in) space.

4. Place a cucumber baton on top of each salad pile and pipe two spots of tamarind paste on each one.

5. Fold the candyfloss strips over each salad to cover the salad completely and cut with a dry knife to produce a candyfloss tube with the salad inside.

6. Remove any excess candyfloss from the edges.

7. Serve immediately on a black slate.

—

This snack is only served when the atmospheric humidity is below 65%.

—

Cutlery:
None.

How to eat:
Pick up the Thai nymph and eat it in 2 mouthfuls. It must be eaten quickly so that the candyfloss does not collapse.

Melón con jamón
(Melon with ham)

Serves 10

Jamón ibérico consommé

- 250 g (9 oz) *jamón ibérico* off-cuts
- 500 g (2 cups) water

—

1. Remove the excess fat from the ham and cut it into uneven pieces roughly 1 cm (½ in) in size.
2. Cover the ham with the water and simmer, skimming continuously to remove fat and scum for 15 minutes.
3. Strain through a Superbag. Do not allow the stock to become cloudy or remove any more fat.
4. Refrigerate.

Cantaloupe melon juice

- 500 g (1 lb 2 oz) cantaloupe melon

—

1. Peel the melon and remove the seeds.
2. Blend the melon flesh in a liquidizer and strain through a Superbag to produce melon juice.

EXTRAS

- Freshly ground black pepper

Jamón ibérico consommé with Xantana

- 250 g (1 cup) *jamón ibérico* consommé, previously prepared
- 0.6 g Xantana

—

1. Mix the Xantana with the ham consommé with a hand-held blender until no lumps remain.
2. Refrigerate.

Spherical melon caviar base

- 250 g (1 cup) melon juice, previously prepared
- 2 g Algin

—

1. While cold, mix the Algin with one third of the juice and process with a hand-held blender to dissolve the Algin completely.
2. Mix in the rest of the juice.
3. Strain and set aside at room temperature.

Calcic mixture

- 500 g (2 cups) water
- 2.5 g Calcic

—

Dissolve the Calcic in the water with a whisk and set aside.

FINISHING AND PRESENTATION

1. Fill four syringes with the melon juice.
2. Drip the melon juice into the water and Calcic solution one drop at a time, and leave to 'cook' for 3 minutes.
3. Strain, then wash the caviar in cold water. Drain.
4. Pour 25 g (2 tbsp) of cold ham consommé with Xantana into each champagne flute.
5. Put 10 g (⅓ oz) spherical melon caviar into each glass and stir to mix it through with the ham consommé.
6. Finish with a little freshly ground black pepper.

—

This dish, like *Melon with ham* from 1994, is a variation on the traditional dish of cured ham with melon.

—

Cutlery:
None.

How to eat:
Drink a little at a time.

Mozzarella sférica-I
(Spherical-I mozzarella)

Serves 10

Mozzarella water

- 4 balls fresh buffalo mozzarella in 500 g (1 lb 2 oz) tubs

—

Open the tubs without breaking the lids (they will be used later as a serving dish). Remove the mozzarella balls and reserve the water from the tubs.

Mozzarella base

- 220 g (7¾ oz) buffalo mozzarella
- 150 g (⅔ cup) mozzarella water, previously prepared
- 70 g (⅓ cup) 35% fat single (light) cream
- 20 g (1⅓ tbsp) double (heavy) cream
- 4 g salt

—

1. Blend the mozzarella with the mozzarella water in the liquidizer until a slightly grainy cream forms.

2. Bring the single cream to the boil and add the mozzarella cream and the double cream. Blend in the liquidizer for 10 seconds.

3. Add the salt, stir and refrigerate.

Algin solution

- 5 g (1 tsp) Algin
- 1 kg (4¼ cups) water

—

1. Blend the Algin with the water in the liquidizer until it is lump-free.

2. Pour into a container to a thickness of 6 cm (2⅓ in).

Spherical-I mozzarella

- 200 g (1 cup) mozzarella base, previously prepared
- 1 kg (4¼ cups) Algin solution, previously prepared

—

1. Using a 15 ml (1 tbsp) measuring spoon, drop the mozzarella base into the Algin solution to form spheres.

2. Leave the mozzarella spheres to 'cook' in the Algin solution for 12 minutes.

3. Remove the mozzarella spheres with a slotted spoon. Rinse them, then keep them submerged in the mozzarella water.

4. Refrigerate.

FINISHING AND PRESENTATION

1. Put the spherical mozzarella balls in the mozzarella water in the tubs they came in. Present the tubs on a stone with spoons. The waiter opens the tub and serves the mozzarella to the guests.

—

Cutlery:
Soup spoon.

How to eat:
In a single mouthful. Break it up inside your mouth to release the liquid inside.

—

A different version of this snack has been created by injecting cold fresh basil water jelly into the centre of the mozzarella spheres, and the *Spherical-I mozzarella* has sometimes been accompanied by a freeze-dried mozzarella ball filled with basil oil.

Salicornia en tempura al azafrán con crema de ostra (Samphire tempura with saffron and oyster cream)

Serves 10

Cleaned oysters

» 3 x 200 g (7 oz) Napoleon oysters

—

1. Open the oysters with an oyster knife. Reserve the liquor.
2. Cut through the muscle holding the oyster to the shell and remove the oyster.
3. De-beard the oysters with a pair of scissors.
4. Strain the liquor through a Superbag and add the oysters. Refrigerate.

—

Napoleon oysters are a variety of large oyster from Galicia.

Tempura batter

» 50 g (½ cup) glutinous rice flour
» 80 g (⅓ cup) water

—

Mix the ingredients with a hand-held blender and refrigerate.

Smoked streaky Spanish bacon fat

» 50 g (2 oz) smoked streaky Spanish bacon

—

1. Slice the bacon into 2 cm (¾ in) pieces and put them in a small pan over a low heat to sweat and release the fat. Do not let them fry.
2. Strain off the fat and set it aside.

Oyster cream with smoked streaky Spanish bacon fat

» 25 g (1 oz) cleaned oysters, previously prepared
» 30 g (2 tbsp) oyster liquor, previously prepared
» 8 g (1½ tsp) melted smoked streaky Spanish bacon fat, previously prepared

—

1. Blend the oysters with the oyster liquor.
2. Emulsify the resulting liquid with the melted bacon fat at room temperature.
3. Strain and refrigerate.

Toasted saffron powder

» 3 g saffron threads

—

1. Toast the saffron threads in a frying pan.
2. Break up the toasted saffron threads to make a coarse powder.

Samphire

» 120 g (4 oz) fresh samphire shoots, 4 cm (1¾ in) long

—

1. Select the best samphire and weigh out 10 x 10 g (¼ oz) servings.
2. Refrigerate.

—

Samphire is a plant that grows in saline soils close to the sea. The branches are fleshy and green, except towards the end of its cycle when the plant turns a reddish colour.

EXTRAS

» 1 kg (4 cups) olive oil

FINISHING AND PRESENTATION

1. Heat the oil to 175°C/345°F.
2. Dip the samphire briefly in the tempura batter and fry in the oil. Do not let the tempura shoots touch, or they will stick together.
3. Drain off any excess oil on paper towel.
4. Arrange them on 10 rectangular slates and lightly dust with toasted saffron powder.
5. Serve 6 g (1¼ tsp) of oyster cream per person in individual bowls.

—

Cutlery:
None.

How to eat:
Pick up the samphire tempura and dip in the oyster cream.

Brioche al vapor de mozzarella al perfume de rosas (Steamed brioche with rose-scented mozzarella)

Serves 10

Brioche dough

- 375 g (3 cups) plain (all-purpose) flour
- 100 g (⅓ cup) sourdough starter
- 67.5 g (⅓ cup) milk
- 32.5 g (2¼ tbsp) sugar
- 6.5 g (¼ oz) fresh pressed yeast
- 140 g (¾ cup) beaten eggs
- 115 g (1 x 4 oz stick) softened butter
- salt

—

1. Place the flour and sourdough starter in the bowl of the mixer.
2. Start the mixer at three quarters of the full speed with dough hook attached.
3. Dissolve the sugar and yeast in the milk and add to the mixer.
4. Wait for one minute before adding the beaten eggs.
5. Knead until the dough is smooth.
6. Add the salt and knead for one more minute.
7. Add the butter in chunks and knead until the brioche dough comes away from the sides of the mixing bowl and the butter is fully incorporated.
8. Keep refrigerated in a covered bowl for 12 hours.

—

A sourdough starter is a mixture of flour and water that is left to ferment and collect natural yeasts. It is used as a raising (rising) agent when making sourdough bread.

Fermented brioches

- 200 g (⅔ cup) brioche dough, previously prepared

—

1. Knead the brioche dough into a long strip.
2. Cut into 10 x 12 g (½ oz) pieces.
3. Shape into balls.
4. Place the 10 brioche balls on parchment paper.
5. Keep at room temperature for 30 minutes, then ferment at 32°C/90°F for 3 hours.
6. Cover well to prevent them from drying out and keep at room temperature until needed.

Crumbled mozzarella

- 2 x 150 g (5 oz) fresh buffalo mozzarella balls

—

1. Remove the outer layer of the mozzarella balls (set this aside for another dish).
2. Break up the creamy interior of the mozzarella by hand.
3. Refrigerate.

Rose air base

- 500 g (2 cups) milk
- 4 drops rose essence
- 2.5 g Lecite

—

Mix all 3 ingredients in a 25 cm (10 in) deep container.

FINISHING AND PRESENTATION

1. Work a hand-held blender over the surface of the rose air mixture until it emulsifies and the air forms.
2. Steam the balls of brioche dough for 16 minutes.
3. Once the brioches are cooked, cut open the top with scissors and put 7.5 g (⅓ oz) crumbled mozzarella into each one.
4. Heat the mozzarella brioches under the salamander grill (broiler) for 30 seconds. Remove and place a spoon of rose air on top of each brioche.
5. Serve on a black slate with satin paper.

—

Cutlery:
None.

How to eat:
Hold the brioche by the base and eat it in 2 mouthfuls.

Making snacks: filling *Steamed brioche with rose-scented mozzarella*; preparing *Mango and black olive discs*; and finishing *Popped Reypenaer* (next page).

Frozen soup with cucumber and rose tonic water is finished at the table by the waiter.

Walnut polvorones, Sea lettuce and white sesame waffle and *Garrapi-nitro banana-LYO with curried sesame.*

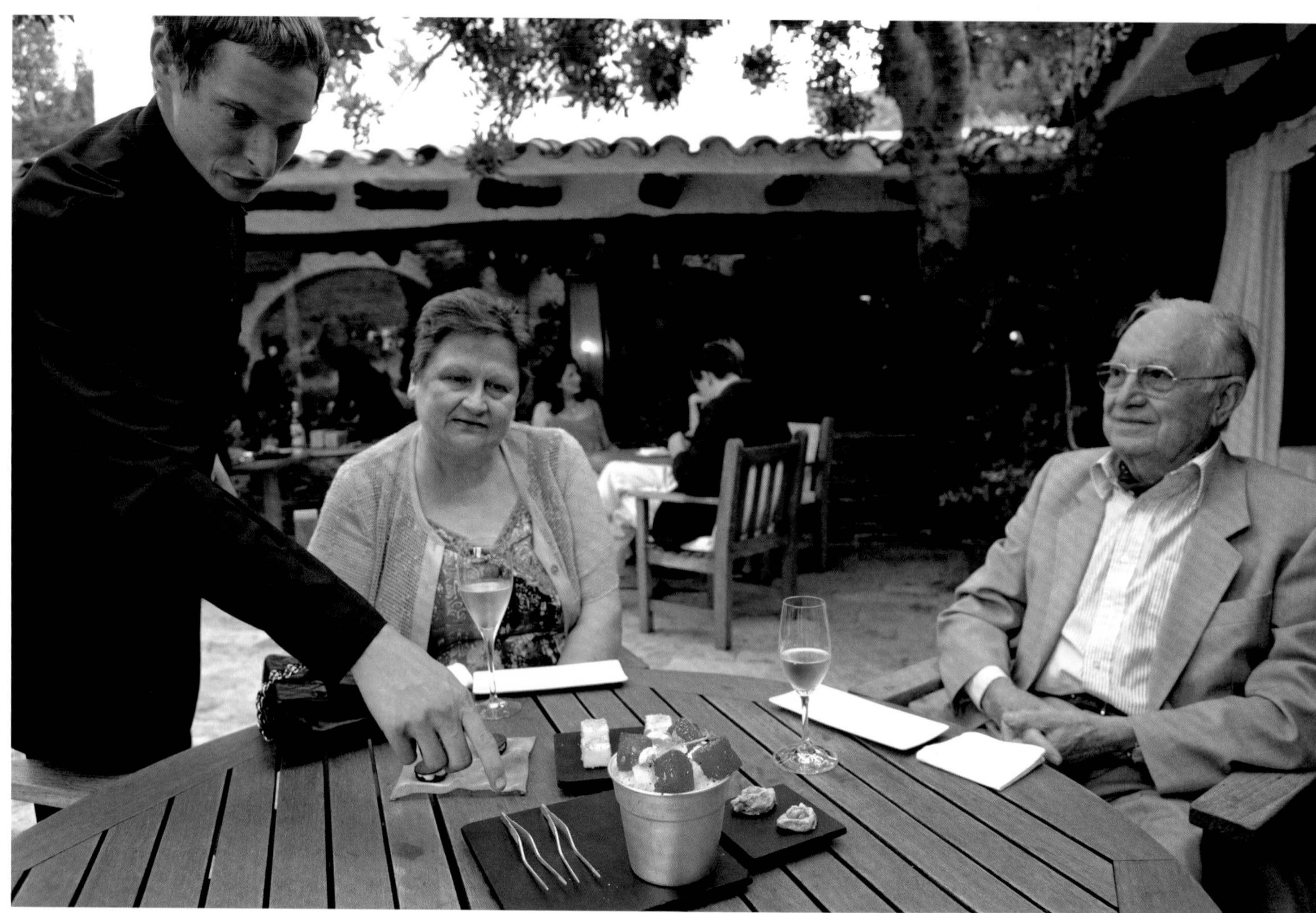

Menthol watermelon-CRU with the tweezers created for it. The waiter explains to the guests how they should be used.

A guest's path through the restaurant

Mango croquanter leaf with tagete flower.

Sight, hearing, touch, smell, taste…
an experience for all five senses.

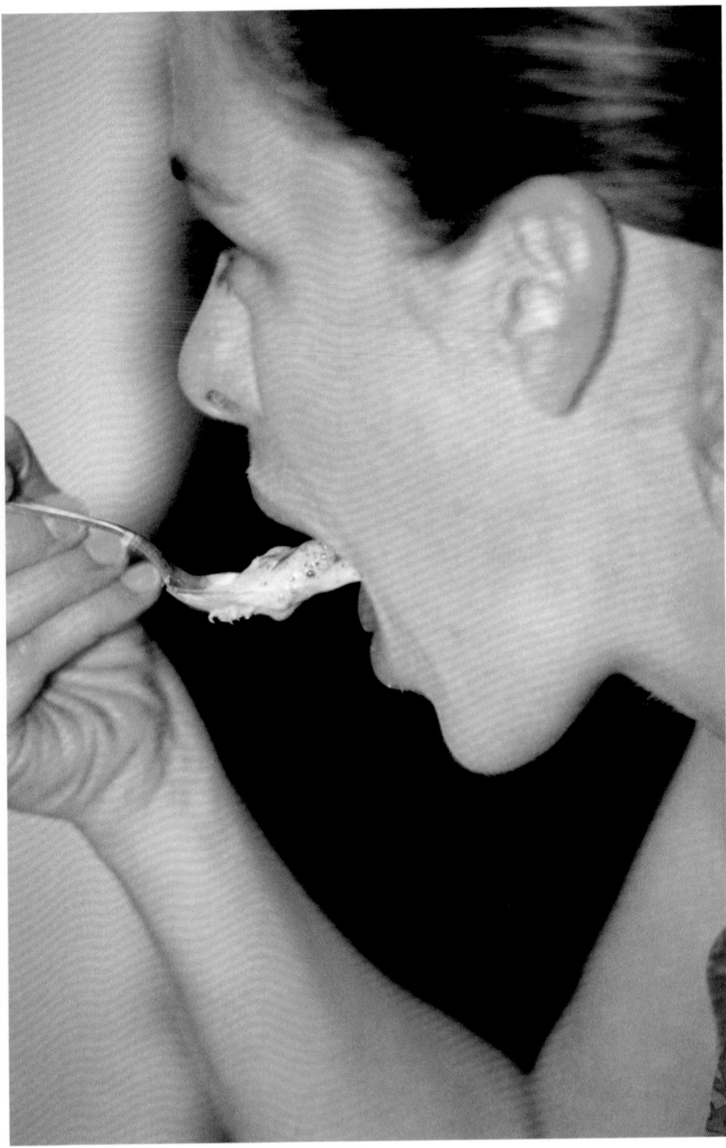

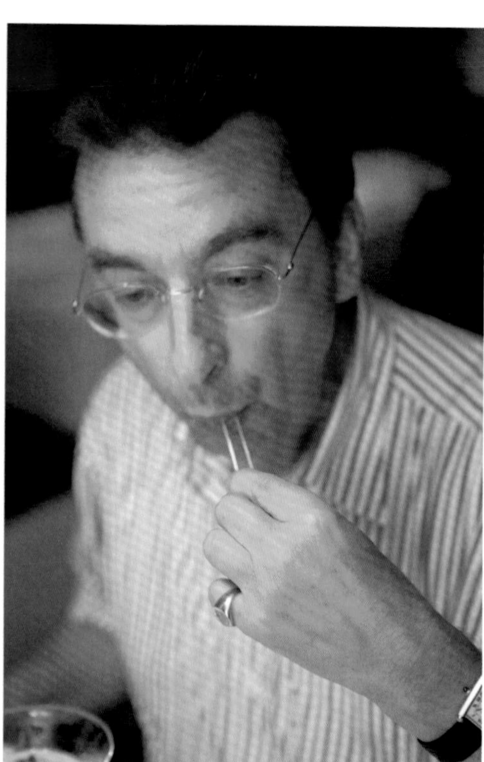

When dining, a guest can experience pleasure on four different levels. First, there is a purely physiological pleasure which comes from satisfying hunger; it is the most fundemental pleasure, but no less important for being so. Secondly, there is the pleasure perceived by the senses, which tells us, for example, if a dish is 'delicious', whether or not we like it, if it is too salty, if we have tasted better in other restaurants or at another time, and so on. Third is the pleasure connected with emotions: everything related to the occasion, such as the attention and generosity with which a guest is treated, the company around the table and the guest's own expectations. Most restaurants are able to satisfy these three types of pleasure.

However, there is another kind of stimulus which is directly related to reason. It is the intellectual pleasure derived from judging the meal according to parameters that are not strictly gastronomic, in which other elements come into play, such as sense of humour, irony, provocation, childhood memories, or – a very important point – the appreciation of the level of creativity of a gastronomic proposal. These are aspects which the guest does not expect to find in a restaurant, but in fact they form an integral part of the dish and of the menu. This is what is known at elBulli as 'the sixth sense'. When a new dish is created, the aim is that the guest will enjoy it on all four levels, and experience all the pleasures that the act of eating can provide.

'There are guests who are capable of seeing what nobody else sees.'

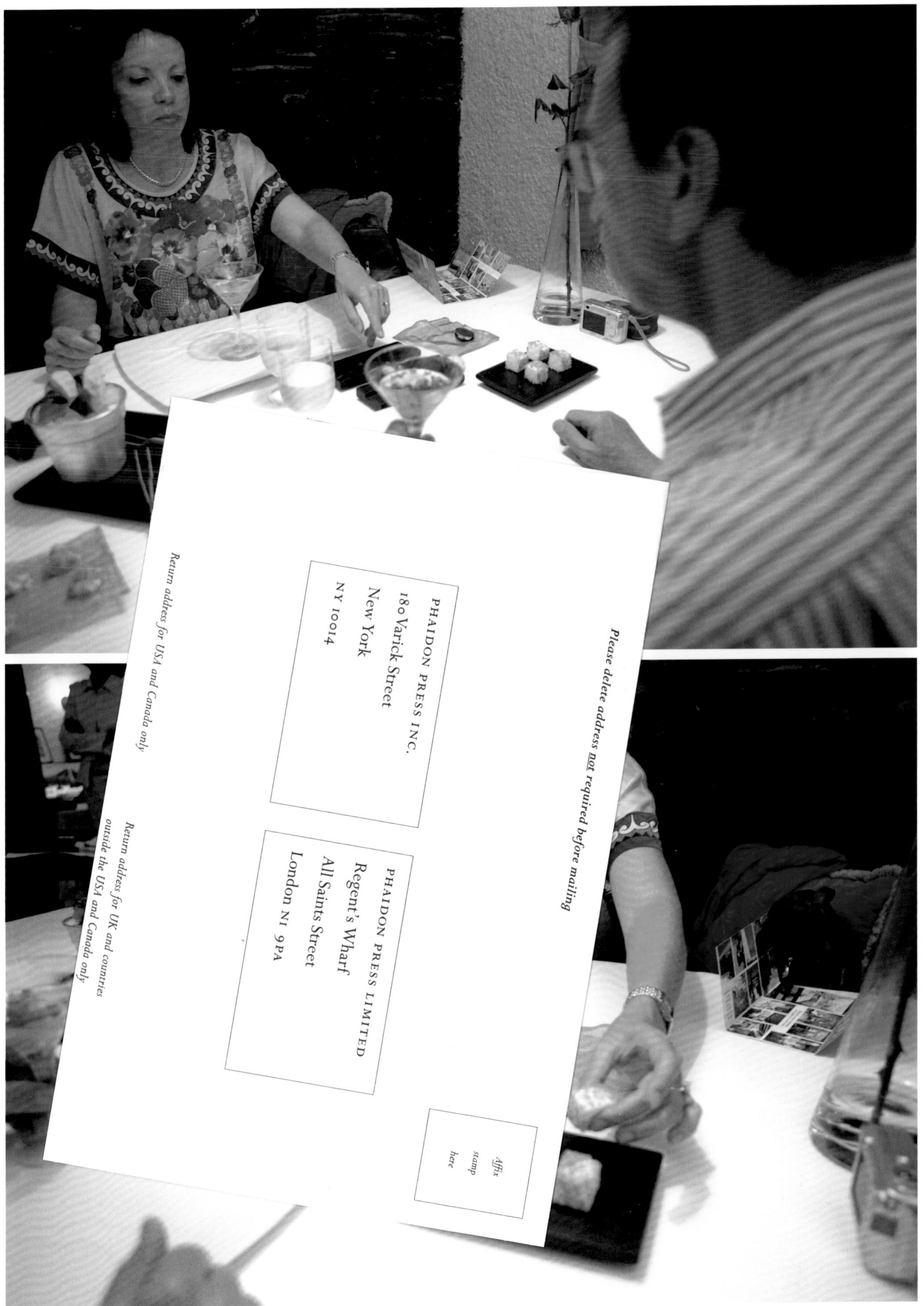
Please delete address not required before mailing
PHAIDON PRESS INC.
180 Varick Street
New York
NY 10014
Return address for USA and Canada only
PHAIDON PRESS LIMITED
Regent's Wharf
All Saints Street
London N1 9PA
Return address for UK and countries outside the USA and Canada only
Affix stamp here

20:45

—

Four hours in the front row

The tension in the kitchen is never transmitted to the dining room, but guests who eat in the kitchen choose to experience elBulli almost as intimately as the staff do.

The chef's table in the kitchen is not always used. At the beginning of the season no one knows who will occupy it, or when. Often the guests who eat there are old friends of elBulli. Observing guests at close hand while they experience new dishes is interesting for the chefs because it allows them to identify problems with the dishes that they might not have foreseen. As a result, they might make improvements to the way a dish is plated or presented by the waiter.

What happens between a restaurant and its guests?

A dish is a conversation between the chef and the guest, and the knowledge and experience of the chef, waiter and guest all inform the part they will play in a meal. The distance between the chef at the kitchen workbench and the guest at the dining room table can be reduced by the care and attention of the waiter, who performs a pivotal role by helping the guests adapt to the rhythm of the kitchen and maximize their experience of the food. The participants bring to the experience their own values, expertise and sensory perceptions, and these can be broadly categorized as follows.

CHEF:
EMITTER

Ability to perceive tastes and flavours

Common sense and judgement

Experience in other fields
- art
- other areas of the food industry
- industrial design
- science and technology

Knowledge
- of history and culture
- of cooking techniques
- of products
- of kitchen technology

Organization

Philosophy

Creative and artistic abilities

WAITER:
TRANSMITTER

Creates a warm atmosphere during dinner

Conveys the philosophy behind the food

Serves the food to the table

Explains the dishes

Controls quality

Controls timing

GUEST: RECEPTOR

Gastronomic experience and knowledge
- of ingredients
- of dishes
- of restaurants and chefs
- of styles and characteristics

Senses
- sight
- hearing
- touch
- smell
- taste

(sight, hearing, touch, smell, taste — flavour)

The sixth sense (the ability to enjoy cooking with the intellect), which can be stimulated in these ways:
- transgression of restaurant conventions
- childhood memories
- magic
- playfulness
- irony and provocation
- decontextualization
- surprise
- a 'knowing wink'
- recognition of a cultural reference
- confounded expectations
- deception

Mind
- guests' unique interpretations of taste

Memory
- of ingredients
- of family meals
- of visits to restaurants

Spirit and emotions

The pressure mounts during service

By this time nearly all the guests have arrived. Cocktails, snacks and the first tapas-dishes are being served.

The pressure is now enormous and the chefs' concentration is at its peak.

In order to appreciate the constant activity of service you would have to immerse yourself in the kitchen for several hours.

There is no good wine without people to drink it

To produce a great wine you need the best grapes and the best winemaking skills. But the wine has to be served with affection and professionalism to express all its qualities.

A wine is only good if there are guests who know how to appreciate it. They do not need to be great experts – it is enough that they have the sensitivity and level of interest to enjoy it.

Once guests have chosen their wine, the wine waiter goes to find it in the cellar or in the wine cooler. He opens it, checks that it is in good condition and leaves it to breathe if necessary. Then it is offered to the guest to taste.

1999
vi
2000
2002

FUJITSU
STYLISTIC
elBullivi - Microsoft Internet Explorer
VER CAJA
añadir a mi caja
tornar
nova recerca
imprimir
fitxa del vi
NOM
Oloroso
CELLER
González Byass
ANY
1969
VOLUM
0.75 litres
DENOMINACIÓ Jerez-Manzanilla de Sanlúcar
TIPUS Generós
PAÍS Espanya
REGIÓ Andalucía
CATEGORIA D.O.
VARIETAT
Palomino Fino >> 100 %
ALCOHOL 22.0 %
PREU 400,00 €
dades del celler
González Byass
Manuel Mª González, 12
Jerez de la Frontera
Cádiz
C.P. 11403
España
956357000
956357043
atencion@gonzalezbyass.es
www.gonzalezbyass.es
elBulli
start

The electronic wine list

Because the menu is imposed upon guests at elBulli, Ferran and Juli believe that they should drink whatever wines they enjoy with their meal. The 2,153-square-foot (200-square-metre) wine cellar has been created and maintained by Juli and the three sommeliers. The length of dinner at elBulli means that guests can try many different wines with the numerous dishes, and guests each have their own opinions and preferences. The sommeliers will have a friendly conversation with the guests at the start of the meal to discuss their likes and dislikes, and will suggest wines they might enjoy, but ultimately guests are encouraged to choose for themselves.

There is now an electronic version of the wine list, which provides a more sensitive and interactive way to choose wines than from a conventional list. The elBullivi project allows guests to make their selection with a portable digital screen after applying different search criteria. The electronic list then provides a shortlist from which guests can order. The only disadvantage of this electronic list is that it is too much fun and guests can spend hours poring over it. However, it is available on the website so they can make and send their choices before they even arrive at elBulli.

On the main menu screen, the wine list can be viewed in the traditional way, or it can be filtered with the following search terms:

- Wine category
- Country
- Region
- Alcohol content
- Grape variety
- Price

POPULAR WINES FROM THE ELBULLI LIST

Fortified

Jerez-Manzanilla de Sanlúcar DO

- Manzanilla Pasada Pastrana, Vinícola Hidalgo
- Fino Antique, Bodegas Rey Fernando de Castilla
- Amontillado Tradición, Bodegas Tradición

Sparkling

Cava-Penedès DO

- Kripta Brut Nature Gran Reserva 2003, Agustí Torelló
- Celler Batlle Brut Gran Reserva 1999, Gramona
- Manuel Raventós Brut Nature Gran Reserva Personal 1999, Josep María Raventós i Blanc

Champagne-Aÿ AOC

- Grand Millésime 1996, Gosset
- R.D. 1990, Bollinger

Champagne-Epernay AOC

- Dom Pérignon 1996, Moët & Chandon

White

- Nun Vinya dels Taus 2006, Vinifera, Penedès DO
- Selección de Añada 2003, Pazo de Señorans, Rías Baixas DO
- Pedrouzos 2005, Val de Sil, Valdeorras DO
- La Pena 2004, Dominio do Bibei, Ribeira Sacra DO
- Pouilly-Fumé Silex 2005, Domaine Didier Dagueneau, Pouilly-Fumé AOC
- Riesling Cuvée Sainte Catherine Schlossberg l'Inédit 2000, Domaine Weinbach-Colette, Alsace Grand Cru
- Corton-Les-Vergennes Cuvée Paul Chanson 2005, elBulli at Hospices de Beaune, Corton-Les-Vergennes Grand Cru
- Terlano Sauvignon Quarz 2005, Cantina Terlano, Terlano DOC

Red

- Clos Mogador 2001, Clos Mogador, Priorat DOQ
- Mas La Plana 1976, Miguel Torres, Penedès DOC
- Ex Ex 6 2004, Castell de Perelada, Empordà DO
- El Pisón 2001, Artadi, Rioja DOCa (Cosecha)
- Pingus 2001, Dominio de Pingus, Ribera del Duero DO (Cosecha)
- Richebourg 2005, Lucien le Moine, Richebourg Grand Cru
- Château Latour 1982, Château Latour, Pauillac 1er Grand Cru Classé
- Insignia 1997, Joseph Phelps, Napa Valley AVA

Sweet

- Oloroso Dulce Matusalem, González Byass, Jerez-Manzanilla de Sanlúcar DO
- Banyuls-Parcé 1952, Domaine du Mas Blanc, Banyuls AOC
- Aszú 6 Puttonyos 1972, Oremus, Tokaji

LEROY
1976

The kitchen at full speed

Because the guests at each table sit down to eat at different times, the order sheets are the only way to track which stage of dinner each guest has reached. The sheets allow the chefs and the waiters to monitor the progress of every table.

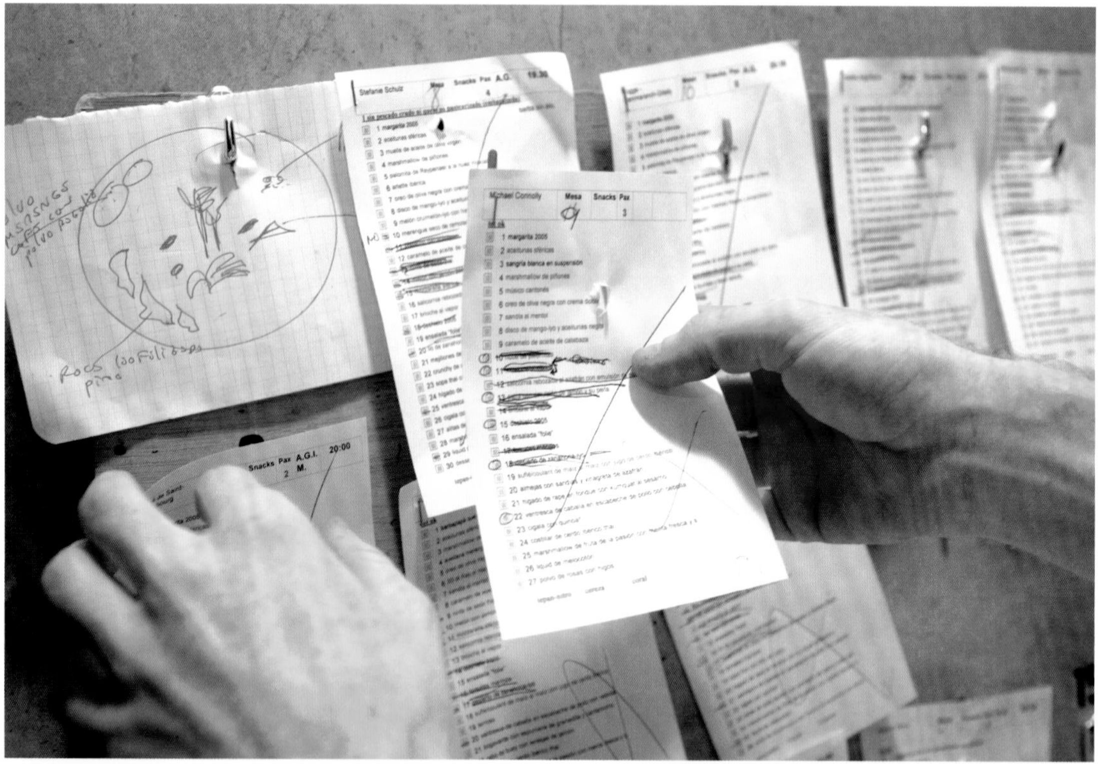

21:10

—

The last guests arrive

Until a few years ago, Ferran used to come into the dining room to say hello, as head chefs do in most restaurants. But more and more guests were going into the kitchen to see Ferran before their meal – first his friends, and then the braver guests. Today the visit to the kitchen has become part of the ritual for everyone.

For some, act one is about to begin

The final guests sit down and begin their meal with cocktails and snacks.

At the same time, other guests are making the transition to act two and receive the first tapas-dishes.

'You know you are experiencing true creativity when you go to a restaurant and have the feeling that you're eating in a country that you've never visited before.'

Deshielo
(Thaw)

Serves 4

Green pine cone infusion

- 480 g (1 lb) green pine cones
- 600 g (2½ cups) water
- 75 g (⅓ cup) sugar
- 0.6 g ascorbic acid

—

1. Soak the green pine cones in hot water for one minute to clean them.
2. Coarsely chop the pine cones into 2 cm (¾ in) chunks.
3. Bring the water to the boil with the sugar and add the chopped green pine cones.
4. Add the ascorbic acid and keep refrigerated for 24 hours.
5. Strain through a Superbag and keep refrigerated.

Frozen green pine cone powder

- 200 g (¾ cup) green pine cone infusion, previously prepared

—

1. Put the green pine cone infusion into a Pacojet beaker and freeze at -20°C/-4°F.
2. Process the frozen green pine cone infusion in the Pacojet for each individual serving until a frozen powder with a snow-like texture is achieved.
3. Store the frozen powder at -20°C/-4°F.

Wild pine nut milk

- 200 g (1⅔ cups) peeled wild pine nuts
- 240 g (1 cup) water

—

1. Process the pine nuts with the water using a hand-held blender until they are well broken up.
2. Stand in the refrigerator for 12 hours.
3. Blend the water and pine nut mixture in a liquidizer until it forms a cream.
4. Squeeze firmly through a Superbag to release all the liquid and create a thick pine nut milk.
5. Strain and keep refrigerated.

Wild pine nut milk sorbet

- 250 g (1 cup) wild pine nut milk, previously prepared
- ¼ x 2 g gelatine leaf, previously rehydrated in cold water
- salt

—

1. Lightly salt the pine nut milk.
2. Heat a quarter of the pine nut milk at 45°C/115°F and dissolve the gelatine leaf in it. Once it has dissolved, add the rest of the milk and mix well.
3. Put the pine nut sorbet mixture in a Pacojet beaker and freeze at -20°C/-4°F.
4. Five minutes before presentation and finishing, process the sorbet with the Pacojet twice and store at -8°C/18°F.

Toasted wild pine nut savoury praline

- 50 g (½ cup) toasted wild pine nuts
- 10 g (⅔ tbsp) olive oil
- salt

—

1. Blend the pine nuts with the oil in the liquidizer until they form a fine, lump-free cream.
2. Strain and season with salt.

Garrapi-nitro pine nuts

- 12 toasted wild pine nuts
- 50 g (3⅓ tbsp) wild pine nut savoury praline, previously prepared
- 500 g (2 cups) liquid nitrogen

—

1. Dip the whole pine nuts into the pine nut praline and then dip them into the liquid nitrogen for 5 seconds to freeze the praline so that the pine nuts are completely coated with it.
2. Keep the garrapi-nitro pine nuts at -10°C/15°F.

—

Liquid nitrogen should not be handled without training in how to use it safely.

Liquorice paste light meringue powder

- 125 g (½ cup) water
- 125 g (½ cup) pasteurized liquid egg white
- 7.5 g (1½ tsp) powdered egg white
- 25 g (1⅔ tbsp) sugar
- 35 g (2⅓ tbsp) liquorice paste

—

1. Mix all the ingredients together while cold and beat in the electric mixer for 5 minutes.
2. Leave to stand for 2 minutes with the mixer switched off.
3. Beat for 10 more minutes and spread over a baking tray lined with a Silpat to a depth of 1 cm (½ in).
4. Dry in the oven at 100°C/210°F for 40 minutes.
5. Raise the oven temperature to 120°C/250°F and leave for a further 40 minutes.
6. When dry, place in a bag and crush to a powder.
7. Store in an airtight container in a cool, dry place.

Rocks and green pine cone light meringue powder

- 125 g (½ cup) green pine cone infusion, previously prepared
- 125 g (½ cup) pasteurized liquid egg white
- 7.5 g (1½ tsp) powdered egg white
- 25 g (1⅔ tbsp) sugar

—

1. Mix all the cold ingredients together and beat in the electric mixer for 10 minutes.
2. Spread the meringue mixture over a baking tray lined with a Silpat to a depth of 1 cm (½ in).
3. Dry in the oven at 90 °C/195°F for one hour and 40 minutes.
4. Cut the light meringue into 8 x 1.5 cm (⅔ in) rocks.
5. Put the remaining meringue in a bag and crush to a powder.
6. Store in an airtight container in a cool, dry place.

Green pine cone jelly

- 200 g (¾ cup) green pine cone infusion, previously prepared
- 1 x 2 g gelatine leaf, previously rehydrated in cold water

—

1. Dissolve the gelatine in a quarter of the green pine cone infusion before mixing with the rest of it.
2. Pour into a container to a depth of 1 cm (½ in) and refrigerate for 2 hours to set.

Freeze-dried green pine cone jelly

- Green pine cone jelly, previously prepared

—

Freeze-dry for 72 hours, then keep in a vacuum-pack bag in a cool, dry place.

Plain caramel slices

- 100 g (3½ oz) fondant
- 50 g (¼ cup) glucose
- 50 g (¼ cup) Isomalt

—

1. Dissolve the fondant and glucose in a pan and boil. Stir until everything has thoroughly dissolved, then add the Isomalt.
2. Keep on a medium heat until the temperature reaches 160°C/325°F. Remove from the heat. (The temperature will increase by another 5°C/9°F).
3. Spread out on parchment paper to a thickness of 1 cm (½ in).
4. When the correct temperature is reached, cut into 5 x 5 cm (2 in) pieces.
5. Store in an airtight container in a cool, dry place.
6. Put a caramel square between two Silpats and heat in the oven until the caramel melts.
7. Remove and quickly roll out into a 1 mm thick caramel sheet.
8. Store the caramel sheets in an airtight container in a cool, dry place.

EXTRAS

- 5 g (1 tsp) freshly ground coffee
- 4 purple shiso shoots
- 4 green shiso shoots
- 4 fresh basil shoots
- 4 borage shoots
- 4 borage flowers

—

Shiso is a kind of Asian herb similar to basil and mint. There are two varieties, purple and green.

If borage flowers are not available, substitute with cucumber flowers.

FINISHING AND PRESENTATION

1. Place half a dessertspoon of pine nut sorbet in the middle of a soup plate.
2. Cover the pine nut sorbet with the frozen green pine cone infusion powder. The surface should be rough.
3. Make a bunch with one shoot of green shiso, one of purple shiso, one of borage and one of fresh basil and place it upright beside the pine nut sorbet.
4. Place a borage flower beside the shoots.
5. Imagining the dish as a clock face, put 1 g of ground coffee at 11 o'clock to the frozen powder.
6. Place a 2 cm (¾ in) piece of freeze-dried green pine cone infusion at 1 o'clock.
7. Stand a 2 cm (¾ in) piece of plain caramel sheet at 3 o'clock.
8. Place 2 rocks made from the light green pine cone infusion meringue and half a teaspoon of light green pine cone infusion meringue powder at 6 o'clock.
9. Place a teaspoon of light liquorice meringue powder at 9 o'clock.
10. Finish by arranging 3 garrapi-nitro pine nuts over the frozen powder.

—

This dish is a variation on the theme of *Thaw* from 2004.

—

Cutlery:
Tapas cutlery, a 14 x 3 cm (5½ x 1¼ in) spoon and fork.

How to eat:
Start with a spoonful of powder and alternate with the different components without mixing them. It is important not to break the structure of the dish so as not to mix flavours.

Espuma de zanahoria-LYO con espuma-aire de avellana y especias Córdoba (Carrot-LYO foam with hazelnut foam-air and Córdoba spices)

Serves 4

Carrot juice

- 1.5 kg (3¼ lb) carrots

—

1. Peel and liquidize the carrots.
2. Pass the juice through a fine strainer and keep refrigerated.

Cold carrot juice foam

- 500 g (2 cups) carrot juice
- 3.5 x 2 g gelatine leaves, previously rehydrated in cold water
- 1 x 0.5 litre (1 pint) ISI siphon
- 1 N^2O cartridge

—

1. Heat a third of the carrot juice and dissolve the gelatine in it.
2. Add the remaining carrot juice. Mix, pass through the fine strainer and fill the siphon with the liquid.
3. Close the siphon and insert the gas cartridge.
4. Keep the siphon in an ice bath in the refrigerator for 6 hours.

Cold carrot juice foam-LYO

- cold carrot juice foam, previously prepared

—

1. Fill 10 x 60 g (2 oz) plastic cups with carrot juice foam and quickly put them into the freeze-dryer.
2. Freeze-dry for 48 hours.
3. Once the foams are completely dried, cut each one into 3 even pieces per person.
4. Keep in the dehydrator so that the freeze-dried foam does not become moist.

Hazelnut cream

- 120 g (4 oz) skinned toasted hazelnuts
- 240 g (1 cup) water

—

1. Blend the hazelnuts with the water in the liquidizer until they have a cream-like consistency.
2. Put the hazelnut cream in a Pacojet beaker and freeze at -20°C/-4°F.
3. Once frozen solid, put through the Pacojet 3 times and leave to thaw in the refrigerator for 3 hours until it has the texture of light cream.
4. Keep refrigerated.

Cold hazelnut foam

- 80 g (⅓ cup) hazelnut cream, previously prepared
- ¾ x 2 g gelatine leaf, previously rehydrated in cold water
- 40 g (2⅔ tbsp) hazelnut paste
- 120 g (½ cup) 35% fat single (light) cream
- 1 g salt
- 1 x 0.5 litre (1 pint) ISI siphon
- 1 N^2O cartridge

—

1. Warm a quarter of the hazelnut cream, dissolve the gelatine in it, then add the rest of the cream and the remaining ingredients.
2. Mix and strain.
3. Fill the siphon with the mixture, close and charge the gas canister.
4. Stand in the refrigerator for 3 hours.

Pink grapefruit segments

» 1 x 300 g (11 oz) pink grapefruit

—

1. Slice off the top and bottom of the grapefruit to expose the segments.

2. Peel the grapefruit in a spiral to expose the flesh so that there are no traces of zest or pith, but without altering the basic shape of the fruit.

3. Remove the segments from their membranes with a sharp knife.

4. Slice each segment down the middle so that each piece measures 2.5 x 1 cm (1 x ½ in). 4 pieces are needed.

5. Keep refrigerated.

Fermented milk *mató* cheese

» 500 g (2 cups) fermented full-cream milk

—

1. Pour the milk into a small pan and heat to 56°C/133°F, stirring constantly with a spatula.

2. Leave to stand for 5 minutes and pour the milk through a sieve so that the whey is drained off and the *mató* cheese remains in the sieve.

3. Collect the *mató* cheese and store in the refrigerator.

Milk air and Córdoba spice base

» 500 g (2 cups) milk
» 1.5 g Lecite
» 3.5 g Fatéma Hal's Córdoba spices

—

1. Heat the milk.

2. Mix in the spices with a hand-held blender and allow to infuse for 24 hours.

3. Strain the infusion through a Superbag over a 25 cm (10 in) deep container. Add the Lecite and process with a hand-held blender.

—

Córdoba spices are a blend that usually contains cinnamon, cloves, cardamom and chilli.

Toasted saffron powder

» 3 g saffron threads

—

1. Toast the saffron threads in a frying pan (skillet).

2. Break up the saffron to make a rough powder.

Fried hazelnuts

» 4 shelled and skinned hazelnuts
» 100 g (⅓ cup) 0.4% olive oil
» salt

—

1. Put the hazelnuts and oil into a cold pan and fry, stirring constantly.

2. Once fried, drain off excess oil on a paper towel and season with salt while hot.

3. Split the hazelnuts in half and set aside.

—

0.4% refers to the acidity level of the olive oil.

EXTRAS

- 2 g virgin fennel seed oil
- 2 g fresh chopped fennel
- 20 g (4 tsp) pure hazelnut paste
- 10 g (¼ oz) coriander (cilantro) shoots
- 4 g Fatéma Hal's Córdoba spices

FINISHING AND PRESENTATION

1. Heat the milk air and Córdoba spice mixture to 50°C/120°F and work a hand-held blender over the surface until it emulsifies and the air forms.

2. Put a drop of virgin fennel seed oil and a pinch of chopped fresh fennel over each grapefruit segment. Place the grapefruit segment in the middle of a plate.

3. Place a teaspoon of *mató* cheese to the right of the grapefruit, but without touching it.

4. Place a spoonful of milk and spice air in the middle of the plate. Then place 4 x 3 g spots of cold hazelnut foam and 3 fried half hazelnuts over it.

5. Apply the hazelnut paste over the foam-air in a zigzag pattern.

6. Place 3 pieces of freeze-dried carrot foam in the upper section of the plate, just above the air.

7. Sprinkle a pinch of saffron powder over the air, lightly place 2 g coriander shoots over one side of the air, and finish by sprinkling a little Córdoba spice around the air.

—

Cutlery:
Tapas cutlery, a 14 x 3 cm (5½ x 1¼ in) spoon and fork.

How to eat:
Alternate the pieces of freeze-dried carrot foam with the other ingredients.

Ensalada 'Folie'
('Folie' salad)

Serves 4

Artichokes-CRU

- » 4 x 60 g (2¼ oz) baby globe artichokes
- » 100 g (½ cup) water
- » 25 g (1⅔ tbsp) extra virgin olive oil
- » 25 g (1⅔ tbsp) 25-year-old sherry vinegar
- » salt

—

1. Remove the leaves from the artichokes, leaving the heart and a small section of the stem.
2. Mix the water with the vinegar and oil to make a vinaigrette and season with salt.
3. Put the vinaigrette in a vacuum-pack bag and add the artichokes.
4. Vacuum seal the bag.
5. Refrigerate for 6 hours.

Garlic-CRU

- » 4 x 6 g (¼ oz) cloves garlic
- » 45 g (3 tbsp) extra virgin olive oil
- » 15 g (1 tbsp) 25-year-old sherry vinegar
- » salt
- » water
- » 1 sprig dried rosemary
- » 1 bay leaf

—

1. Peel the garlic cloves and blanch 3 times in boiling water.
2. Cool in iced water and dry.
3. Make a vinaigrette with the oil and vinegar and season with salt.
4. Put the vinaigrette in a vacuum-pack bag and add the garlic and herbs.
5. Vacuum seal the bag.
6. Refrigerate for 48 hours.

Algin solution

- » 1 kg (4¼ cups) water
- » 5 g (1 tsp) Algin

—

1. Mix the 2 ingredients in a liquidizer until a lump-free mixture is obtained.
2. Strain and set aside.

Spherical-I goats' milk yoghurt nodules

- » 50 g (¼ cup) goats' milk yoghurt
- » 500g (2 cups) Algin solution, previously prepared

—

1. Pour the Algin solution into a container to a depth of 4 cm (1¾ in).
2. Beat the yoghurt to produce a smooth, lump-free cream. Do not whip it.
3. Take a syringe with a 2 mm opening and fill with the beaten goats' milk yoghurt.
4. Pipe the goats' milk yoghurt into the Algin solution to form 4 nodules with a 1 cm (½ in) diameter.
5. Allow them to 'cook' in the Algin solution for one minute.
6. Take the nodules out of the mixture and dip them in water to clean them.
7. Drain the nodules without breaking them and keep them in a container lined with parchment paper.
8. Refrigerate.

Black olive juice

- » 500 g (1 lb 2 oz) black Aragón olives

—

1. Stone (pit) the olives.
2. Process the olives in the liquidizer and strain through muslin. Squeeze well to release all of the juice from the olives.
3. Refrigerate the juice.

Spherical-I black olive solution

- » 100 g (⅓ cup) black olive juice, previously prepared
- » 0.5 g Calcic
- » 0.2 g Xantana

—

1. Dilute Calcic in the olive juice.
2. Add Xantana to the juice and process with a hand-held blender until it is lump-free. Stand for 2 hours to release any air bubbles that may have formed during the blending.

Spherical-I black olives

- » 500 g (2 cups) Algin solution, previously prepared
- » 100 g (⅓ cup) spherical-1 black olive solution, previously prepared
- » 100 g (⅓ cup) extra virgin olive oil

—

1. Using a 1 cm (⅓ in) diameter hemispherical measuring spoon, make 8 spherical black olive balls and place them into the Algin solution.
2. Leave them for one minute.
3. Take the olives out of the Algin solution and submerge them in water.
4. Remove from the water and place in the extra virgin olive oil.
5. Do not refrigerate.

Fermented milk *mató* cheese

- » 500 g (2 cups) fermented full-cream milk

—

1. Pour the milk into a small pan and heat to 56°C/133°F, stirring constantly with a spatula. Leave to stand for 5 minutes.
2. Gently pour the milk through a sieve to drain away the whey, leaving the *mató* cheese in the sieve.
3. Refrigerate.

Preserved tuna water and oil

- 1 kg (2¼ lb) canned tuna preserved in olive oil
- 300 g (1⅓ cups) water

—

1. Pour the oil from the can and set aside.
2. Combine the tuna with the water and gently break it up with a hand-held blender.
3. Strain through a Superbag and collect the tuna water that is released.
4. Refrigerate.

Preserved tuna oil air

- 400 g (1⅔ cups) preserved tuna oil, previously prepared
- 400 g (1⅔ cups) preserved tuna water, previously prepared
- 2.5 g Lecite

—

1. Mix the three ingredients together in a 25 cm (10 in) deep container with a hand-held blender.

Preserved cat's claw shoots

- 4 preserved cat's claw shoots

—

1. Cut the cat's claw shoots into 2 cm (¾ in) lengths.
2. Refrigerate.

—

Cat's claw is a creeper that grows in areas of Peru, Colombia and Bolivia, as well as in the Alicante region of Spain. It grows in tall forests in sunny areas and is known to have medicinal properties.

Peeled green walnuts

- 2 whole green walnuts

—

1. Break the walnuts in half with a nutcracker.
2. Remove the nut halves in one piece and peel them with a short pointed knife to obtain 4 half walnuts.
3. Refrigerate.

Flowering mini-cucumbers

- 4 flowering mini-cucumbers

—

1. Remove the bumps from the cucumber skin by hand.
2. Clean the cucumbers with a paper towel and refrigerate.

'Air-bag' dough

- 250 g (2 cups) plain (all-purpose) flour
- 70 g (⅔ cup) strong bread flour
- 190 g (¾ cup) cold milk
- 10 g (2 tsp) fresh yeast
- 5 g (1 tsp) salt

—

1. Combine all the ingredients (except the salt) in a mixer with a dough hook.
2. Knead for 9 minutes at medium speed.
3. Add the salt and knead for 2 more minutes.
4. Knead by hand for one minute. Keep the dough well covered in a bowl in the refrigerator.
5. Leave to rise for 4 hours.

—

This is the minimum recommended quantity to ensure a good result.

'Air-bags'

- 200 g (7 oz) 'air-bag' dough, previously prepared

—

1. Roll the dough out through a rolling machine at maximum thickness.
2. Leave the dough to stand for approximately one minute, covered with a damp cloth.
3. Roll the dough out twice more to 0.5 cm (¼ in).
4. Cut into 1.5 cm (⅔ in) rounds.
5. Bake in the oven at 240°C/475°F for one minute. Turn over and bake for another minute until the dough has risen and is golden brown.
6. Take out of the oven, leave to cool and keep in an airtight container in a cool, dry place.

Savoury macadamia nut praline

- 50 g (2 oz) raw macadamia nuts
- 10 g (2 tsp) sunflower oil
- salt

—

1. Process the macadamia nuts with the oil in the liquidizer until a lump-free cream is obtained.
2. Strain, season with salt and put in a squeezy bottle.

Tuna roe vinaigrette

- 20 g (¾ oz) dry tuna roe
- 30 g (2 tbsp) extra virgin olive oil

—

1. Peel the roe.
2. Chop the peeled roe in the liquidizer. Use short, sharp bursts to obtain a granular powder.
3. Mix with the extra virgin olive oil and refrigerate.

Shaved toasted hazelnuts

» 30 g (1 oz) peeled hazelnuts

—

1. Toast the hazelnuts and shave them with a Microplane grater to produce the longest threads possible.

2. Place the threads in an airtight container without piling them up, so as not to alter the texture.

3. Store in a cool, dry place.

EXTRAS

» 8 pickled daisy buds
» 8 fresh *ficoïde glaciale* shoots
» 4 purslane shoots
» 4 fresh bergamot flowers
» 10 g (2 tbsp) 25-year-old sherry vinegar
» Maldon sea salt

—

Ficoïde glaciale is a green, fleshy-leaved plant often eaten raw in salads, also known as ice plant.

Purslane is a smooth, fleshy-leaved plant that can be eaten both raw and cooked.

Dressed *pa-ha*

» 1 *pa-ha* stem
» extra virgin olive oil
» 25-year-old sherry vinegar
» salt

—

1. Peel the *pa-ha* stem with a short, pointed knife.

2. Cut the stem into 4 x 2 cm (¾ in) pieces on a slight angle at one of the ends.

3. Dress the *pa-ha* pieces with extra virgin olive oil, 25-year-old sherry vinegar and salt.

—

Pa-ha is a long and thick-stemmed vegetable with a very porous interior and an unusual texture.

Bread with oil

» 4 x 2.5 cm (1 in) slices rustic bread, crusts removed
» 30 g (2 tbsp) extra virgin olive oil

—

1. Soak the bread in the oil.

—

The bread must be soaked just before presentation and finishing.

FINISHING AND PRESENTATION

1. Work a hand-held blender over the surface of the preserved tuna oil air mixture until it emulsifies and the air forms.

2. Cut the artichokes-CRU in half lengthways and stand them on the right-hand side of the base of a concave oval dish.

3. Place a garlic-CRU clove on the left-hand side of the plate. Place a teaspoon of home-made *mató* cheese in the upper section of the plate.

4. Place an 'air-bag' beside the *mató* cheese. Place a flowering mini-cucumber opposite the garlic.

5. Place an oil-soaked piece of bread opposite the 'air-bag', and the cat's claw and a halved green walnut beside it.

6. Place a piece of dressed *pa-ha* in the middle of the plate.

7. Place one spherical-I nodule and 2 pickled daisy buds in the lower part of the plate, to the left of the artichoke.

8. Cover the base of the dish with 2 spoons of preserved tuna oil air.

9. Arrange 2 spherical olives, 2 *ficoïde glaciale* shoots, one purslane shoot and a bergamot flower over it.

10. Without touching any other ingredients, make a 4 cm long (1¾ in) and 1 cm (½ in) wide line of shaved hazelnut on one side of the dish.

11. Place a 3 g pile of savoury macadamia nut praline beside the 'air-bag', ensuring that they do not touch.

12. Dress the artichokes with a spoon of tuna roe vinaigrette.

13. Finish by sprinkling a pinch of salt over the bread, garlic and *pa-ha*, and 3 drops of sherry vinegar over the air.

—

If any of the ingredients are not available, they can be substituted by other ingredients that resemble them, as long as the flavour and texture are similar. This dish has also been made with home-made caviar from *serla* roe, and with tuna foam and air-foam instead of tuna air.

Serla is a local Catalan fish that contains a lot of roe.

—

Cutlery:
Tapas cutlery, a 14 x 3 cm (5½ x 1¼ in) spoon and fork.

How to eat:
Eat each component separately, combined with the air, in order to appreciate the different textures and flavours.

Mejillones de roca con algas a las hierbas frescas (Rock mussels with seaweed and fresh herbs)

Serves 4

Rock mussels

» 32 x 15 g (½ oz) rock mussels

—

1. Plunge the rock mussels a few at a time into boiling water for 10 seconds.

2. Remove the mussels from the water and leave them to cool at room temperature.

3. Use a short, pointed knife to cut the muscle joining each mussel to its shell.

4. Lift the rock mussels out, taking care they do not break.

5. Cover the mussels with their own liquor, which has been previously strained through a Superbag. Refrigerate.

Thickened mussel water

» 100 g (½ cup) rock mussel liquor, previously prepared
» 0.4 g Xantana

—

1. Strain the mussel liquor through a Superbag to remove any impurities.

2. Mix the mussel liquor and Xantana in a container.

3. Process with a hand-held blender to obtain a smooth, lump-free cream.

4. Refrigerate.

Sliced *shiraita* kombu in rice vinegar syrup

» 2 slices of *shiraita* kombu measuring 6 x 19 cm (2½ x 7⅔ in)
» 120 g (½ cup) water
» 80 g (⅓ cup) rice vinegar
» 1.5 g salt
» 4 g sugar

—

1. Mix the water with the rice vinegar, salt and sugar.

2. Place the sliced *shiraita* kombu in a small pan and cover with the vinegar mixture.

3. Bring to the boil and then remove from the heat.

4. Keep refrigerated for 24 hours.

5. Cut the seaweed into 12 x 2 cm (¾ in) squares.

—

Shiraita kombu is the Japanese name for the slices taken from the middle section of kombu seaweed.

Seaweed

» 20 g (¾ oz) fresh nori seaweed
» 20 g (¾ oz) fresh samphire
» 20 g (¾ oz) fresh wakame seaweed
» 20 g (¾ oz) dulse seaweed
» 20 g (¾ oz) red tosaka seaweed
» 20 g (¾ oz) green tosaka seaweed
» 8 stems fresh purple glasswort
» 4 x 3 cm (1¼ in) stems pasteurized sea grapes

—

1. Clean all the seaweed (apart from the sea grapes) under running water to remove excess salt.

2. Refrigerate.

3. Select the 8 x 4 cm (1½ in) purple glasswort stems.

4. Hydrate the sea grapes under plenty of running water until it is smooth and moist.

—

Purple glasswort is an annual plant that grows in saline soils. The branches are fleshy and green.

Sea grapes (*umi budo*) take their name from the clusters of liquid-filled globules along the seaweed. They have a crisp texture and originate from Japan. The sea grapes should be hydrated just before presentation and finishing.

EXTRAS

» 4 fresh basil shoots
» 4 fresh 1.5 cm (⅔ in) chervil leaves
» 4 fresh mint shoots
» 4 fresh tarragon shoots

FINISHING AND PRESENTATION

1. Arrange the seaweed salad on the right-hand side of a moon-shaped dish in the following order: kombu, green tosaka, dulse, kombu, samphire, nori, purple glasswort, wakame, red tosaka and finally kombu.

2. Arrange the 8 mussels on the left-hand side following the edge of the dish to complete the circle started by the seaweed.

3. Arrange the fresh herbs over the seaweed.

4. Cover each mussel with a spoon of thickened mussel water and fill the middle of the dish with another spoon of the same sauce.

5. Finally, place a sea grape stem in the space between the rock mussels and the seaweed salad.

—

Cutlery:
Tapas cutlery, a 14 x 3 cm (5½ x 1¼ in) spoon and fork.

How to eat:
Alternate the mussels with each type of seaweed. Take a little mussel water with every mussel.

Caracolines en caldo corto con nécora en escabeche y amaranto al hinojo
(Baby snails in court bouillon with crab escabeche and amaranth with fennel)

Serves 4

Crab legs and claws

» 8 x 100 g (3½ oz) velvet crabs
» water
» salt

—

1. Boil the crabs for 55 seconds in salted water.
2. Remove them from the water and leave to cool at room temperature.
3. Remove the legs and claws from the bodies.
4. Remove the meat from the claws in one piece, leaving behind the cartilage.
5. Set aside the meat from four claws per person and refrigerate.

Crab escabeche

» crab bodies and legs, previously prepared
» 20 g (4 tsp) dried garlic
» 60 g (2½ oz) onion
» 50 g (2 oz) ripe tomatoes
» 200 g (¾ cup) olive oil
» 200 g (¾ cup) water
» 30 g (2 tbsp) 25-year-old sherry vinegar
» 3 g dried thyme
» 3 g dried rosemary
» 1 bay leaf

—

1. Chop the crab bodies into 8 pieces each.
2. Peel and crush the garlic cloves.
3. Peel and julienne the onion into very thin slices.
4. Roughly grate the tomatoes.
5. Brown the garlic in a pot with 75 g (¼ cup) oil. Add the onion and stir until soft. Add the tomato and fry gently until well sautéed.
6. Add the crab and fry lightly.
7. Add the remaining oil and water, and cook until the sauce is well flavoured.
8. Add the vinegar. Leave to evaporate for a few minutes and then strain through a chinois, pressing through well.
9. Strain through fine-meshed cloth and refrigerate.

Escabeche air base

» 200 g (¾ cup) crab escabeche, previously prepared
» 0.4 g Lecite

—

Combine the ingredients in a 25 cm (10 in) deep container.

Snails and their court bouillon

» 250 g (9 oz) baby snails
» salt
» 1 sprig fresh thyme
» 1 sprig fresh rosemary
» 1 bay leaf
» 1 sprig fresh fennel fronds

—

1. Wash the baby snails in water 3 times and drain.
2. To get rid of the slime, add salt and wash once again in water. Repeat until they are no longer slimy.
3. Put the snails in a pot and cover with lukewarm water. Gradually bring to a simmer.
4. Season the water with salt and add the herbs.
5. Cook over a medium heat for 5 minutes, skimming continuously to remove the scum. Leave to cool in the same water.
6. Rinse the snails and cover with the strained court bouillon.

Boiled amaranth

» 20 g (4 tsp) amaranth grains
» 300 g (1⅓ cups) water
» salt

—

1. Bring the water to the boil. Add the amaranth, season and cook for 30 minutes.
2. Strain to remove as much liquid as possible, and keep refrigerated.

—

Amaranth is an ancient grain commonly eaten in Mexico and the Himalayas.

Fresh fennel seeds

» 4 small bunches fresh fennel flowers

—

1. Snip the seeds from the fennel flowers with scissors.
2. Refrigerate.

Fresh herbs

» 8 sprigs fresh basil
» 12 x ½ cm (¼ in) fresh mint leaves
» 12 x 1 cm (½ in) fresh tarragon leaves
» 8 fresh fennel flowers
» 12 x 1 cm (½ in) fresh chervil leaves
» 16 fresh thyme flowers

—

Divide the fresh herbs and flowers into 4 portions.

EXTRAS

» olive oil
» freshly ground black pepper
» salt

FINISHING AND PRESENTATION

1. Work a hand-held blender over the surface of the escabeche base until it emulsifies and the air forms.
2. Heat the snails in their court bouillon.
3. Heat the crab claw meat in a little of the escabeche. Do not let the meat overcook.
4. Sauté the cooked amaranth in a little oil with the fresh fennel seeds and season with salt.
5. Stand 4 warm crab claws in a row on one side of a bowl.
6. Arrange the snails at the base of the bowl in one layer.
7. Season the snails with freshly ground black pepper.
8. Arrange the fresh flowers and herbs over the snails.
9. Place a long quenelle of 6 g (1¼ tsp) amaranth and fennel seeds beside the crab claws, without touching the snails.
10. Pour a spoon of court bouillon over the snails.
11. In a separate bowl serve 3 spoons of escabeche air per person.

—

Cutlery:
Tapas cutlery, a 14 x 3 cm (5½ x 1¼ in) spoon and fork.

How to eat:
Alternate the baby snails with the amaranth and the crab. Dip the crab into the escabeche air.

Terroso
(Earthy)

Serves 4

Summer truffle *empanadillas*

- 1 x 35 g (1¼ oz) peeled summer truffle
- 20 g (4 tsp) summer truffle purée, previously prepared
- 20 g (4 tsp) Metil solution, previously prepared
- salt

—

1. Slice the truffles into 1 mm slices.
2. Place the slices on clingfilm (plastic wrap) lightly coated with the Metil solution to form 4 x 4 cm (1¾ in) circles. The slices should overlap slightly.
3. Lightly coat the circle with Metil solution and a little salt.
4. Put 5 g (1 tsp) of summer truffle purée in the middle of the summer truffle circle.
5. Seal the disc as if it were a turnover, and refrigerate.

—

Empanadillas are a type of Spanish pasty similar to a turnover.

Metil solution

- 100 g (⅓ cup) water
- 3 g Metil

—

1. Mix the ingredients at room temperature in a liquidizer until they form a smooth, even mixture.
2. Strain and stand in the refrigerator for 24 hours.

Summer truffle purée

- 50 g (2 oz) peeled summer truffle
- 15 g (1 tbsp) 35% fat single (light) cream
- 15 g (1 tbsp) white truffle oil
- salt

—

1. Heat the cream and blend it with the truffle and the white truffle oil in the liquidizer until it forms a smooth purée.
2. Strain and season with salt to taste.
3. Refrigerate.

Venus rice stock

- 50 g (¼ cup) Venus rice
- water

—

1. Cook the rice in the recommended amount of water for 30 minutes.
2. Strain and reserve the cooking liquid.

—

Venus rice is a black rice variety from Italy.

Venus rice stock jelly

- 100 g (⅓ cup) Venus rice stock, previously prepared
- 0.4 g Agar
- ⅓ x 2 g gelatine leaf, previously rehydrated in cold water
- salt

—

1. Season the Venus rice stock with salt.
2. Add Agar to the stock and bring to the boil, stirring constantly with a whisk.
3. Remove from the heat, add the drained gelatine and pour into a container to a depth of 2 cm (¾ in).
4. Refrigerate for 3 hours.
5. Once it has set, cut the jelly into 2 cm (¾ in) cubes. This will give one cube per person.

Fresh liquorice infusion

- 50 g (2 oz) fresh liquorice stick
- 300 g (1⅓ cups) water
- 1 g ascorbic acid

—

1. To prevent oxidization, peel the liquorice and place in the water into which the ascorbic acid has been dissolved.
2. Break up the liquorice and the water in the liquidizer and infuse for 24 hours in the refrigerator.
3. Strain through a Superbag.

Fresh liquorice infusion jelly lasagne

- 200 g (¾ cup) fresh liquorice infusion, previously prepared
- 2.3 g Agar
- 1½ x 2 g gelatine leaves, previously rehydrated in cold water
- 5 g (1 tsp) liquorice paste

—

1. Mix the Agar with half of the liquorice infusion and bring to the boil, stirring constantly with a whisk.
2. Remove from the heat, add the remaining infusion and dissolve the gelatine into it.
3. Pour the jelly onto a 20 x 20 cm (8 x 8 in) flat tray to a depth of 1 mm.
4. Wait 5 minutes and pour the jelly onto the tray again to create another 1 mm thick layer.
5. Repeat this operation twice more to create 4 x 0.1 cm gelatine layers.
6. Refrigerate for one hour and cut into 3 cm (1¼ in) squares. There should be one lasagne per person.
7. Place one drop of liquorice paste between the third and fourth layers. Refrigerate.

Cep (porcini) *albóndigas*

- 50 g (2 oz) ceps (porcini)
- 8 g (1½ tsp) Metil solution, previously prepared

—

1. Clean the ceps and cut the stems into 3 mm cubes.
2. Mix 25 g (1 oz) of the cubes with 8 g (1½ tsp) of Metil solution.
3. Make 4 *albóndigas* weighing 8 g (¼ oz) each.
4. Refrigerate.

—

Albóndigas are Spanish meatballs.

Peanut oil marshmallow

- 250 g (1 cup) milk
- 5 x 2 g gelatine leaves, previously rehydrated in cold water
- 40 g (2⅔ tbsp) virgin peanut oil

—

1. Put 200 g (¾ cup) of milk in the freezer to cool to 3°C/37°F.
2. Meanwhile, mix the gelatine with the remaining 50 g (¼ cup) milk in a pan.
3. Dissolve the gelatine leaves at 40°C/105°F and pour into the electric mixer bowl.
4. Start to whip. After 30 seconds, add all the cooled milk in one go.
5. Continue to whip for 3 minutes and add the virgin peanut oil.
6. Keep whipping for another 30 seconds and spread out over a transparent tray to a thickness of 2 cm (¾ in).
7. Refrigerate for 2 hours.
8. Cut into cubes with 2 cm (¾ in) sides.
9. Store refrigerated in an airtight container.

Grated peanuts

- 40 g (1½ oz) peeled toasted peanuts

—

1. Grate the peanuts with a Microplane grater.
2. Keep in an airtight container.

Toasted black sesame savoury praline

- 50 g (2 oz) black sesame seeds
- 5 g (1 tsp) sunflower oil
- salt

—

1. Toast the black sesame in a frying pan (skillet).
2. Process the toasted black sesame seeds with the sunflower oil in a liquidizer until a fine, lump-free cream is obtained.
3. Strain, season with salt and put in a squeezy bottle.

Beetroot shoot juice

- 300 g (11 oz) beetroot shoots

—

1. Put the beetroot shoots through a juice extractor.
2. Set aside the juice obtained.

Beetroot shoot juice air base

- 100 g (⅓ cup) beetroot shoot juice, previously prepared

—

Pour the beetroot shoot juice into a 15 cm (6 in) deep container.

Freeze-dried cold white miso foam

- 35 g (2⅓ tbsp) white miso paste
- 125 g (½ cup) water
- 1 x 2 g gelatine leaf, previously rehydrated in cold water
- 1 x 0.5 litre (1 pint) ISI siphon
- 1 N^2O cartridge

—

1. Dilute the white miso paste in the water with a whisk and strain.
2. Heat a third of the liquid obtained and dissolve the gelatine into it.
3. Add the remaining liquid, strain and put in the siphon.
4. Close it and insert gas cartridge.
5. Refrigerate for 3 hours.
6. Fill 5 x 60 g (2 oz) cups with chilled miso foam and freeze-dry for 48 hours.
7. Remove the freeze-dried foam from the cup moulds and cut each one in half vertically.
8. Keep vacuum sealed until just before serving.

Potato stock

- 400 g (14 oz) potatoes
- 500 g (2 cups) water
- salt

—

1. Clean and cut the potatoes, skin on, into ½ cm (¼ in) slices.
2. Cover with water and boil over a medium heat for one hour. Remove the froth continuously.
3. Strain carefully to prevent the stock from becoming cloudy.
4. Season with salt and set aside.

EXTRAS

- 20 g (¾ oz) red cabbage shoots
- olive oil
- salt

FINISHING AND PRESENTATION

1. Work a hand-held blender over the top of the beetroot shoot juice air base so it emulsifies and the air forms.
2. Steam the Venus rice jelly.
3. Cook the cep *albóndigas* for 30 seconds in lightly salted water at 80°C/175°F. Drain and season with salt.
4. Sauté the red cabbage shoots in a little olive oil and season with salt.
5. Coat the peanut marshmallow with grated peanut.
6. Place a summer truffle *empanadilla* in the 11 o'clock position on a large oval dish. Place a cube of hot Venus rice jelly at 12 o'clock and a liquorice lasagne at 2 o'clock.
7. Put a sesame praline at 4 o'clock.
8. Place a coated peanut marshmallow at 5 o'clock. Put a teaspoon of beetroot shoot air at 7 o'clock.
9. Place a piece of freeze-dried miso foam at 8 o'clock.
10. Arrange in the middle of the plate a small pile of sautéed red cabbage shoots on the left and a cep *albondiga* on the right.
11. Present the hot potato broth separately so that the waiter can serve it in front of the diners.

—

Cutlery:
Tapas cutlery, a 14 x 3 cm (5½ x 1¼ in) spoon and fork.

How to eat:
Eat the *empanadilla* whole and alternate with the other components, without mixing them.

Fondue al hígado de rape, al ponzu y kumquat al sésamo blanco (Monkfish liver fondue with ponzu and white sesame-flavoured kumquat)

Serves 4

Ponzu sauce

- 6 g (1¼ tsp) dried kombu seaweed
- 150 g (⅔ cup) water
- 15 g (½ oz) sliced *katsuobushi*
- 60 g (¼ cup) fresh lime juice
- 75 g (⅓ cup) soy sauce

—

1. Combine the water with the kombu and bring to the boil.

2. Remove from the heat and leave to infuse for 2 minutes.

3. Take the kombu out and bring the kombu-infused water to the boil. Then add the shaved *katsuobushi*. Take off the heat and infuse for 5 minutes.

4. Squeeze through a Superbag and cool at room temperature.

5. Add the lime juice and soy sauce when cold.

6. Keep refrigerated.

—

Katsuobushi is the Japanese name for dried *bonito* (tuna) that has been smoked and cured with the *Aspergillus glaucus* fungus.

Ponzu sauce air base

- 200 g (¾ cup) ponzu sauce, previously prepared
- 0.4 g Lecite

—

Combine both ingredients in a 25 cm (10 in) deep container.

Soy sauce vinaigrette, toasted sesame oil and *yuzu*

- 150 g (⅔ cup) soy sauce
- 100 g (½ cup) toasted sesame oil
- 15 g (1 tbsp) rice vinegar
- 10 g (2 tsp) *yuzu* juice

—

1. Mix all the ingredients together with a whisk.

—

Yuzu is an Asian citrus fruit that tastes like a cross between mandarin and lemon. It is used particularly for its highly aromatic zest.

Monkfish liver slices

- 1 x 500 g (1 lb 2 oz) piece of monkfish liver
- ice

—

1. Cut off the ends of the liver and remove the outer veins.

2. Cover the liver with water and plenty of ice and leave in the refrigerator for 48 hours for the blood to drain away. Change the water and ice every 8 hours.

3. Drain and dry the liver well. Cut into 2 mm slices.

4. Divide into 4 servings of 6 slices each. Slightly overlap each slice over the next.

5. Keep refrigerated.

Dashi stock

- 40 g (1½ oz) dried kombu seaweed
- 1 kg (4¼ cups) water
- 50 g (2 oz) shaved *katsuobushi*

—

1. Cut the kombu into 1 cm (½ in) pieces and bring to the boil in the water.

2. Remove from the heat. Leave to stand for 5 minutes, then take out the kombu.

3. Bring the resulting stock back to the boil. Add the *katsuobushi* shavings and when it comes back from the boil, remove from heat.

4. Leave to stand for 5 minutes and strain through a Superbag.

5. Set aside.

Candied kumquats

- 150 g (⅔ cup) water
- 45 g (¼ cup) sugar
- 4 x 30 g (1 oz) kumquats

—

1. Mix the sugar and water and bring to the boil, simmering until the sugar dissolves completely.

2. Clean the kumquats and remove any stems.

3. When the syrup boils, add the kumquats to the boiling syrup and remove from heat.

4. Cool the kumquats in the syrup in the refrigerator.

Kumquat juice

- 6 x 30 g (1 oz) kumquats

—

1. Clean the kumquats, cut into quarters and remove any seeds from inside.

2. Liquidize the kumquat pulp and keep refrigerated.

Candied kumquats filled with kumquat juice and sesame

» 4 candied kumquats, previously prepared
» 40 g (3 tbsp) kumquat juice, previously prepared
» 10 g (2 tsp) toasted sesame oil
» 15 g (1 tbsp) toasted Japanese white sesame seeds

—

1. Make a cut in the top of each kumquat with a knife.

2. Use tweezers to remove the flesh from the fruit.

3. Using a syringe, fill the kumquats with previously prepared kumquat juice.

4. Put 2 drops of sesame oil inside each kumquat.

5. Finish by covering the cut with the toasted Japanese white sesame seeds.

FINISHING AND PRESENTATION

1. Work a hand-held blender over the surface of the ponzu sauce air mixture until it emulsifies and the air forms.

2. Put 2 spoons of soy and sesame vinaigrette into 4 bowls.

3. Cover the vinaigrette with 2 spoons of ponzu sauce air.

4. Place the 4 filled kumquats on 4 individual serving trays.

5. Place the monkfish liver on 4 slates accompanied by tweezers.

6. Heat the dashi stock well and place in a jug.

7. The waiter will bring a spirit burner and a hot pan separately, and will pour the hot dashi into the pan at the table.

—

Cutlery:
Silver tweezers.

How to eat:
Take a slice of monkfish liver and dip into the boiling dashi for 2 seconds. Remove from the dashi and dip into the bowl with vinaigrette and the ponzu sauce air. Eat the whole filled kumquat last.

Ventresca de caballa en escabeche de pollo con cebolla y caviar de vinagre (Belly of mackerel in chicken escabeche with onions and vinegar caviar)

Serves 4

Mackerel belly confit

- 8 x 200 g (7 oz) mackerel
- salt
- 500 g (2 cups) extra virgin olive oil

—

1. Use a very sharp knife to remove the bellies from the mackerel. Be careful not to pierce internal organs, as this will give the fish a bitter taste.
2. Use paper towels to remove any nerves or tissue that may have stuck to the belly. Ensure that there are no bones left.
3. Lightly salt the bellies.
4. Place the bellies on a non-stick tray, skin side down.
5. Cover with extra virgin olive oil and heat the confit at 70°C/160°F for 2 minutes.
6. Store the bellies in the oil until presentation and finishing.

Sherry vinegar caviar

- 10 g (¼ oz) basil seeds
- 120 g (½ cup) water
- 10 g (2 tsp) 25-year-old sherry vinegar

—

1. Put the basil seeds in the water and leave to hydrate for 20 minutes.
2. Take 50 g (2 oz) hydrated basil seeds and add the sherry vinegar.
3. Mix well and refrigerate.

Roast onion

- 1 x 100 g (3½ oz) Figueres onion

—

1. Wrap the onion in foil and bake at 180°C/350°F for 25 minutes.
2. Peel and cut into 8 x 1.5 cm (⅔ in) pieces.
3. Store at room temperature.

—

Figueres onions are a variety of onion native to Catalunya.

Chicken escabeche jus and fat

- 2 kg (4½ lb) cleaned chicken cut into 3 cm (1¼ in) pieces
- salt
- 100 g (3½ oz) onion, julienned
- 50 g (2 oz) garlic cloves crushed in their skin
- 2 sprigs dried thyme
- 2 sprigs dried rosemary
- 1 bay leaf
- 500 g (2 cups) olive oil
- 50 g (¼ cup) 25-year-old sherry vinegar
- 750 g (3¼ cups) water
- 15 g (½ oz) black peppercorns

—

1. Salt the chicken.
2. Brown the chicken in a pan with oil.
3. Once the chicken is well browned, add the onion and garlic and cook until they are browned.
4. Add the dried herbs and peppercorns and cook for one more minute.
5. Add the vinegar, reduce for one minute and add the water.
6. Cook for 20 minutes.
7. Refrigerate for 24 hours.
8. Heat the escabeche and strain. Press well to release all the jus.
9. Set aside 50 g (⅓ tbsp) for presentation and finishing.
10. Decant the escabeche jus into a tall, narrow container to allow the fat to separate.
11. Store the escabeche jus and fat separately.

Chicken escabeche air base

- 200 g (¾ cup) chicken escabeche jus, previously prepared
- 50 g (3⅓ tbsp) chicken escabeche fat, previously prepared
- 1 g Lecite

—

Combine all three ingredients in a 25 cm (10 in) deep container

EXTRAS

- 10 g (2 tsp) chopped chives
- 8 x 1 cm (½ in) fresh chervil leaves
- 8 fresh tarragon shoots
- freshly ground black pepper

FINISHING AND PRESENTATION

1. Heat the chicken escabeche air base at 40°C/104°F. Work a hand-held blender over the top of the liquid until it emulsifies and the air forms.
2. Place a soupspoon of chicken escabeche air on each side of a rectangular dish.
3. Sprinkle freshly ground black pepper on the meat side of the mackerel bellies and arrange them over the air with the skin side down.
4. Sprinkle chopped chives over the roast onion and top each piece with one chervil leaf and one tarragon leaf.
5. Place 2 teaspoons of chicken escabeche air between 2 mackerel belly pieces and arrange two pieces of roast onion with herbs over it.
6. Put 2 teaspoons of sherry vinegar caviar on top of the onion pieces.
7. Finish by lightly sprinkling a few drops of chicken escabeche jus over the mackerel bellies and the onion pieces.

—

Cutlery:
Tapas cutlery, a 14 x 3 cm (5½ x 1¼ in) spoon and fork.

How to eat:
Eat the mackerel belly and the air together, and after each mouthful eat a piece of roast onion with fresh herbs and sherry vinegar caviar.

—

Another version of this dish has also been created in which the roast onion is substituted with *pa-ha* dressed with sherry vinegar, extra virgin olive oil and salt.

Cigala con quinoa[3]
(Langoustine with quinoa[3])

Serves 4

Puffed quinoa

- 50 g (¼ cup) quinoa
- 250 g (1 cup) olive oil
- salt

—

1. Boil the quinoa for 25 minutes in plenty of water.
2. Drain, rinse in cold water to stop the cooking process, then drain well.
3. Spread the cooked quinoa out over trays lined with parchment paper; ensure the grains are not overlapping.
4. Leave the quinoa in a warm place for 24 hours until it is completely dry.
5. Once dry, cook the quinoa in oil at 180°C/350°F until it puffs up.
6. Drain, soak up the excess oil on paper towel and season with salt while still hot.

Langoustine tails

- 4 x 140 g (5 oz) langoustines

—

1. Remove the heads from the langoustines, and set these aside for preparing the essence.
2. Peel the tails up to the last ring of the shell.
3. Remove the intestinal tract and store the tails in the refrigerator.

Langoustine essence

- langoustine heads (already prepared)
- olive oil

—

1. Sauté the langoustine heads in a little olive oil in a frying pan (skillet).
2. Crush the heads one by one to obtain their jus.
3. Add a few drops of olive oil to the essence obtained, without emulsifying it.

—

This preparation should be made immediately before presentation and finishing.

Metil solution

- 3 g Metil
- 100 g (½ cup) water

—

1. Blend the ingredients together at room temperature in a liquidizer until they form a smooth, even mixture.
2. Strain and leave in the refrigerator for 24 hours.

Cooked quinoa

- 50 g (¼ cup) quinoa
- 200 g (¾ cup) water
- salt

—

1. Boil the quinoa in lightly salted water for 14 minutes.
2. Drain and lay out on a tray to cool quickly and halt the cooking process.
3. Refrigerate.

Quinoa-coated langoustine

- 4 langoustine tails, previously prepared
- 100 g (3½ oz) cooked quinoa, previously prepared
- 20 g (4 tsp) Metil solution, previously prepared

—

1. Mix the cooked quinoa with the Metil solution.
2. Coat the langoustine tails with this mixture so that each langoustine is completely covered with a fine layer of it, with only the tail shell remaining uncovered.
3. Lay out on parchment paper and put in the refrigerator.

Spring onion (scallion) rings

- 2 x 50 g (2 oz) spring onions (scallions)
- ice cubes

—

1. Peel and cut the spring onions into 2 mm rings.
2. Choose 36 rings with a 1.5 cm (⅔ in) diameter and soak them in water filled with ice cubes for 2 hours.
3. Remove from the water and drain on a paper towel.
4. Refrigerate.

Diced tomato

- 1 x 100 g (3½ oz) ripe tomato

—

1. Blanch the tomato in boiling water, plunge it into iced water and then remove the skin.
2. Cut the tomato into quarters and remove the seeds.
3. Dice the tomato flesh into 0.5 cm (¼ in) cubes. Refrigerate.

Lime cubes and chopped zest

- 2 x 150 g (5 oz) limes

—

1. Slice off the top and bottom of the limes to reveal the segments.
2. Peel them in a spiral to expose the flesh and so that there are no traces of rind or pith, without altering the basic shape of the limes.
3. Remove the segments from their membranes with a sharp knife.
4. Cut the segments into 12 x 0.5 cm (¼ in) cubes.
5. Remove the zest and chop it into tiny 1 mm cubes.
6. Refrigerate each ingredient separately.

Chilli oil

- 1 g dried chilli
- 50 g (¼ cup) sunflower oil

—

1. Chop the chilli and leave to infuse in the oil for 2 hours at 70°C/160°F.

2. Strain and put into a squeezy bottle.

Quinoa shoots

- 60 g quinoa shoots
- 20 g (1⅓ tbsp) water
- salt

—

1. Boil the quinoa shoots for 5 minutes in the measured water.

2. Season with salt and keep hot.

EXTRAS

- 160 g (⅔ cup) *kefir*
- 12 fresh, small coriander (cilantro) leaves
- extra virgin olive oil
- olive oil
- salt

—

Kefir is a fermented milk product from the Caucasus region.

FINISHING AND PRESENTATION

1. Lightly salt the quinoa-coated langoustine and fry both sides in olive oil.

2. On the right-hand side of the plate, arrange a vertical salad made up of 9 spring onion (scallion) rings, 9 tomato cubes, 3 lime cubes, 4 small coriander (cilantro) leaves and a little chopped lime zest. Finish with 4 drops of chilli oil, salt and a few drops of extra virgin olive oil.

3. Mix 60 g (2 oz) of cooked quinoa shoots with 30 g (1 oz) of puffed quinoa and heat under the salamander grill (broiler).

4. Divide the mixture among the 4 dishes. Place as a bouquet in the base of the dishes.

5. Cut the upper part of the tail off the quinoa-coated langoustine so that the top part of the tail is bare.

6. Place a langoustine tail vertically on the left-hand side of the salad, leaving a space of 4 cm (1¾ in) in which to arrange vertically a spoon of langoustine essence and oil.

7. The *kefir* comes in a separate jug so that the waiter can serve it in front of the diner.

—

Cutlery:
Spoon, fork and fish knife.

How to eat:
Each ingredient alternately.

Alitas de pollo tandoori con germinado de borraja, crema de ostra y mató aéreo (Tandoori chicken wings with borage shoots, oyster cream and frothy *mató* cheese)

Serves 4

Tandoori chicken sauce

- 500 g (1 lb 2 oz) cleaned chicken, cut into 3 cm (1¼ in) pieces
- 30 g (1 oz) onion, julienned
- 2 g tandoori paste
- 1 g tandoori powder
- 200 g (¾ cup) water
- olive oil
- salt

—

1. Heat the oil in a pan, add the seasoned chicken pieces and brown well.

2. Add the julienned onion and stir until it caramelizes.

3. Add the tandoori paste and powder. Cook everything together for one minute and add the water.

4. Cook on a medium heat until the sauce is reduced and well flavoured.

5. Use a fine mesh sieve to strain and season with salt if necessary.

Chicken wing confit

- 6 x 100 g (3½ oz) free-range chicken wings
- 20 g (1⅓ tbsp) olive oil

—

1. Cut off the wing tips at the joint and use the middle section.

2. Remove any remaining feathers with tweezers.

3. Place the cleaned chicken wings into a vacuum-pack bag with the oil and vacuum seal.

4. Slow cook the chicken wings at 63°C/145°F in a Roner for 24 hours.

5. Take the wings out of the Roner and trim one end slightly to expose the bone.

6. Remove the bones carefully by hand, keeping them whole and without breaking the meat.

Fermented milk *mató* cheese

- 500 g (2 cups) fermented full-cream milk

—

1. Pour the milk into a small saucepan and heat to 56°C/133°F, stirring continuously with a spatula.

2. Leave to stand for 5 minutes.

3. Pour the milk through a sieve to drain off the whey. The *mató* cheese curds will remain in the sieve.

4. Refrigerate.

Milk air with Córdoba spice base

- 500 g (2 cups) milk
- 2.5 g Sucro
- 3.5 g Fatéma Hal's Córdoba spices

—

1. Mix the 3 ingredients with a hand-held blender and strain through a Superbag.
2. Pour the mixture into a 25 cm (10 in) deep container.

Smoked streaky Spanish bacon fat

- 50 g (2 oz) smoked streaky Spanish bacon

—

1. Slice the bacon into 2 cm (¾ in) chunks and put in a small pan over a low heat to sweat and release the fat. Do not let it fry.
2. Strain off the fat and set aside.

Cleaned oysters

- 3 x 200 g (7 oz) Napoleon oysters

—

1. Open the oysters with an oyster knife. Retain the liquor.
2. Cut through the muscle holding the oyster to the shell and remove the oyster.
3. De-beard the oysters with a pair of scissors.
4. Strain the liquor through a Superbag and add the oysters.
5. Refrigerate.

Oyster cream

- 25 g (1 oz) cleaned oysters, previously prepared
- 30 g (2 tbsp) oyster liquor, previously prepared
- 8 g (1½ tsp) melted smoked streaky Spanish bacon fat, previously prepared

—

1. Blend the oysters with the oyster liquor.
2. Emulsify the resulting liquid with the melted bacon fat at room temperature.
3. Strain and refrigerate.

Green almonds in almond oil

- 12 green almonds
- 10 g (2 tsp) toasted almond oil

—

1. Peel and split the almonds in half.
2. Pour the toasted almond oil over them. Cover and refrigerate.

Borage shoots

» 2 punnets (2 oz) borage shoots

—

1. Use scissors to remove the base of the borage shoots. The stem should be left as long as possible.
2. Make 8 bunches of 5 borage shoots.
3. Refrigerate.

—

If borage shoots are not available, they can be substituted with shoots of wild purslane.

EXTRAS

» freshly ground black pepper
» salt
» olive oil

FINISHING AND PRESENTATION

1. Work a hand-held blender over the surface of the milk and Córdoba spice mixture until it emulsifies and the air forms.
2. Season the cooked chicken wings with salt and freshly ground black pepper and fry over a medium heat in a non-stick frying pan with a little oil, keeping the skin in contact with the base of the pan.
3. Once the skin is well browned and crisp, turn the wings over and fry for 30 seconds.
4. Take the wings out of the pan and trim them on each side. Cut each wing into 2 x 2 cm (¾ in) pieces. Divide into portions with 3 pieces of wing in each one.
5. On a rectangular dish make 2 small piles of 3 half almonds in almond oil at each end of the plate.
6. Put a small bunch of borage shoots beside each pile of almonds.
7. Pour a small amount of oyster cream over the borage shoots.
8. Put a teaspoon of *mató* cheese in the upper central part of the dish.
9. Place one portion of chicken wings diagonally across the middle of the dish, leaving a space of 1 cm (½ in) between each piece of wing.
10. Pour hot tandoori chicken sauce over the wings.
11. Finish by putting a spoon of milk and Córdoba spice air over the home-made *mató* cheese. Make a hole in the air so that the *mató* can be seen.

—

Cutlery:
Tapas cutlery, a 14 x 3 cm (5½ x 1¼ in) spoon and fork.

How to eat:
Alternate the chicken wings with the other components.

—

Maintaining the intense concentration needed to serve 1,500 dishes over five hours is as challenging as ever

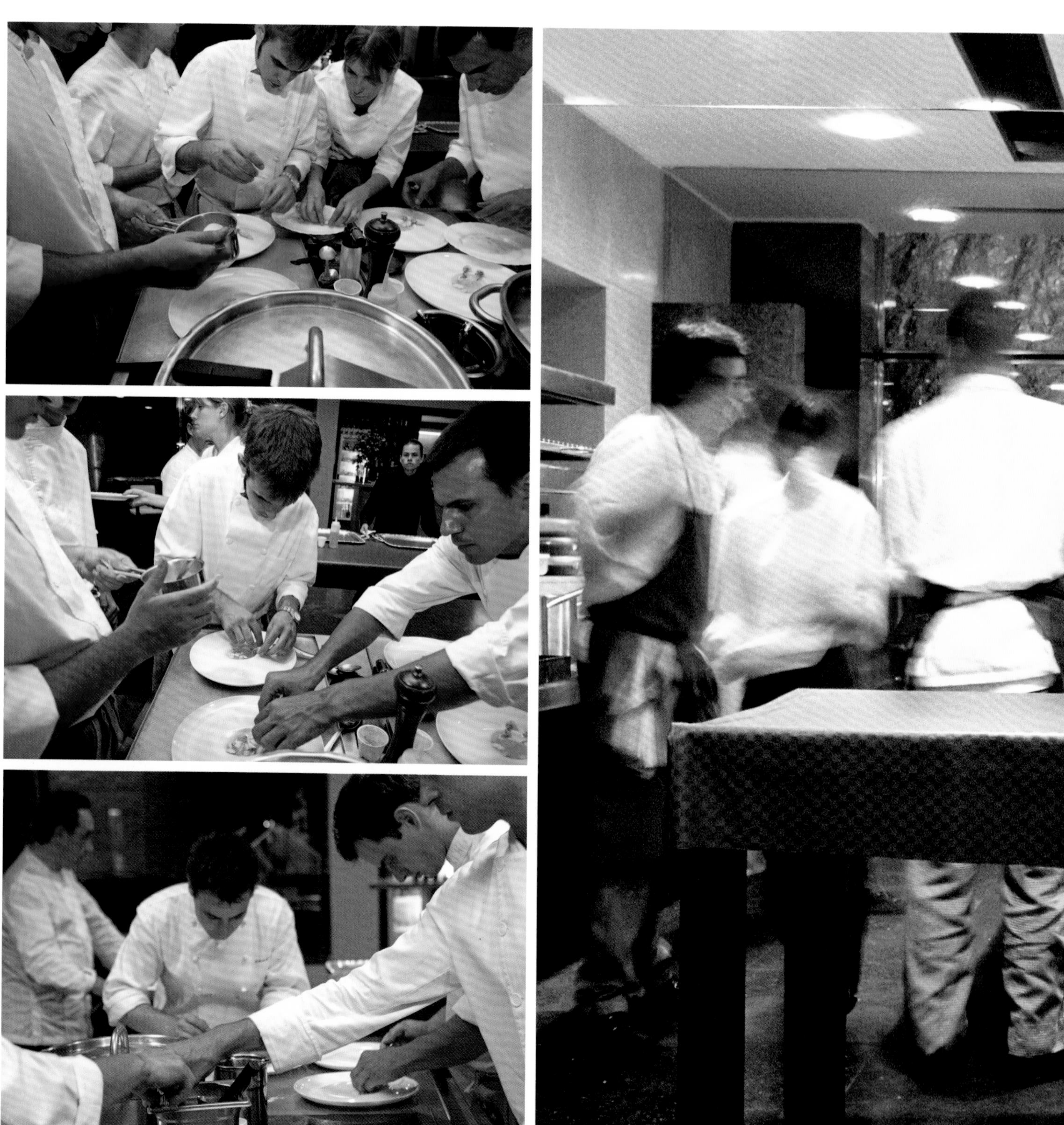

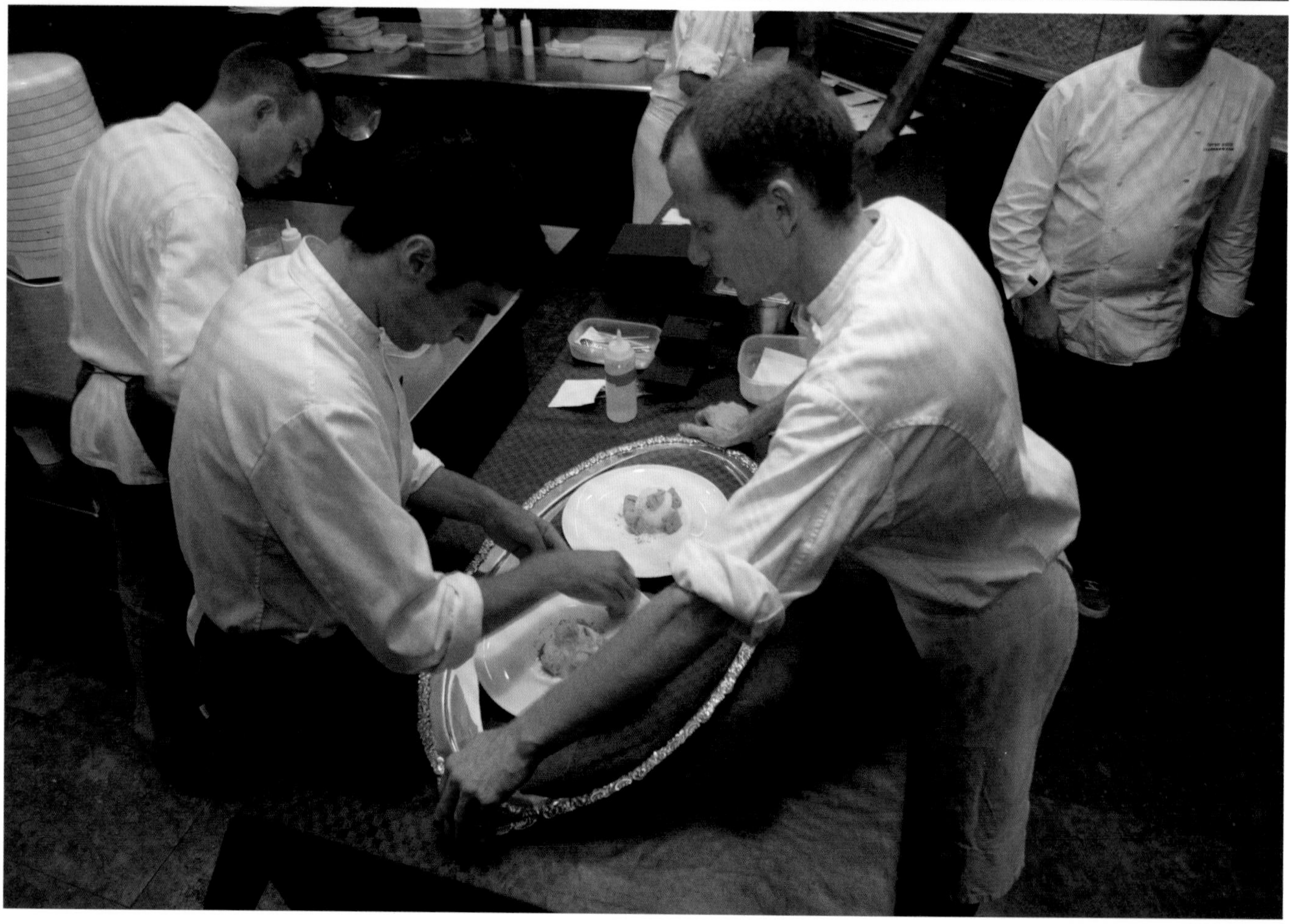

The kitchens at elBulli

There are two kitchens at elBulli, a large one and a small one, covering about 350 square metres (3,770 square feet) in total. They are only a few metres apart, but have different purposes: the small kitchen houses the large stock pots that simmer all day, the staff meal is prepared there, and chefs send their dishes from there during service. The large kitchen is where the morning creative sessions take place, where most of the *mise en place* is done, and where the dishes are prepared.

The kitchens were created in 1993 after months of planning and research, which included a visit to the kitchen of the Troisgros brothers in Roanne, France. They were designed according to Ferran's plans and models by architect Dolors Andreu using natural materials from the surrounding area, such as slate from the Cap de Creus. In the middle of the pass (the front bench from which the food is served) stands a large bull's head by the Catalan sculptor Xavier Medina Campeny, one of several sculptures in the kitchen. But despite what many people think, the bull's head sculpture is not the reason behind the name of the restaurant.

The hobs (stoves) in the elBulli kitchen are all electric. They are large, flat built-in induction hobs and the temperature can be regulated from either side of the unit. Using induction hobs facilitates very exact, precise control of the cooking, which is essential in preparing the creations that make up the menu at elBulli.

'L'amant de cap norfeo digue: pèsol, ploma, barca. La veu respongué: tongue, tongue, tongue. L'amant afegí: nap, gerd, trufa. Finalment la papil. La s'obri.'

This motto runs along the workbench in the kitchen at the elBulli workshop in Barcelona, and translates as: 'The lover of Cap Norfeo says: "Pea, feather, boat." The voice answers: "Tongue, tongue, tongue." The lover responds: "Turnip, raspberry, truffle." At last, the taste buds open.'

The kitchens at elBulli contain specialist cooking equipment that is not seen in many restaurants, but it is a kitchen first and foremost. When it comes to service, the only way of getting all the dishes out is through sheer hard work, technical skill, concentration and many pairs of hands.

'If technology were that advanced, we would not need forty chefs for fifty guests.'

Synchronization between the dining room and kitchen is the key to everything running smoothly

The waiters' work is not limited to carrying plates from the kitchen to the dining rooms. Each waiter is assigned to a table and will take care of those guests, ensuring they are neither rushed nor left waiting, and that every dish is introduced correctly so that the guests know how to eat it. The waiter may even give a finishing touch to a dish in front of the guest, for example when a frozen 'peach' is sliced at the table, or a few drops of essential oil are added to an air to release a last-minute fragrance.

The same story at two different speeds

The frenetic speed the chefs work at during service is confined to the kitchen, and they try not to allow it into the dining room. Here, the distance between the tables and the air of tranquillity mean that guests can relax with their friends. A peaceful atmosphere is also essential for experiencing the full sensory impact of each dish.

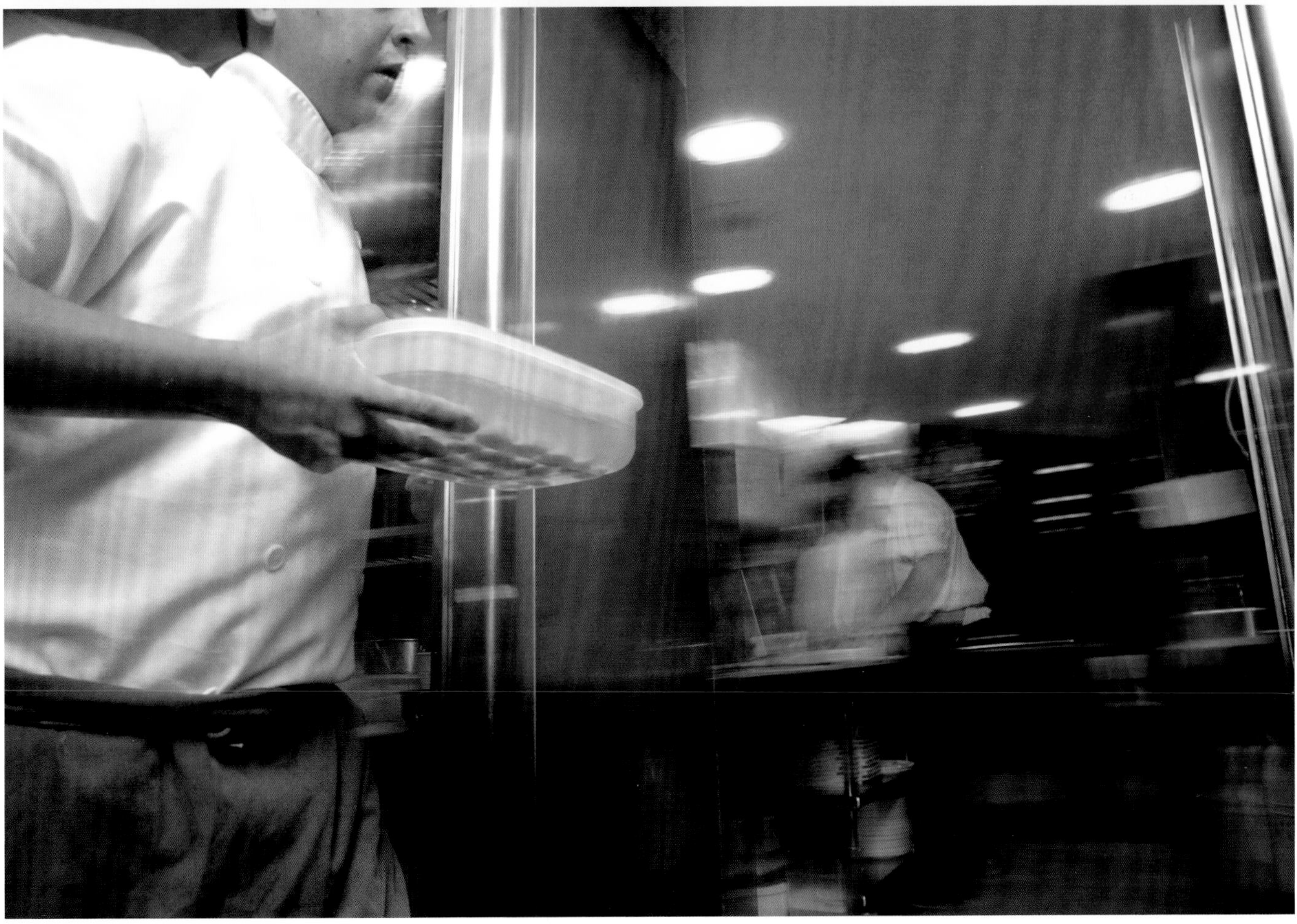

A perfectly coordinated team

Ferran has compared the action in the kitchens to that of a Formula One race, because every dish that is sent out requires the same level of precision and speed as a pit stop – the difference being that in the elBulli kitchen there is a pit stop every few minutes.

23:15

—

The pace slows down as act three approaches

Cooking and art

Comparisons drawn between art and cookery are not new and have frequently been debated over the last few years. Throughout the twentieth century, there have been attempts to combine the two, which have usually originated in the artistic community. However, now the debate is about whether the cuisine of Ferran Adrià and other chefs can be considered an artistic phenomenon. This concept has attracted much controversy and discussion, which culminated in an invitation for Ferran to participate in the Documenta 12 exhibiton in Kassel in 2007.

Roger Buergel, organizer of Documenta 12, asked Ferran to help him answer the question of whether cookery can be art because of his creative intelligence and the fact that his dishes provoke an aesthetic emotional response. Buergel made it clear that Ferran was invited as an artist who considers the interaction between materials and the immaterial, not as the cook for the exhibition. The elBulli restaurant became a satellite pavilion of the show, during which two people were flown to Cala Montjoi each day to experience the food at the restaurant.

Ferran's relationship with the art world began in the early 1990s through his friendship with the Catalan sculptor Xavier Medina Campeny. While elBulli was closed for the winter, Ferran worked in Medina Campeny's workshop in Barcelona, dedicating himself, for the first time, to creativity in the widest sense of the word. This experience helped to define his point of view on the relationship between cookery and art. He resolved that cookery has its own rules and history, and so generates its own language. This language takes the shape of a dish, or a combination of different dishes in the form of a menu, which provoke analysis and reflection and make it possible to 'say' something. Cooking not only satisfies a physiological need or provides sensory pleasure, it also elicits important aesthetic responses, anchors them in a story, and establishes an evolution, which can be translated into intellectual concepts. The British Pop artist Richard Hamilton wrote, "Ferran's genius lies in his intention to develop and perfect a language made from what we eat. [...] Ferran's art is linguistic because he manipulates ingredients like a language which he can model and revitalize so that his creations take a place among other artistic forms."

Any attempt to bring together cookery and other creative disciplines is important because it establishes the foundation from which to learn, to advance, to create debate and to discover limits. Despite the debate, Ferran has always maintained that cookery is cookery and it must be developed within the parameters of the discipline, a discipline that is rich and complex enough to generate its own evolution and its own path.

The technique of spherification is the controlled setting of a liquid with a concentrated flavour, mixed with Algin, which, when submerged in a Calcic bath, produces spheres with a liquid interior. Depending on the dose, the length of time it spends in the Calcic bath and the utensil used to apply it (such as different-sized spoons and syringes) these spheres can be created with different textures, consistencies and diameters: ravioli, bubbles, marbles, or caviar, as shown on these pages.

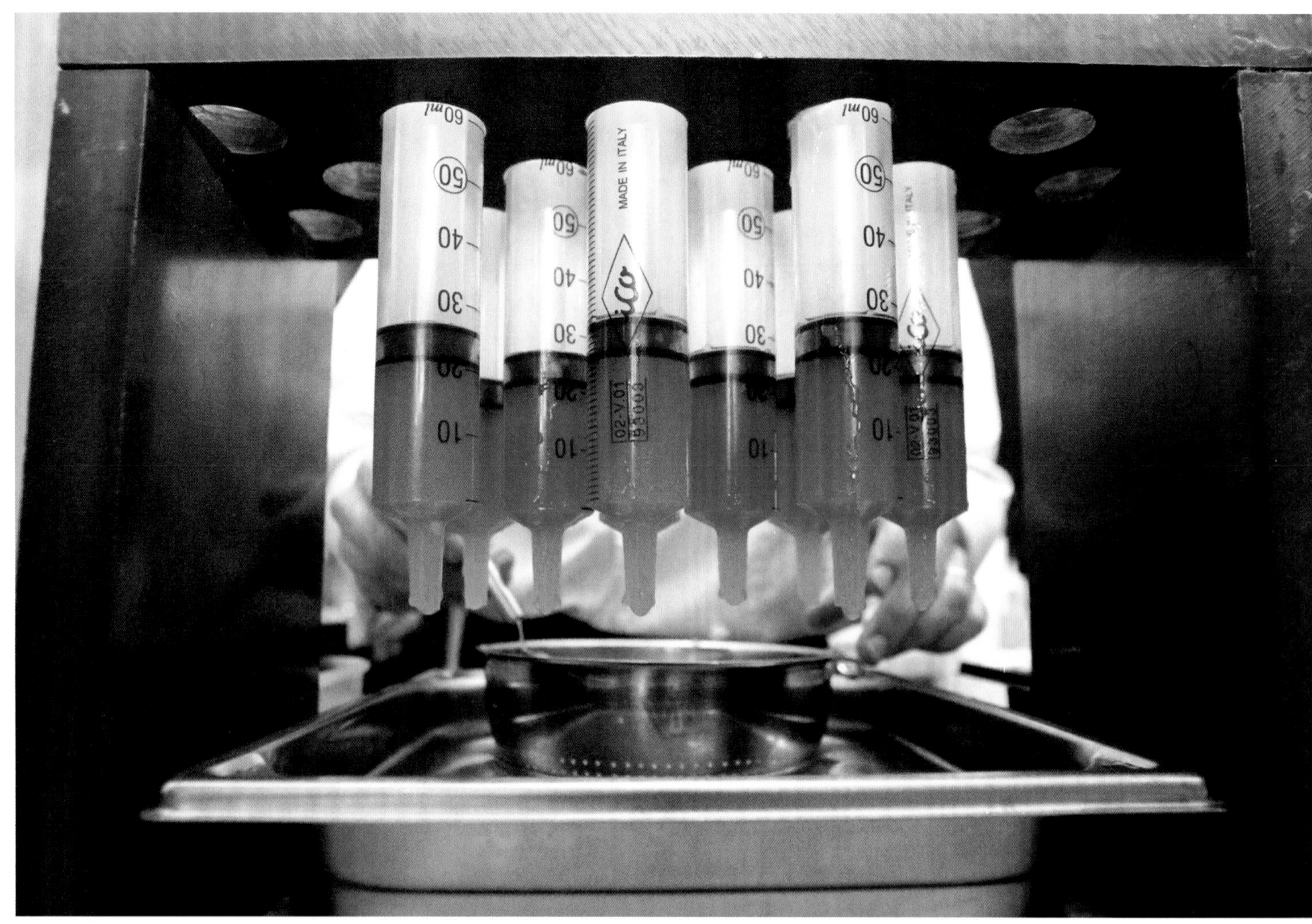

This syringe rack, which was designed especially for elBulli to help with spherification, allows many droplets to be formed simultaneously, which means that several portions can be made at once. Without this it would take several minutes to make enough for one dish.

This is the most dangerous moment

After nearly four hours of maximum concentration, slowing down can lead to the loss of attention to detail. The head chef is responsible for making sure this does not happen.

Like the conductor of an orchestra, he must have all his senses alert. The order sheets are just the musical score. He must be able to control the whole process and make decisions on the spur of the moment.

23:35

Jean Jacques y Montse Lambert
Mesa
Snacks
Pax
6
20:00
1 margarita 2005
2 olivas sféricas
3 marshmallow de parmegiano
4 oreo de oliva negra con crema doble
5 baguette de malta con crocant de especias
6 melón cru con hierbas y almendra tierna
7 palomita de Reypenaer a la nuez moscada
8 caramelo de aceite de calabaza
9 ninfa de algodón
10 caviar sférico de melón
11 mozzarella casera con albahaca
12 huevos de series
13 brioche al vapor
14 deshielo 2005
15 nudos sferificados de yogur con ficoide glaciale, alcapar
16 mejillones de roca con "gargillou" de algas
17 tortilla de gelatina de trufa negra
18 sopa thai con tofu de coco

23:40

Creativity does not stop

Although it is nearly the end of the meal and tension in the kitchen is still high, Ferran finds a moment to try a new preparation that his head chefs want him to consider. Creativity has had to take a back seat since 19.30, but that does not mean it has stopped.

ferran adrià
by ARMAND BASI

Ferran monitors the order sheets throughout service and checks the flow of dishes being served to each table.

Liquid de melocotón
(Peach liquid)

Serves 4

Peach liquid

- 100 g (½ cup) Kuhri peach liqueur
- 100 g (½ cup) 35% fat single (light) cream
- 1 kg (4¼ cups) liquid nitrogen

—

1. Freeze a 5 ml (1 tsp) hemispherical measuring spoon, then fill it with peach liqueur and dip it inside the liquid nitrogen tank without letting the nitrogen touch the liqueur, so that only the spoon freezes.

2. When the inside edge of the spoon is frozen (about 8 seconds), dip the spoon in completely so that the top layer of liqueur also freezes.

3. Freeze for 8 more seconds. Remove from the nitrogen and tap the spoon so that the peach liqueur is released as a hemispherical ice cube.

4. Quickly dip the ice cube in the cream, ensuring that no part is uncovered, then put back into the liquid nitrogen for 3 seconds.

5. Remove from the nitrogen and store in the freezer at -20°C/-4°F.

—

Liquid nitrogen should not be handled without training in how to use it safely.

Wild peach juice

- 100 g (⅓ cup) Garnier wild red peach juice

—

Thaw the juice. Strain it and put it in a squeezy bottle.

FINISHING AND PRESENTATION

1. Fifteen minutes before serving, remove the peach liquids from the deep freezer at -20°C/-4°F and put in the freezer at -8°C/18°F so that the liqueur inside melts.

2. Fill a measuring spoon with wild peach juice and place it over one of the slots on a frozen rectangular slate with 2 holes.

3. Place the peach liquid over the other slot and serve quickly.

—

Cutlery:
None.

How to eat:
Eat the liquid whole. Break it gently inside the mouth. Finish with the spoon containing wild peach juice.

Coulant/suflé de granadilla al toffee y cardamomo (Coulant/soufflé of granadilla with cardamom toffee)

Serves 4

Granadilla juice

» 15 x 100 g (3½ oz) sweet granadillas

—

1. Cut the granadillas in half and scoop out the flesh with a teaspoon over a chinois to catch and strain the juice.

2. Process the flesh and seeds with a hand-held blender on the lowest speed so that they release all their juice without being crushed.

3. Strain the juice through a Superbag and refrigerate.

—

The sweet granadilla (*Passiflora ligularis*) is related to the passion fruit and is native to tropical areas of South and Central America. It is a round, orange fruit with black spots and juicy seeds.

Chilled cardamom toffee foam

» 2 g cardamom seeds
» 175 g (¾ cup) 35% fat single (light) cream
» 150 g (¾ cup) sugar
» 1 x 0.5 litre (1 pint) ISI siphon
» 1 N^2O cartridge

—

1. Powder the cardamom seeds in a grinder.

2. Put the sugar in a small pan and heat to make a dark caramel.

3. Heat the cream, add to the caramel and stir continuously to create a smooth, even mixture.

4. Add the powdered cardamom and leave to infuse for 30 minutes. Strain and allow the toffee to stand in the refrigerator for 12 hours.

5. Fill the siphon with the toffee.

6. Close it and insert the gas cartridge.

7. Refrigerate.

Granadilla juice Metil cloud

» 250 g (1 cup) granadilla juice, previously prepared
» 3 g Metil
» 3 x 2 g gelatine leaves, previously rehydrated in cold water

—

1. Blend 200 g (¾ cup) granadilla juice with the Metil with a hand-held blender until lump-free.

2. Place the mixture in the freezer to reduce the temperature quickly to 3°C/37°F.

3. Drain the rehydrated gelatine sheet and heat to dissolve in 50 g (¼ cup) granadilla juice.

4. Once the granadilla and Metil solution has reached 3°C/37°F, remove from the freezer and leave in a warm place until the temperature increases to 14°C/57°F.

5. Put the solution into the mixer and begin beating at medium speed.

6. When it starts to foam, add the granadilla and gelatine mixture, which has been heated to 39°C/102°F.

7. Beat for about 7 minutes until the mixture forms peaks like beaten egg whites.

Toffee and granadilla coulant/soufflé

» granadilla juice Metil cloud, previously prepared
» chilled cardamom toffee foam, previously prepared
» 4 x 4.5 cm (1¾ in) round moulds, 6 cm (2½ in) deep and lined with parchment paper

—

1. Put the Metil cloud into a piping bag with a No. 8 plain nozzle.

2. Place the moulds on a flat tray lined with parchment paper.

3. Pipe the Metil cloud into the base of the mould to form a 1 cm (½ in) layer. Continue to pipe the cloud around the walls of the mould, leaving a 1.5 cm (⅔ in) diameter space in the middle.

4. Freeze for 5 minutes until the cloud sets, then fill the space with toffee foam.

5. Finish by covering the moulds with a 1 cm (½ in) layer of cloud.

6. Set in the freezer for 5 minutes.

Cardamom powder

» 20 g (1⅓ tbsp) cardamom pods

—

1. Break open the cardamom pods and take out the seeds.

2. Powder the seeds in a grinder.

EXTRAS

» 2 x 50 g (2 oz) passion fruits

—

Cut the passion fruits in half.

FINISHING AND PRESENTATION

1. Lift the soufflé with a spatula and place it in the middle of a 21 cm (8½ in) dish.

2. Carefully remove the mould without breaking the soufflé.

3. Heat the soufflé under the salamander grill (broiler) until hot on the outside and the inside is almost liquid.

4. Sprinkle powdered cardamom over the surface of the soufflé.

5. Serve the halved passion fruit separately so that the waiter can spoon out the passion fruit seeds around the soufflé in front of the diner.

—

Alternatively, the soufflé could be heated in a microwave at full power for 5 seconds.

—

Cutlery:
Tapas cutlery, a 14 x 3 cm (5½ x 1¼ in) spoon and fork.

How to eat:
Break the soufflé and eat it alternately with the passion fruit seeds.

Aire-LYO de chocolate con sorbete crispy de frambuesa y granizado de eucalipto (Chocolate air-LYO with crisp raspberry sorbet and eucalyptus water ice)

Serves 4

Chocolate and hazelnut praline air base

- 400 g (14 oz) chocolate
- 50 g (3⅓ tbsp) Piedmont hazelnut praline
- 5 g (1 tsp) Lecite
- 1 kg (4¼ cups) water

—

1. Crush the chocolate and place it in a bowl.
2. Add the praline and Lecite.
3. Heat the water to 90°C/195°F and add the chocolate, praline and Lecite solution.
4. Allow to stand for one minute, then process with a hand-held blender.
5. Maintain the temperature at 50°C/120°F.

Freeze-dried chocolate and hazelnut praline air

- frozen chocolate and hazelnut praline air, previously prepared

—

1. Place in the freeze-dryer for 48 hours.
2. Once the freeze-drying process is complete, store in an airtight container in a cool, dry place.

Frozen chocolate and hazelnut praline air

- Chocolate and hazelnut praline air base, previously prepared

—

1. Work the hand-held blender over the top of the chocolate and praline mixture until it emulsifies and the air forms on top of the liquid.
2. Fill two 10 x 20 x 5 cm (5 x 8 x 2 in) containers with this air and freeze immediately.
3. Leave in the freezer for 2 hours with an airtight lid to prevent the frozen air from absorbing other flavours.

100% syrup

- 50 g (¼ cup) sugar
- 50 g (¼ cup) water

—

1. Mix the ingredients in a small pan and bring to the boil.
2. Refrigerate.

Raspberry sorbet

- 200 g (1¼ cups) raspberries
- 25 g (1 oz) glucose
- 50 g (¼ cup) 100% syrup, previously prepared
- 1 g sorbet stabilizer

—

1. Combine the glucose and 100% syrup in a pan at a medium heat.
2. When the temperature reaches 40°C/105°F, add the powdered stabilizer and turn the heat up to 85°C/185°F.
3. At the same time, purée the raspberries in the liquidizer.
4. When the base containing the stabilizer is warm, add the raspberry purée and strain.
5. Mix and then allow to stand in the refrigerator for 8 hours.
6. Transfer to a Pacojet beaker and freeze at -20°C/-4°F.

Eucalyptus leaf infusion

» 25 g (1 oz) young eucalyptus leaves
» 500 g (2 cups) water
» 65 g (⅓ cup) sugar

—

1. Combine the water and sugar in a small pan and bring to the boil.
2. Chop the eucalyptus leaves and add to the pan.
3. Cover and infuse for 5 minutes.
4. Strain.

Eucalyptus leaf water ice

» 300 g (1⅓ cups) eucalyptus leaf infusion, previously prepared
» ½ x 2 g gelatine leaf, previously rehydrated in cold water

—

1. Dissolve the gelatine in a quarter of the eucalyptus infusion.
2. Add the remaining infusion and freeze in a shallow container to a depth of 1 cm (½ in).
3. Freeze at -10°C/15°F.

Kataifi pastry skein

» 15 g (½ oz) kataifi pastry

—

1. Shape 4 x 1 g skeins from the kataifi pastry.
2. Bake at 210°C/410°F for 5 minutes.
3. Store in an airtight container in a cool, dry place.

—

Kataifi is very thin pastry in long threads.

Chocolate-sprayed kataifi skeins

» 150 g (5 oz) chocolate
» 50 g (2 oz) cocoa butter
» 4 kataifi skeins, previously prepared

—

1. Melt the chocolate in a microwave on medium power.
2. Add the cocoa butter and let it dissolve. The mixture should be kept at 35°C/95°F.
3. When it is free of lumps and the cocoa butter is well melted, fill a chocolate spray gun.
4. Spray the kataifi skeins with chocolate and place in the freezer for 20 seconds.
5. Repeat this step twice.
6. When complete, store in an airtight container in a cool, dry place.

Chocolate-sprayed raspberries

» 150 g (5 oz) chocolate
» 50 g (2 oz) cocoa butter
» 4 x 2.5 g raspberries

—

1. Melt the chocolate in a microwave.
2. Add the cocoa butter and let it dissolve. The chocolate and cocoa butter mixture should be kept at 35°C/95°F.
3. When the mixture is lump-free and the cocoa butter is melted, fill a chocolate spray gun.
4. Place the 4 raspberries on a tray in the freezer for 3 minutes.
5. Spray until evenly coated.
6. Refrigerate in an airtight container.

EXTRAS

» 20 g (4 tsp) freeze-dried raspberry crisp

FINISHING AND PRESENTATION

1. Process the raspberry sorbet with a Pacojet and store in the freezer.

2. Scrape the eucalyptus water ice with a spatula to obtain frozen shavings and store them in the freezer.

3. Place a little freeze-dried chocolate air in the middle of an oval dish.

4. Mix 7.5 g (¼ oz) raspberry sorbet with 1 g freeze-dried raspberry crisp.

5. Place in the middle of the dish.

6. Imagining the plate as a clock face, place a skein of chocolate-sprayed kataifi pastry at 11 o'clock.

7. Place 20 g (4 tsp) eucalyptus water ice shavings from 10 o'clock to 5 o'clock.

8. Spread 1 g freeze-dried raspberry crisp along the edge of the water ice, bordering the freeze-dried chocolate air.

9. Scatter 5.5 g (1 tsp) freeze-dried frozen chocolate air over the part of the dish that is not covered by the water ice.

10. Place a chocolate-sprayed raspberry opposite the kataifi pastry, where the freeze-dried chocolate air meets the eucalyptus water ice.

—

Cutlery:
Tapas cutlery, a 14 x 3 cm (5½ x 1¼ in) spoon and fork.

How to eat:
Eat each element separately and alternately.

The chefs prepare the *Raspberry sorbet with lemon verbena, haba tonka toffee and raspberry crunchy.* After drawing a line of cocoa sauce, they add a little haba tonka foam, on top of which they place some broken-up raspberry biscuit and a few frozen raspberry drops. Finally, the chocolate shell containing the raspberry sorbet with lemon verbena is positioned so that it leans against the foam.

Fruit has been treated in different ways – in syrup, candied, fresh, CRU, freeze-dried – in preparation for the avant-dessert *Natura*.

DOLCE

23:55

The chefs of the sweet world start to plate *Apricot palet with milk chocolate ice cream and passion fruit…*

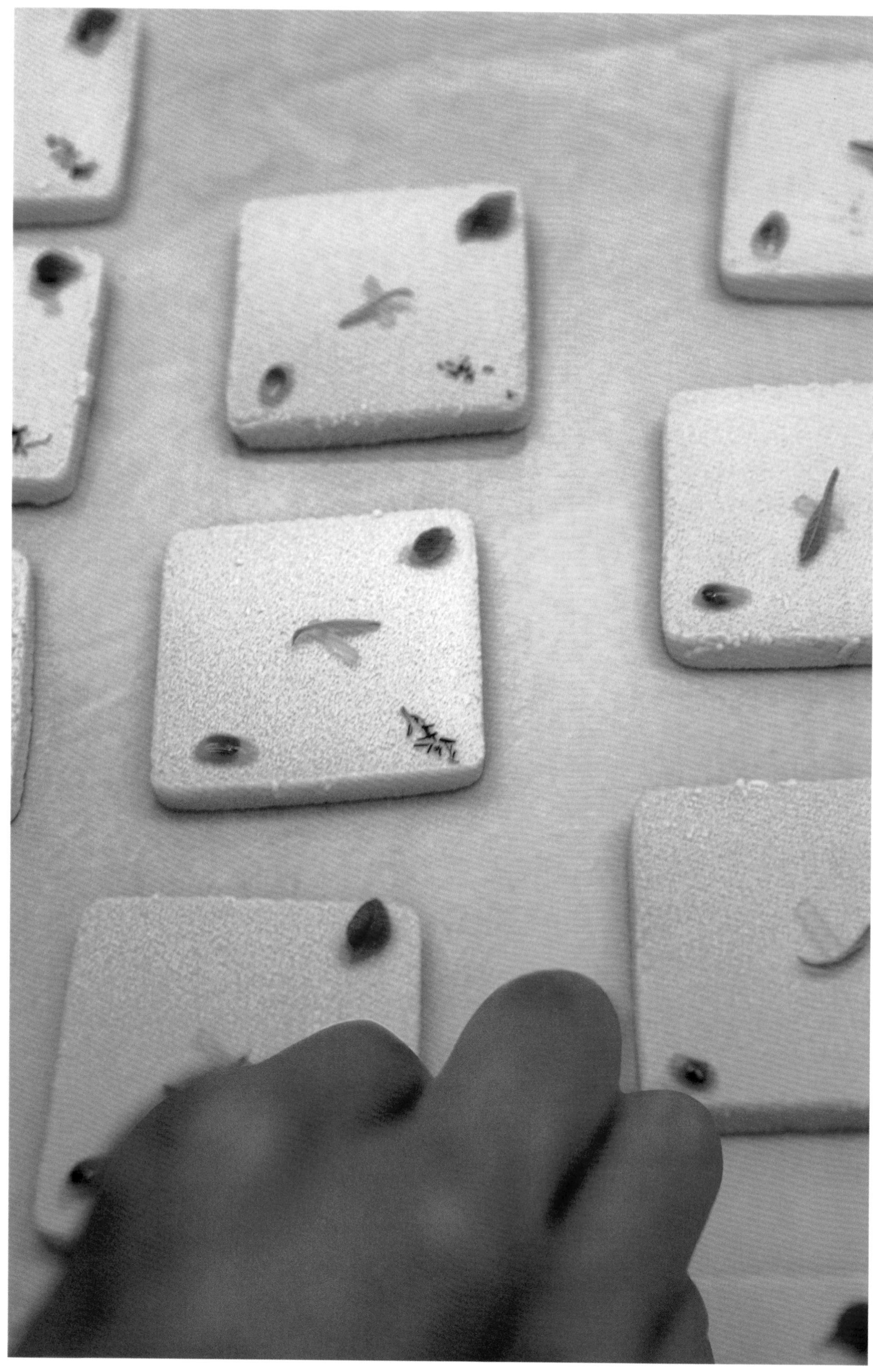

...and the *Pistachio croquanter flower with grapefruit, yuzu and tea.*

Mateu
El Bulli

Act four begins

It is the intention at elBulli that sensitivity to the guests' needs and preferences should create a close bond between waiters and guests. This is a philosophy that the waiters are skilled at putting into practice: they pay the greatest possible attention to their guests and guide them expertly through the experience of the meal.

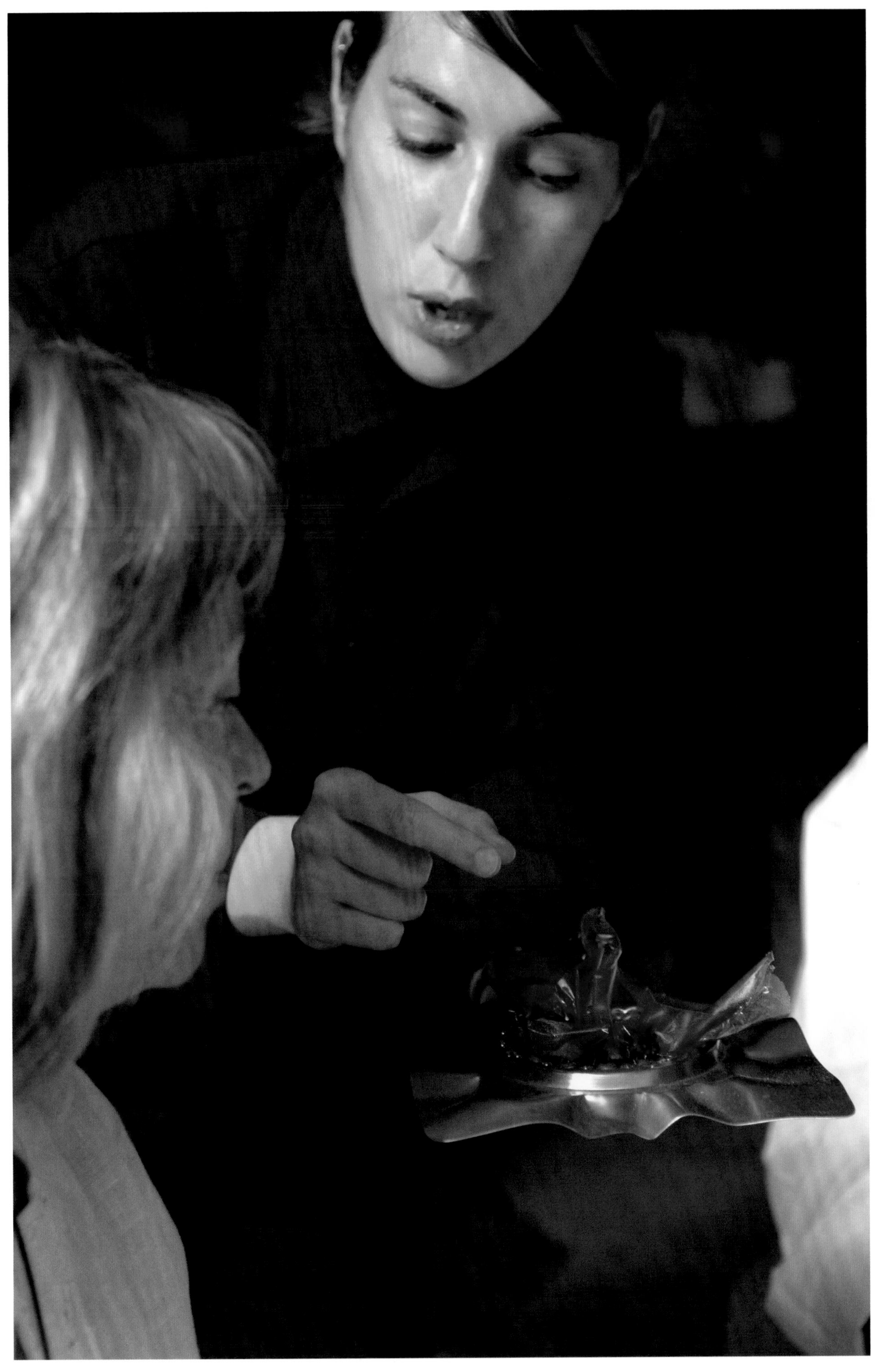

Frutas-LYO en chocolate
(Fruit-LYO in chocolate)

Serves 10

Freeze-dried raspberries dipped in chocolate

» 10 freeze-dried raspberries
» 250 g (1 cup) tempered chocolate

—

1. Dip each raspberry into the tempered chocolate with a long-pronged fork.

2. Put the dipped raspberries on a sheet of parchment paper.

3. Leave in a cool, dry place for 30 minutes and then repeat the operation.

4. When dry, store in an airtight container.

Freeze-dried strawberry slices with white chocolate

— **Yoghurt sugar**

» 60 g (½ cup) Pral yoghurt powder
» 35 g (1¼ oz) dextrose
» 5 g (1 tsp) powdered citric acid

—

1. Mix all the ingredients in a bowl and store in an airtight container in a cool, dry place.

— **Freeze-dried strawberry slices dipped in white chocolate and yoghurt sugar**

» 10 freeze-dried strawberry slices
» yoghurt sugar, previously prepared
» 250 g (1 cup) tempered white chocolate
» rose essential oil

—

1. Put 50 g (¼ cup) yoghurt sugar in a container.

2. Mix the tempered white chocolate with a drop of rose essential oil.

3. Dip the strawberry slices one by one in the chocolate with a long-pronged fork and put on top of the yoghurt sugar.

4. Sprinkle the rest of the yoghurt sugar over the dipped strawberries before the chocolate crystallizes.

5. Leave in a cool, dry place for 3 hours.

6. Store in an airtight container in a cool, dry place.

Freeze-dried apricot chunks with white chocolate and mint

— **Freeze-dried apricot chunks**

» 2 x 75 g (2¾ oz) apricots

—

1. Peel and halve the apricots.
2. Cut each half into 3 chunks.
3. Freeze on a tray lined with parchment paper.
4. Put in the freeze-dryer for 48 hours.
5. Once the freeze-drying process is complete, store in an airtight container in a cool, dry place.

— **Dehydrated mint powder**

» 10 fresh mint leaves

—

1. Place in the dehydrator for 2 hours at 60°C/140°F until completely crisp.
2. Place in a bag and crush lightly by hand to produce a fine powder.
3. Store in an airtight container in a cool, dry place.

— **Freeze-dried apricot chunks dipped in white chocolate**

» 10 freeze-dried apricot chunks, previously prepared
» 400 g (1¾ cups) tempered white chocolate
» dehydrated mint powder, previously prepared

—

1. Dip each apricot chunk in the tempered white chocolate with a long-pronged fork.
2. Put each dipped apricot chunk on a sheet of parchment paper.
3. Before the chocolate crystallizes, sprinkle each chunk with a little dehydrated mint powder.
4. Leave in a cool, dry place for 3 hours.
5. Store in an airtight container.

Freeze-dried peach chunks with milk chocolate and lemon verbena

— **Freeze-dried peach chunks**

» 2 x 180 g (6¼ oz) peaches

—

1. Peel and halve the peaches.
2. Cut each half into 4 chunks.
3. Freeze on a tray lined with parchment paper.
4. Place in the freeze-dryer for 48 hours.
5. Once the freeze-drying process is complete, store in an airtight container in a cool, dry place.

— **Dehydrated lemon verbena powder**

» 10 leaves of fresh lemon verbena

—

1. Put in the dehydrator for two hours at 60°C/140°F until completely crisp.
2. Put in a bag and crush lightly by hand to create a fine powder.
3. Store in an airtight container in a cool, dry place.

— **Freeze-dried peach chunks dipped in milk chocolate**

» 10 freeze-dried peach chunks, previously prepared
» 400 g (1¾ cup) tempered milk chocolate
» dehydrated lemon verbena powder, previously prepared

—

1. Dip each peach chunk in the tempered milk chocolate using a long-pronged fork.
2. Put each dipped peach chunk on a sheet of parchment paper.
3. Before the chocolate crystallizes, sprinkle each chunk with a little dehydrated lemon verbena powder.
4. Leave in a cool, dry place for 3 hours.
5. Store in an airtight container.

FINISHING AND PRESENTATION

—

Cutlery:
None.

—

Freeze-dried apricot chunks with white chocolate and mint are served in June, July and August.

Freeze-dried peach chunks with milk chocolate and lemon verbena are served in June, July, August and September.

Árbol de fruta de la pasión
(Passion fruit tree)

Serves 10

Freeze-dried passion fruit powder

» 25 g (1 oz) freeze-dried passion fruit crisp

—

1. Grind the passion fruit crisp into a fine powder.

2. Store in an airtight container in a cool, dry place.

Trees

» 1 kg (5 cups) Demerara sugar
» 3 attractive branches without leaves
» 3 flowerpots

—

Fill the flowerpots with sugar and stick a branch in each of one so that they look like little trees without leaves.

EXTRAS

» 50 g (¼ cup) sugar

FINISHING AND PRESENTATION

1. Put 8 g (1½ tsp) sugar into the candyfloss (cotton candy) machine and carefully remove the resulting floss.

2. Sprinkle the candyfloss with the powdered freeze-dried passion fruit crisp.

3. Carefully shape into 6 cm (2½ in) balls.

4. Put the balls onto the branches of all 3 trees, taking care not to crush them.

—

This morphing cannot be served if the atmospheric humidity is over 60%.

—

Cutlery:
None.

How to eat:
Pick the floss with your fingers without crushing it, and eat in several mouthfuls.

Piña/hinojo
(Pineapple/fennel)

Serves 10

Pineapple batons

- 1 x 650 g (1 lb 7 oz) pineapple

—

1. Slice off both ends of the pineapple and cut off the skin.
2. Cut into 40 5 x 1.2 cm (½ in) batons.
3. Refrigerate.

Pineapple infused with fennel and star anise

- 40 pineapple batons, previously prepared
- 1 handful fresh fennel fronds
- 5 star anise seeds, separated into 6 points each

—

1. Wash the fennel thoroughly in cold water.
2. Put the fennel and star anise points in a container.
3. Place the pineapple batons over the fennel and star anise, leaving space between them so that they will be completely infused with the aroma. Then cover the pineapple with another layer of fennel and star anise.
4. Cover the container with an airtight lid and refrigerate for 7 hours.

FINISHING AND PRESENTATION

1. Just before serving, open the container and separate the pineapple batons.
2. Take some fennel sprigs from the container and fill 10 black bowls.
3. Arrange 4 pineapple batons in each bowl so that they nestle among the fennel and do not touch one another.
4. Finish by placing 3 star anise points between the fennel and the pineapple.
5. Serve on a slate accompanied by silver tweezers.

—

There is another version of this dish using peach instead of pineapple and fresh lavender instead of fresh fennel.

—

Cutlery:
Silver tweezers.

Moshi de yogur y frambuesa (Yoghurt and raspberry *mochi*)

Serves 10

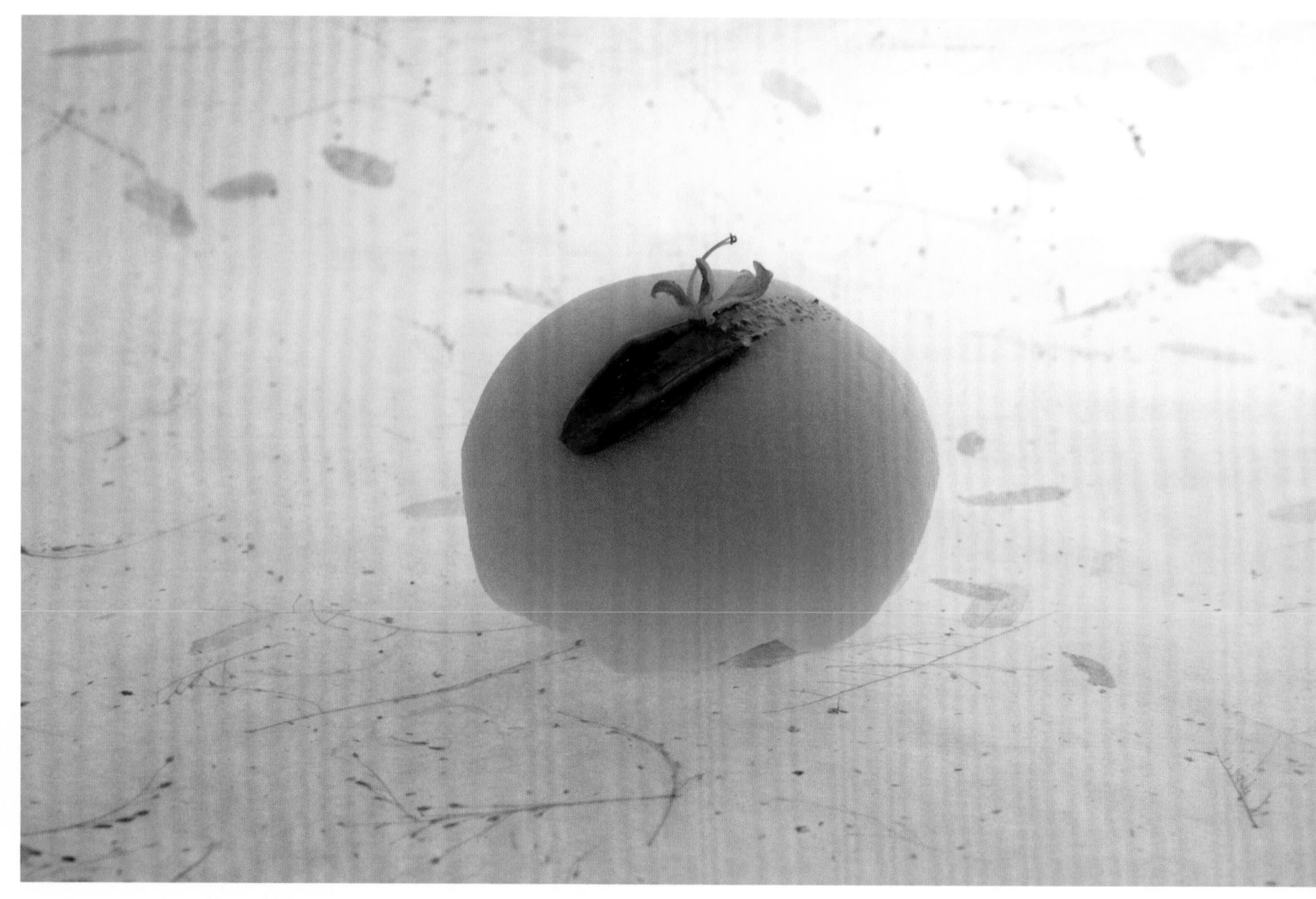

Mochi dough

elBulli cannot reveal the *mochi* dough recipe because of a confidentiality agreement with Mr Sakai, who taught the chefs how to make it.

Mochi discs

- *mochi* dough, previously prepared
- 200 g (1⅔ cups) potato starch

—

1. Store the *mochi* dough at room temperature for one hour before rolling it out.
2. Roll out the *mochi* dough between 2 sheets of parchment paper to a thickness of 0.2 cm. Sprinkle potato starch over it so that it does not stick.
3. Put it in the freezer for 30 minutes.
4. Cut out ten 11 cm (4½ in) *mochi* discs.
5. Refrigerate the *mochi* discs in an airtight container with parchment paper between them to prevent sticking.

—

As this dough is very elastic, care must be taken when rolling.

—

Mochi are Japanese sticky rice cakes, usually filled with a paste of some kind.

Cold yoghurt mousse

- 140 g (⅔ cup) plain (natural) yoghurt
- 140 g (⅔ cup) Greek yoghurt
- 120 g (½ cup) 35% fat single (light) cream
- 60 g (¼ cup) sugar
- 0.5 g citric acid
- 1¾ x 2 g gelatine leaves, previously rehydrated in cold water

—

1. Put a quarter of the plain yoghurt, half of the sugar and the citric acid in a pan and heat gently.
2. Dissolve the gelatine in this mixture, then add the remaining plain yoghurt.
3. Mix with the Greek yoghurt and leave to set in the refrigerator.
4. Meanwhile, semi-whip the cream with the rest of the sugar.
5. When the yoghurt jelly is half set, fold in the semi-whipped cream.
6. When it is evenly mixed, pour the mixture into an airtight container.
7. Refrigerate for 3 hours.

Matcha tea syrup

- 25 g (1⅔ tbsp) x 100% syrup, made with equal quantities of sugar and water
- 5 g (1 tsp) *matcha* tea

—

1. Mix both ingredients and keep in the refrigerator.

—

Matcha is Japanese powdered green tea.

EXTRAS

- 10 raspberries
- 10 rosemary flowers

FINISHING AND PRESENTATION

1. Lay out the *mochi* discs on a table.
2. When they are at room temperature, put each one in a small bowl to create a better shape.
3. Using a piping bag, pipe 15 g (1 tbsp) of yoghurt mousse in the middle of the *mochi* disc.
4. Place a fresh raspberry in the middle and pipe another 15 g (1 tbsp) more of yoghurt mousse.
5. Carefully close the *mochi*.
6. Once you have the folded up the edges in your hand, seal carefully without tearing the dough.
7. Turn the *mochi* over and brush off the excess potato starch.
8. Place on a square of paper.
9. Using a fine brush, apply a teardrop of *matcha* tea syrup to the top of the *mochi* and put a fresh rosemary flower on top.

—

Cutlery:
None.

How to eat:
Hold the *mochi* with the paper and eat in 2 mouthfuls.

Happy birthday!

More than two hundred birthdays a year are celebrated at elBulli, but nobody wants a piece of cake after eating thirty dishes.

00:15

—

Sometimes a large birthday card is brought out, which opens into the shape of a birthday cake – with a candle, of course.

But a birthday without a cake is not really a birthday, so later the waiter brings in a real cake, which is small and light and in the shape of a candle.

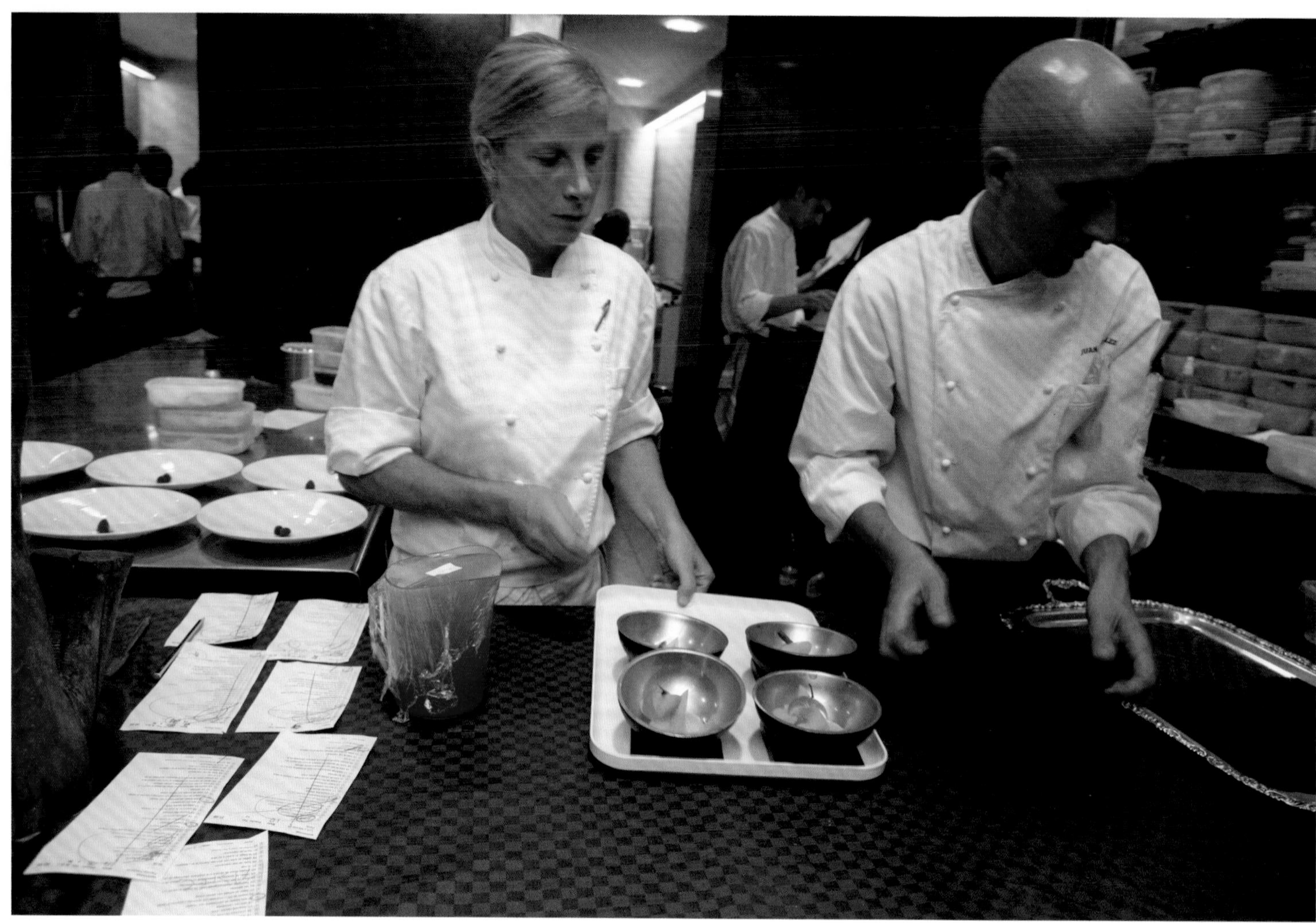

The chefs are about to serve *Peach, cinnamon, lime and fruit-CRU.*

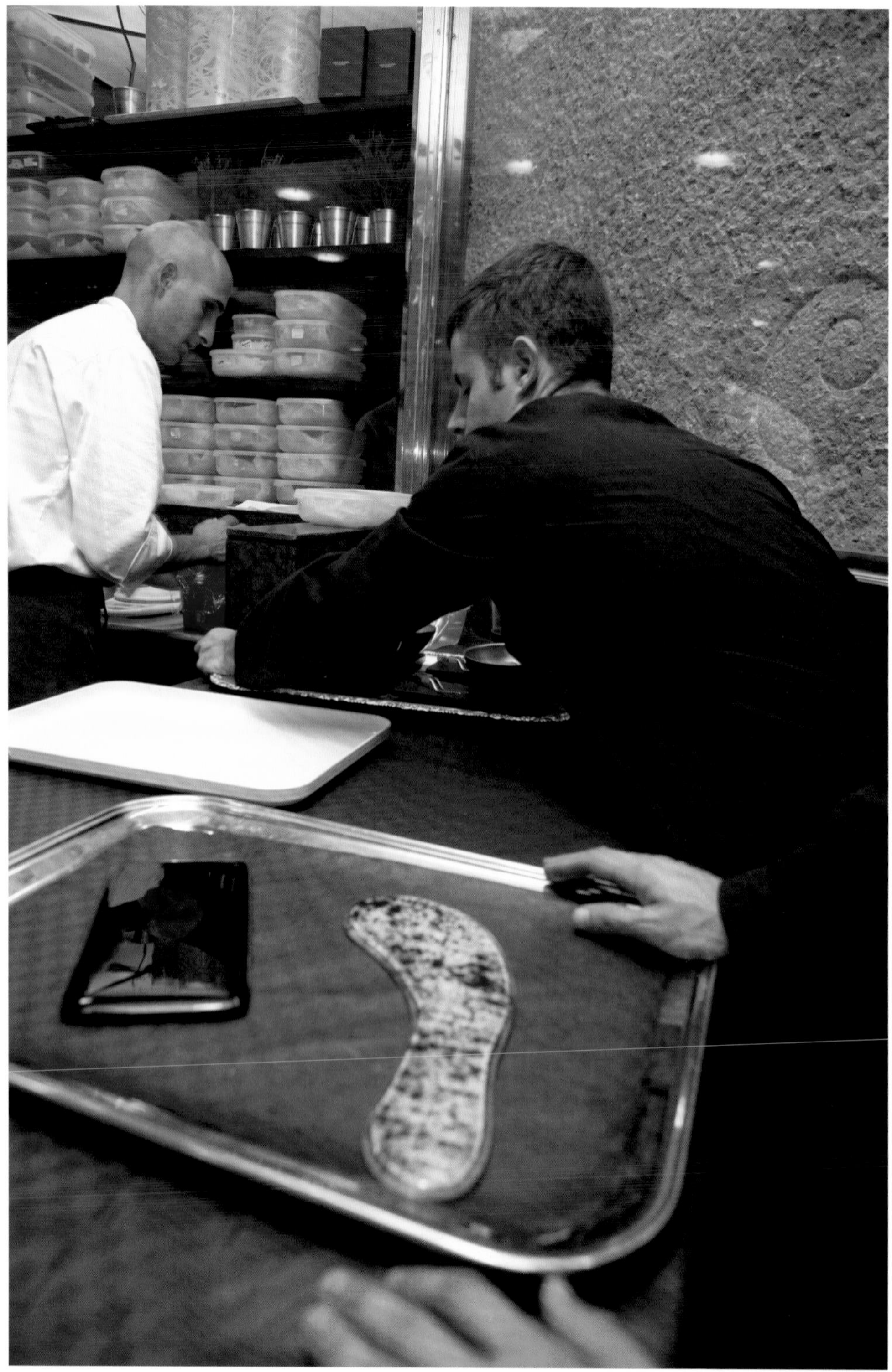

Passion fruit, chocolate and hazelnut palet-croquant.

Morphings about to be served: sheets of chocolate, which could be flavoured with eucalyptus or coriander (cilantro), quenelles of sorbet served on spoons and sweet waffle sandwiches.

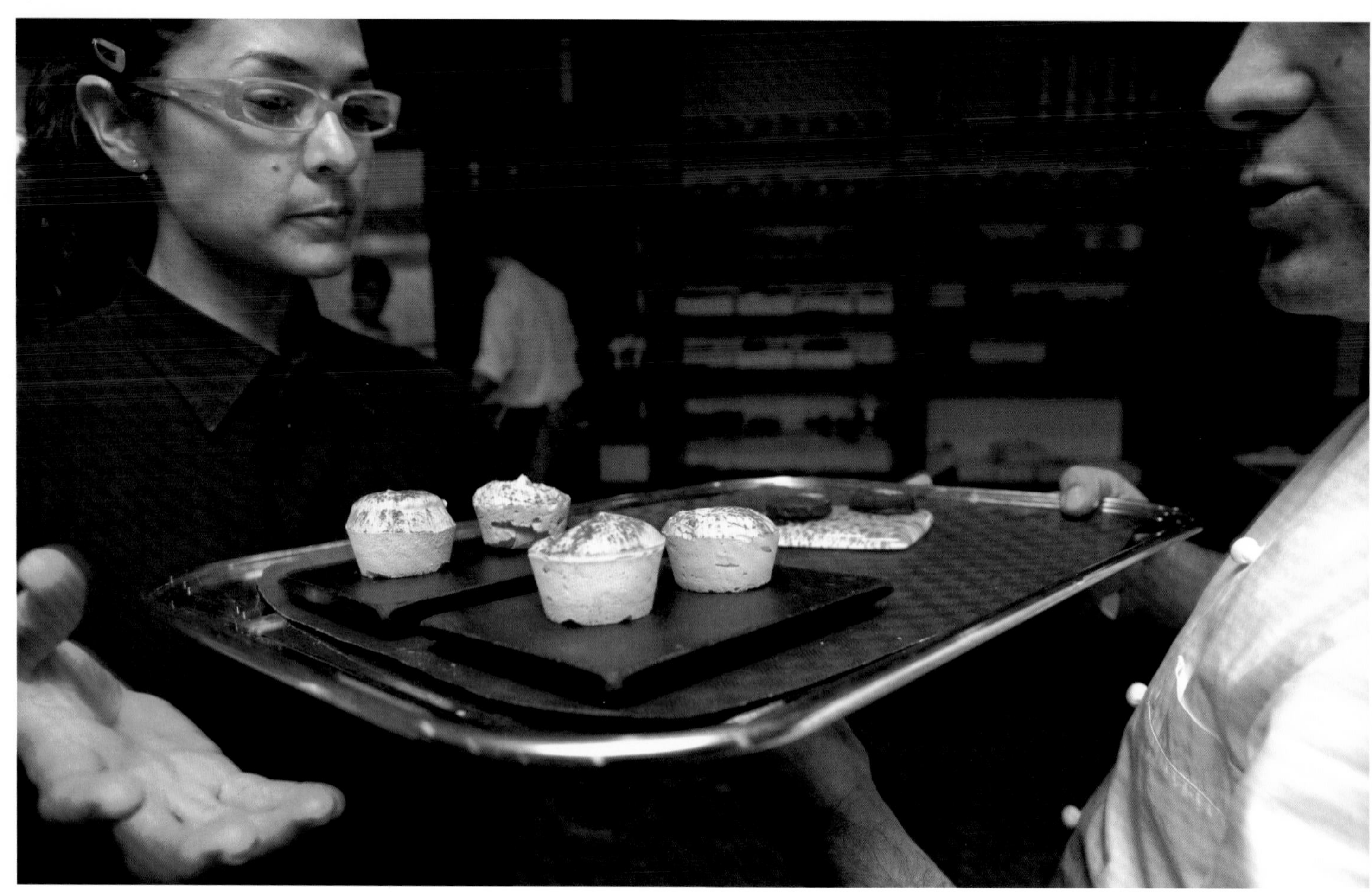

Freeze-dried cappucino with lemon sorbet, Peach-CRU and *Mandarin borracho.*

Creative methods III

THE SENSES AS A STARTING POINT

Eating involves the use of all the senses. Each sense can be seen as a separate creative method, but in many cases it is the interaction between different senses that produces the most interesting results. This can occur not just within one dish, but also over the course of a sequence of dishes that engages the senses in different ways.

SIGHT

Often the first sense to transmit information about a dish, sight helps a diner to identify the ingredients that compose it and sets up expectations about how it will taste. The diner might also recognize the concept of a dish (as a soufflé, for example), or know the signature style of a particular restaurant, type of cuisine or chef through the colours, shapes, proportions or presentation of a dish. Of course, a chef will always try to make the dish visually appealing, and each element should justify its presence by its flavour, but sight can convey far more than just aesthetic pleasure. At elBulli it is one of the principal ways in which the chef can engage with a guest through humour or decontextualization. A dish might resemble one thing but actually be another, or it may be aesthetically beautiful but not resemble anything a diner has eaten before. Both these properties have the effect of diverting the guest's attention towards the other sensory experiences when the first mouthful is being eaten.

HEARING

Although it is certainly the least important sense for the act of eating, hearing can still play an interesting role. The sounds associated with eating a dish, such as biting into an apple or a brittle sheet of caramel, do affect a diner's perception and expectations. The importance of crunching sounds has been thoroughly investigated by food manufacturers. Potato crisps (chips), for example, are intentionally made large because eating them with the mouth slightly open amplifies the sound of the initial crunch. Less directly, other aural stimulation, such as sound levels or conversation, waiting staff or other background activity, can also affect the sensations of eating.

TOUCH

This can be divided into two main sensations: temperature and texture. Temperature is the diner's first tactile sensation. Apart from the fact that food should not exceed the temperature extremes that the mouth can withstand (from -20°C/-4°F to 65°C/149°F), subtle variations in temperature can be very revealing. Contrasting extremes, too, can be effective, as in *Pea soup 60°/4°*, in which there is no visual clue to the presence of unexpectedly different temperatures, that highlight different aspects of the flavour of peas.

Texture can transmit many different sensations. Some ingredients, such as frogs' legs, pasta and pigs' trotters, are highly prized for their texture, and others can be transformed into many different textures. A purée or liquid can become a mousse, a foam, a granita, a sorbet or a jelly, and altering an ingredient's natural texture can radically alter a diner's perceptions of it. One of the milestone dishes at elBulli, possibly one of its finest, makes great use of the interplay of liquid-derived textures and is the perfect expression of some of the restaurant's best-known innovations. *Textured vegetable panaché* was a response to Michel Bras's iconic dish *Gargouillou de jeunes légumes*, in which thirty different vegetables at their very best are perfectly cooked, seasoned and presented. Tasting Bras's dish stimulated in Ferran the desire to invent his own ultimate vegetable dish, and *Textured vegetable panaché* incorporated all the new techniques for creating different savoury textures that were being developed in 1994. The elBulli dish is composed of an almond sorbet, cauliflower mousse, purée of tomato, beetroot foam, raw avocado, basil jelly and sweet corn mousse.

Temperature and texture can also be combined, and may be perceived with the hands as well as the mouth. *Mastic +60/spoonful -20* involves a hot mastic gelatine that is eaten with a frozen teaspoon, and *Pressed green olives with fennel* includes a bowl of fresh fennel fronds into which diners can submerge their hands.

SMELL

Three roles are played by smell in the act of eating: it triggers the production of gastric juices, enables the appreciation of the characteristic aromas of an ingredient, dish or cooking process, and can help the chef to judge the quality of a product. Smell is a vital component of flavour, but its role is often undervalued – one does not often see guests inhaling the aromas of a dish in the same way that they might with a glass of wine. In fact, smell's potential can be explored beyond the natural aromas that a food will emit and can be introduced as an added stimulus or component of the dish. Many cold desserts have no distinctive smell of their own, so in 1997 the *Chocolate sponge with mint ice cream and orange-blossom flavoured liquorice* was created. It was presented covered by a *cloche*, which just before serving had been warmed and sprayed with orange blossom water so that, when the waiter removed it at the table, the aroma was released and intensified the experience of the dessert. Another example of this technique is a dish of langoustines presented with a branch of rosemary for the diner to smell while eating the dish. Including the rosemary in this way, rather than infusing its sometimes overpowering flavour into the sauce, highlights the close and complex interaction between the senses of smell and taste, and allows diners to draw their own conclusions.

TASTE

Taste lies at the heart of the act of eating. Taste buds identifies the basic tastes: sweet, salt, bitter, sour. 'Flavour' is the range of sensory perceptions yielded by the food, including aroma, texture and, to a lesser extent, sound. The taste buds identify the basic tastes present in the dish, but the sensory judgement about whether the combination is pleasing or jarring is made in the mind. This two-stage process is exploited by *Green almonds 'basic tastes'*, which presents the almonds in sweet, sour, bitter and salty variations.

THE SIXTH SENSE

Physical pleasure through the five senses can be experienced in many restaurants. There is also pleasure related to the emotions, which can result from a warm, friendly atmosphere and good service. But a type of intellectual satisfaction, too, can be experienced if a dish provokes a deeper response or analysis on the part of the guest: if it brings back a childhood memory, for example, confounds expectations, makes a guest laugh, draws on their knowledge of other cuisine styles or invites them to join in a game. These sensations are perceived and enjoyed by what elBulli has termed the 'sixth sense': pleasure experienced by the mind. The sixth sense often relies on setting up a tension or a contrast between the guest's own knowledge and experiences, and the elements in the dish in front of him. The objective of this creative method is for elBulli's food to be enjoyed by all six senses, in the mind as well as in the mouth and nose. There are many restaurants one can visit in order to eat well, but creative cooking that engages the sixth sense is much harder to find.

Creating dishes that stimulate the sixth sense is a process that often draws on other creative methods and on the other five senses to create a dialogue between the chef and the guest. Different techniques can be employed, such as irony, referencing childhood memories, playfulness, provocation and removing dishes from their usual context. In *Morels à la crème pipette* a knowing wink is made to the classic French dish *Morilles à la crème*. The morels are presented on a device designed especially for this dish, a skewer-pipette from which the cream sauce can pass directly into the mouth. The form of the classic dish of mushrooms in cream sauce has been changed, and the diner does not recognize the dish when first presented with it. It is only in the flavour that the original dish can be detected. Transgressing the traditional boundaries of cuisine is an important part of the sixth sense, but it is crucial to preserve the distinction between playfulness and gratuitous provocation, and for the dish to give pleasure in conventional ways as well as through the sixth sense. The *Spice dish* consists of a Granny Smith apple jelly with twelve tiny piles of spices around the edge for the guests to identify. Instructions from the waiter and a written list of the spices in random order turn the dish into a game to be enjoyed by food enthusiasts, but it is not simply an identification puzzle; it is also a way of exploring how different spices interact with the jelly, with each other and with the guest's expectations.

SYMBIOSIS OF THE SWEET AND SAVOURY WORLDS

Restaurants and cookbooks have always traditionally distinguished starters and main courses (savoury) from desserts and pastry (sweet). At elBulli these two strands are called the savoury world and the sweet world, and their symbiosis has largely come about through the close working relationship between Ferran and Albert. Albert was influenced by the great chefs Jacques Maximin and Jacques Torres, among others, and their work towards fusing of the roles of main course chef and pastry chef. Pastry work requires precision, rigour and technical skill, and applying this discipline to the savoury world can open up many new possibilities. The sweet world chef can benefit from the immediacy of service in a kitchen: traditionally, their painstaking creations are made in advance and can feel remote from the act of eating, but the last-minute finishing techniques of a chef can also inform the work of the pastry chef.

The symbiosis of the two worlds was particularly important at elBulli in the mid-1990s, and it was characterized by an exchange of techniques and concepts as well as of dishes and ingredients. Creating new textures and applying different processes to an ingredient – such as making a sorbet or mousse out of fresh fruit – has always been an important part of the sweet world, but less so in the savoury. At elBulli these techniques were applied to savoury dishes too, and it opened up a whole new realm of possibilities, most famously the savoury ice creams that elBulli has pioneered. Caramels and croquants also began to appear in the savoury world in 1995, and some savoury dishes, like *Two ways of presenting chicken curry*, were strongly influenced by desserts in their presentation style. Many savoury world concepts, like lasagne, stews, salads and soups, began to appear in the sweet world, and specific savoury dishes were adapted, as in the *Sweet version of the textured vegetable panaché*, which included smoked Idiazábal cheese. The dish that made the symbiosis between sweet and savoury most apparent to the guest was *Biscuit glacé*. Although it contains no sugar and was served amongst the savoury dishes, the use of hazelnuts and vanilla made the dish seem sweet, and led guests to expect to taste sugar. The dish encapsulated the fact that the traditional sweet and savoury categories imposed upon dishes are not absolute, and that sometimes a dish is simply what it is, rather than what one expects it to be.

Finally, in 1996, the creation of avant-desserts formed a bridge and at the same time blurred the boundaries between the two worlds. An early avant-dessert was *Apple tart tatin with duck foie gras,* which paired a savoury ingredient with a classic sweet dish. Once they were firmly established, these dishes allowed guests to embark on an exploration of the transition between sweet and savoury.

COMMERCIAL FOOD IN HIGH-END CUISINE

The use of commercial foods and preparations in fine dining cuisine is often closely connected with the sixth sense. The appearance of well-known products (or dishes that resemble them) can provoke childhood memories or use a visual reference to make a joke. They enable the chef to send diners back to their childhoods or to situations that have nothing to do with fine dining in order to create new and surprising connections. The method has such potential that it can stand as a creative method in its own right. It can be employed in two basic ways: first, the direct use of commercial preparations as an ingredient in cooking (at elBulli these have included Actimel, Oreo cookies, Fisherman's Friend lozenges and pork scratchings), and second, making new versions and forms of commercial products, such as ice cream wafer sandwiches, candyfloss (cotton candy), marshmallows, lollipops and Soleros (a brand of ice cream).

NEW WAYS OF SERVING FOOD

In contemporary cooking, using new receptacles and dishes that may not previously have been used for food has been a fertile creative method and a fruitful way of transcending the boundaries of traditional cuisine. Before the emergence of nouvelle cuisine, it was very rare that high-end restaurants would present food on anything other than a bone china plate or bowl. At elBulli some of the more radical new receptacles have included spoons made from plastic or paper (materials that would never previously have been considered smart enough for a fine dining restaurant), pipettes, scent spoons, 'slurps' (wide straws filled with a soft set jelly that is designed to be sucked), frozen slates and stones. Many of the new dishes and cutlery have been created specifically for a particular dish by Luki Huber, industrial designer and collaborator since 2001. This method also creates new roles for waiters when serving. The waiter might complete a dish at the table, or make suggestions about how a dish should be eaten. These instructions are intended to help the guest enjoy the dish to the full, particularly if it is a new concept for which there is no reference point. Of course, there is nothing to stop guests from eating the dish in a different way if they so choose, in the same way that they might read a novel in alternating chapters or look at a painting upside-down, but they will not experience the dish in the way that its creator intended. Any instructions offered are intended not to inhibit guests' freedom but to help them experience the maximum pleasure from the dish.

The practice of a waiter finishing a dish at the table is not a new one. Traditionally, many classic restaurants have provided the spectacle of a waiter carving a rib of beef or flambéing *crêpes Suzette* at the table, or just serving cheese from a trolley. This practice has been developed and expanded in contemporary cuisine as a way of shortening the distance between chef and guest. 'Cooking' with liquid nitrogen, in which a preparation is rapidly frozen by being briefly submerged in liquid nitrogen (at around -196°C/-321°F), is one of the most spectacular ways in which a dish can be finished at the table. Other elBulli dishes finished at the table include *Tamarillo and eucalyptus jelly with frozen peach sphere*, in which the peach is 'segmented' by the waiter in front of the guest.

In a more radical step that narrows the gap between chef and diner even further, sometimes it is the guest who adds the finishing touch to the dish, a practice that has very few precedents in the history of fine dining. *Hot monkfish liver with baby onions and honey caramel* requires the guest to add the sheet of honey caramel to the dish immediately before eating it. This requirement has practical origins, as the caramel would melt in contact with the heat of the dish and therefore could not survive the walk to the table; but the act of participating in the construction of the dish also heightens the guest's awareness of what they are eating.

CHANGING THE STRUCTURE OF DISHES

The basic structure of classic dishes has for many decades been the French model of main ingredient plus sauce and side dish. The creative method of changing the structure of dishes questions this traditional arrangement and looks at the composition of dishes in a new way, and many factors have contributed to its emergence as a highly rewarding creative method. The nouvelle cuisine concept of the tasting menu (or *menu dégustation*), in which a fixed menu of five or six smaller, lighter dishes would be served to showcase the style of a particular chef, had already begun to dispense with the traditional French structure of a dish. The re-evaluation of the merits of ingredients, ignoring the automatic prestige of luxury ingredients like truffles and caviar, also questioned

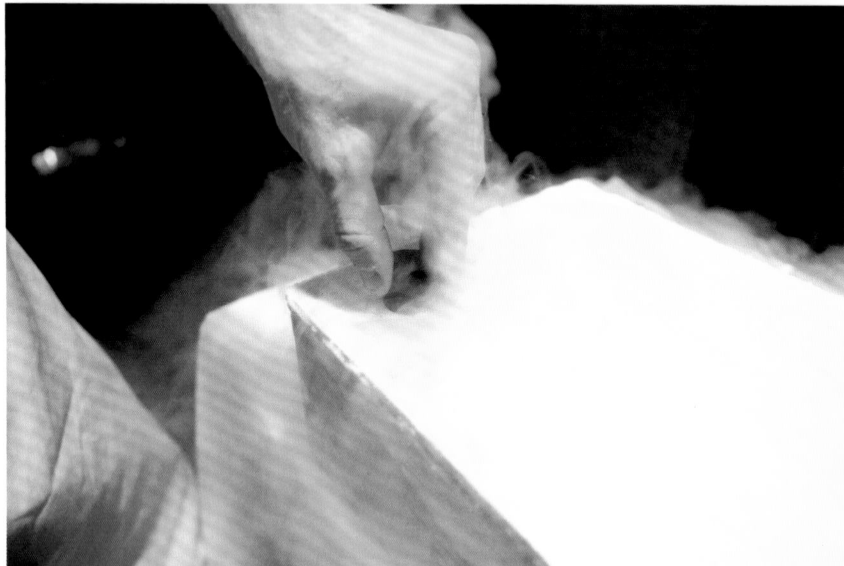

What do you call a grill that 'cooks' by freezing?

'Teppan-nitro' is a word that doesn't appear in any dictionary. If the staff at elBulli don't know what to call a method of preparation, a piece of equipment or a utensil, it means that it hasn't existed until now – at least, not as far as they know.

At elBulli many new concepts and techniques have been developed, and the equipment needed to carry them out has been invented. Later on they had to be given names.

Inventing a new language is a sign of creativity. Now that elBulli has started to develop one, the task lies not just in creating it, but in making the language better.

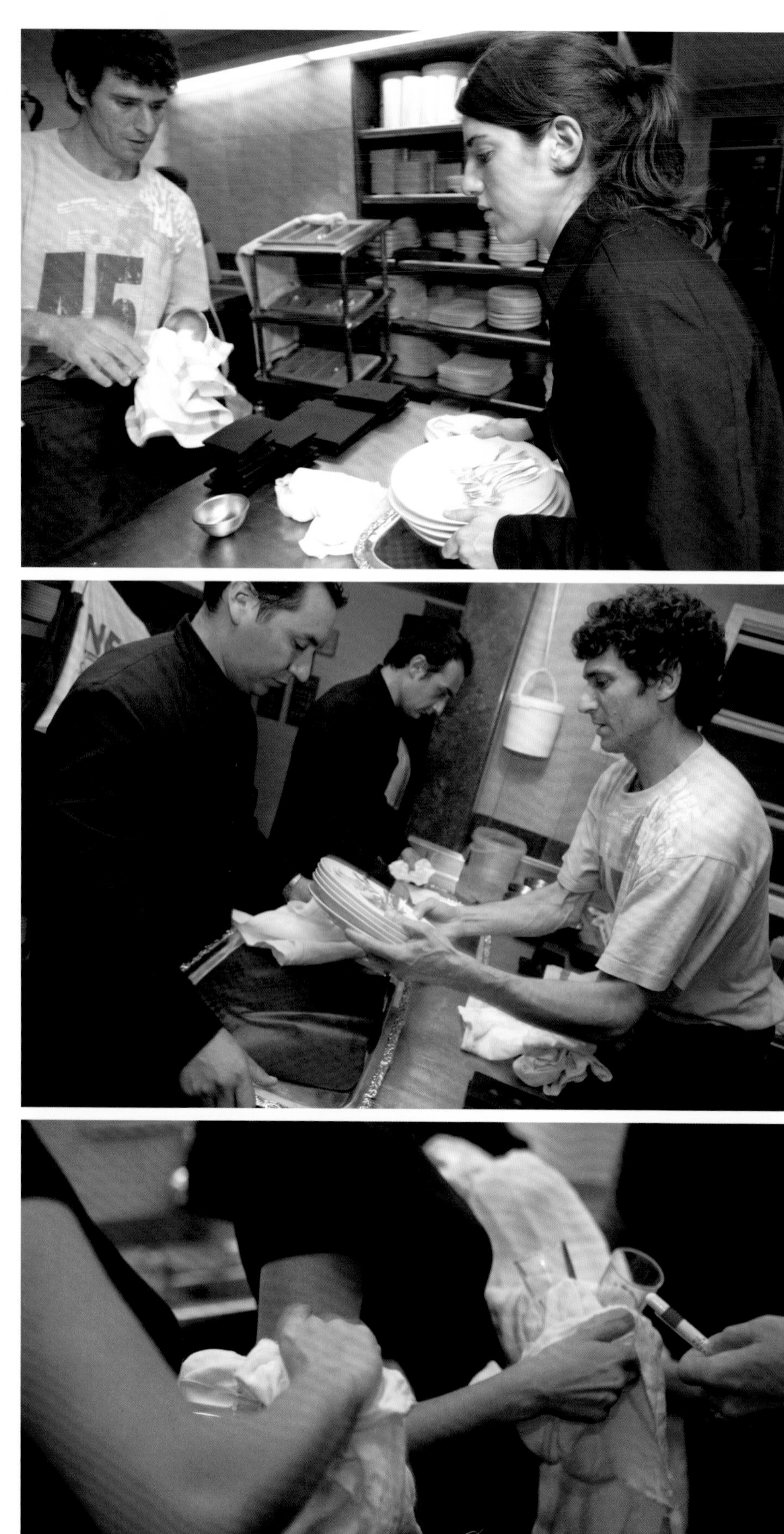

Every evening, four people in the pot wash (dishwashing area) face a mountain of over 2,500 pieces of crockery, cutlery and pans.

Tomorrow starts now

The refrigerators are tidied. A list of produce needed for the next day's menu is compiled. Afterwards, Eduard will begin to make the shopping list.

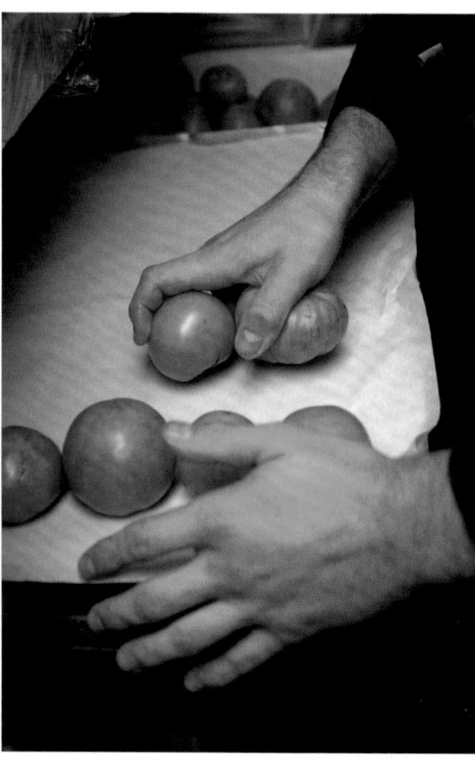

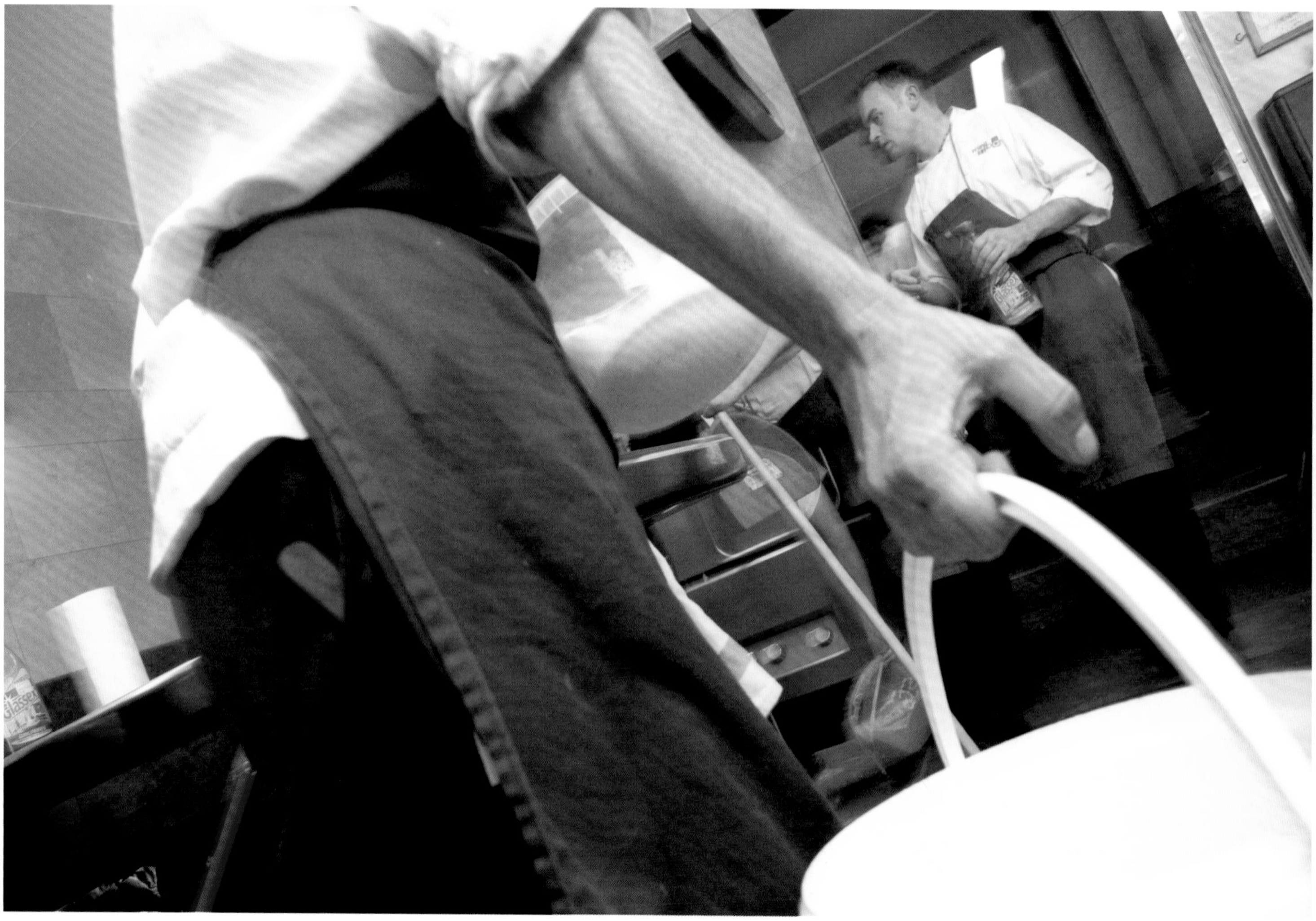

How do you clean a kitchen measuring 3,770 square feet (350 square metres) in half an hour? With good organization and forty chefs to share the work.

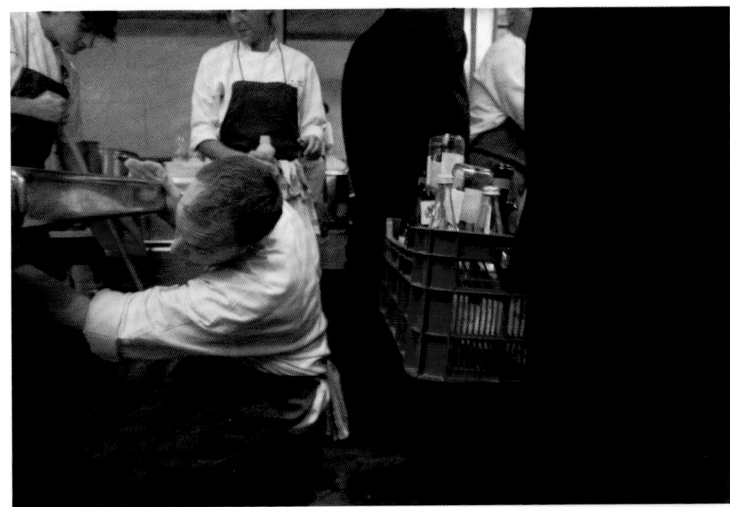

granini
Schweppes
Schweppes
Schweppes
Schweppes
Heineken
Heineken
Heineken
ACEITUNAS

Tapioca
MILD
5 Kg
BORGES
SUAU

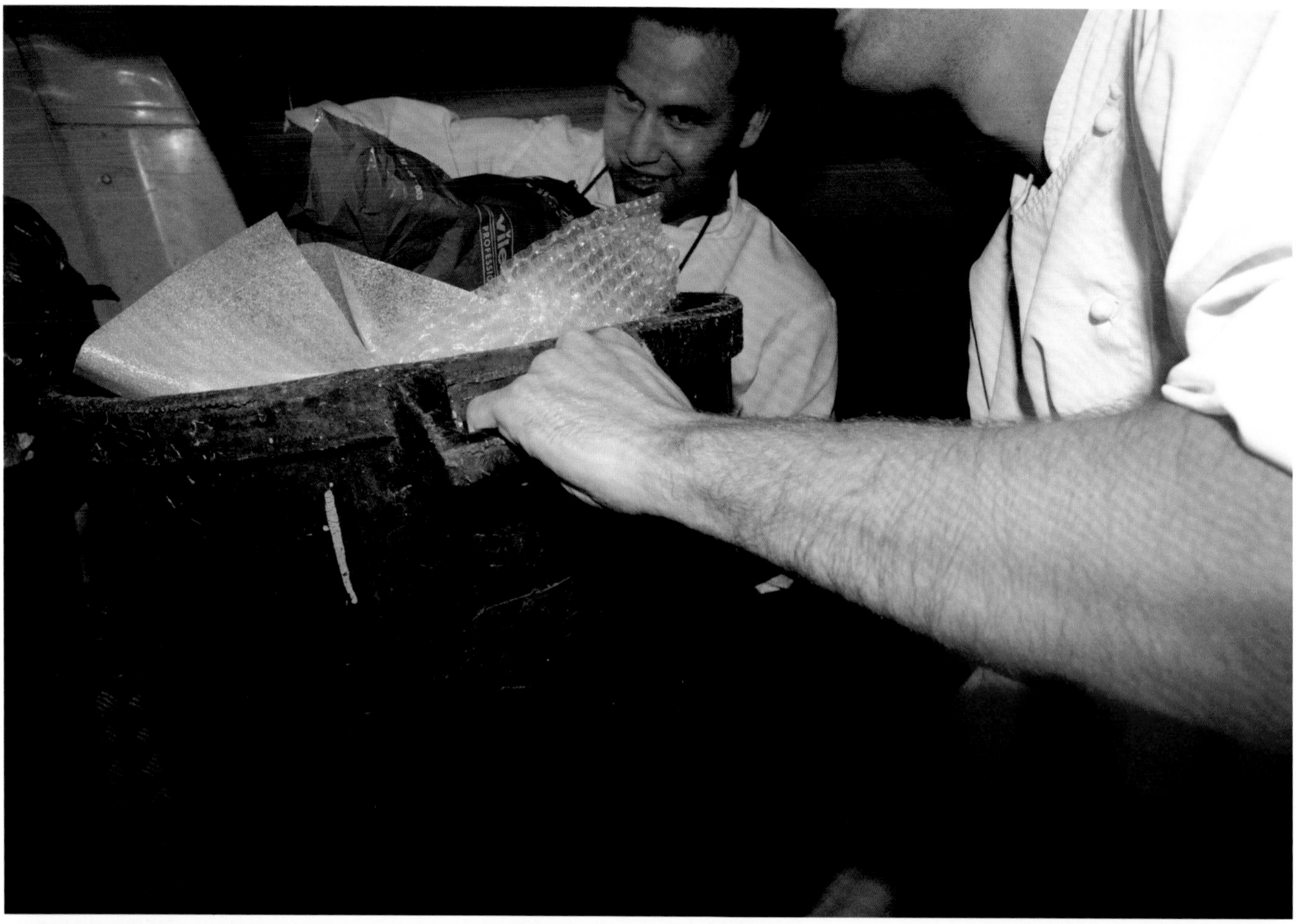

No one comes to collect the twelve bins of rubbish generated at elBulli every day

After service, four of the staff spend half an hour loading the rubbish into the van and take it to the refuse container next to the staff car park. One of the disadvantages of not being in a city is having to be self-sufficient when it comes to disposing of the waste.

Service is over for the savoury world

Now it is time to get everything cleaned up and ready for tomorrow. The sooner everyone finishes, the sooner they can go home.

—

The guests decide when act four will end

The final stages of the meal often take place on the terrace. It is time for coffee, liqueurs and conversation, and the guests receive a copy of the menu they have eaten.

Time to say goodnight

01:00

—

Going home with elBulli on your mind

01:05

—

Who is coming tomorrow?

When service is over, and with the reservations sheet in front of him, Ferran checks the details for tomorrow to find out if there are guests who have never been to elBulli before, and whether any regulars are coming. All these details are essential for preparing the order sheets for the following day. Every day around fifty people come to dinner, but no guest is the same as another.

elBulli in numbers

15	-	Tables per day
50	-	Guests per day
160	-	Days open for business
8,000	-	Guests per year
7 – 20,000 (4 – 12,400)	-	Kilometres (miles) travelled by guests to eat at elBulli
70	-	Staff members working at the height of the season
40	-	Chefs
26	-	People working in the dining room
8 (5)	-	Kilometres (miles) walked per day, on average, by each waiter
11,200	-	Staff meals per year
12,000 (129,165)	-	Square metres (square feet) of land by the sea
80 (860)	-	Square metres (square feet) of terrace
350 (3,770)	-	Square metres (square feet) of kitchen space
250 (2,690)	-	Square metres (square feet) of dining room space
€215	-	per meal in 2009
€300	-	per person including drinks in 2009 (on average)
170 – 200	-	Ingredients in the menu
1,500	-	Cocktails, snacks, tapas-dishes, avant-desserts, desserts and morphings served per day
700 (25)	-	Grams (ounces) of food per meal per guest
5,600 (5½)	-	Kilograms (tons) total weight of food consumed per year
200	-	Kitchen cloths and aprons used every night
1,000	-	Pieces of cutlery used every night
10,000	-	Bottles opened per year
55	-	Types of glassware
750	-	Glasses moved around the restaurant daily
1,666	-	Wines on the list
40	-	Different vintages
216	-	Grape varieties
325	-	Different DOCs on the wine list
2	-	Wine ageing cellars
4,000	-	Hours of creative work per year

—

Everybody lends a hand in the pot wash and the utility room

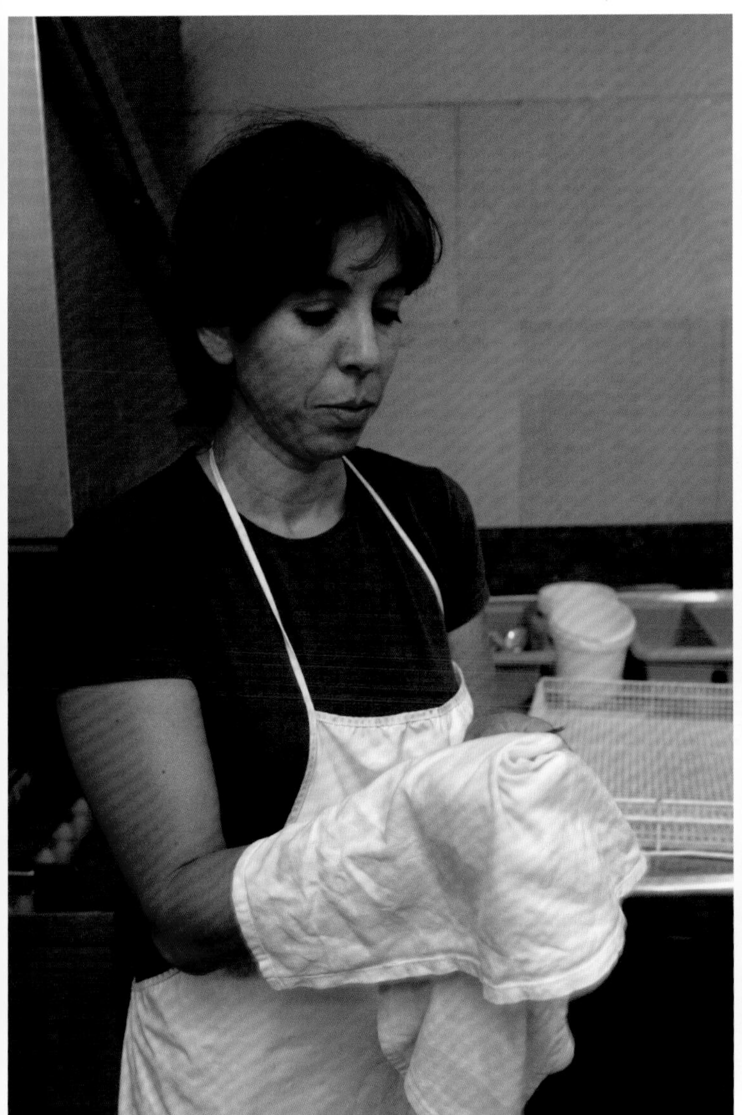

Round-up of the day

When the other chefs have left, the head chefs and managers discuss everything that has happened, organize tasks for the next day, help to compile the shopping list and discuss the menu for the following evening.

This is all done in a more or less relaxed manner, depending on how the day has gone.

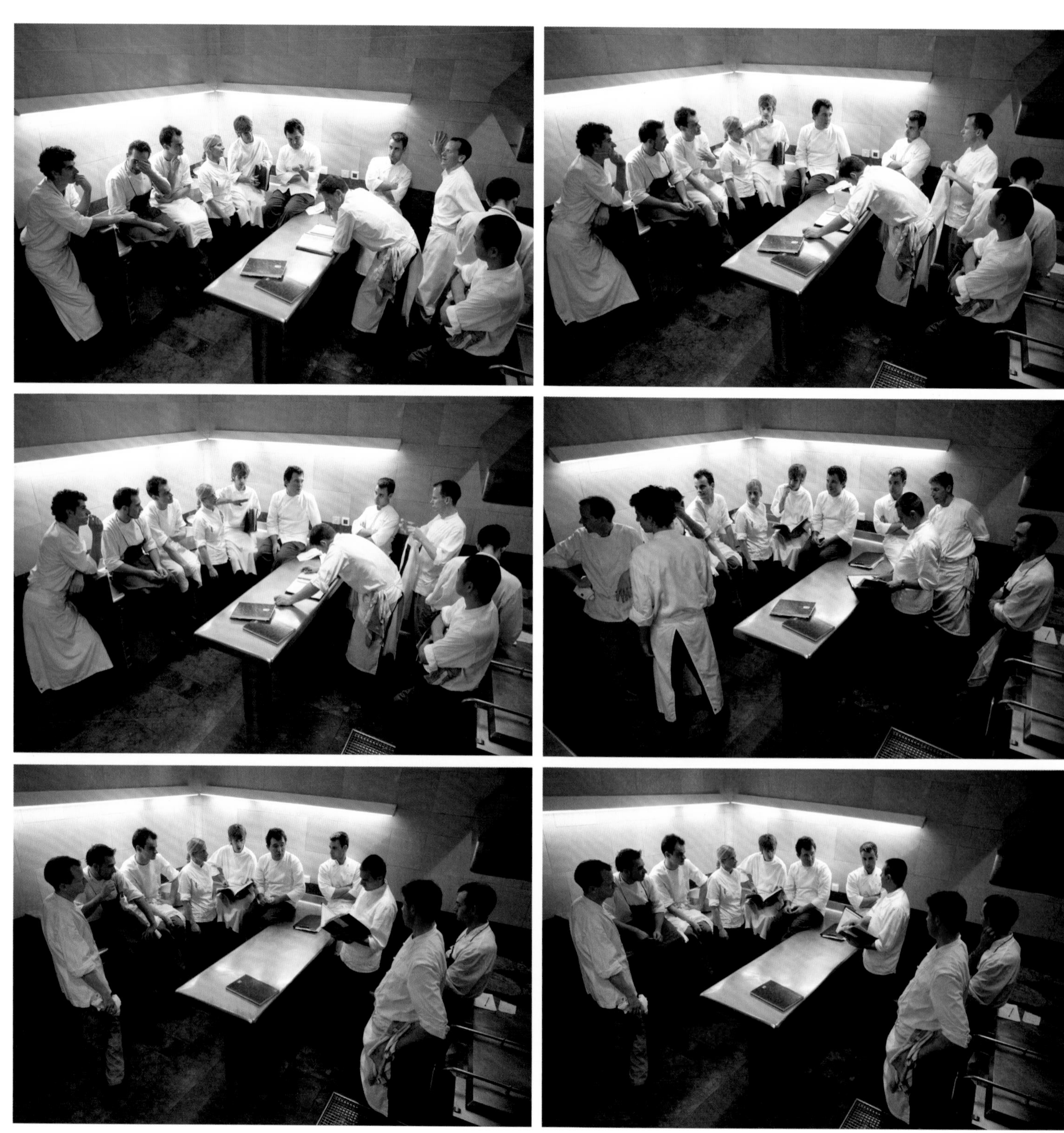

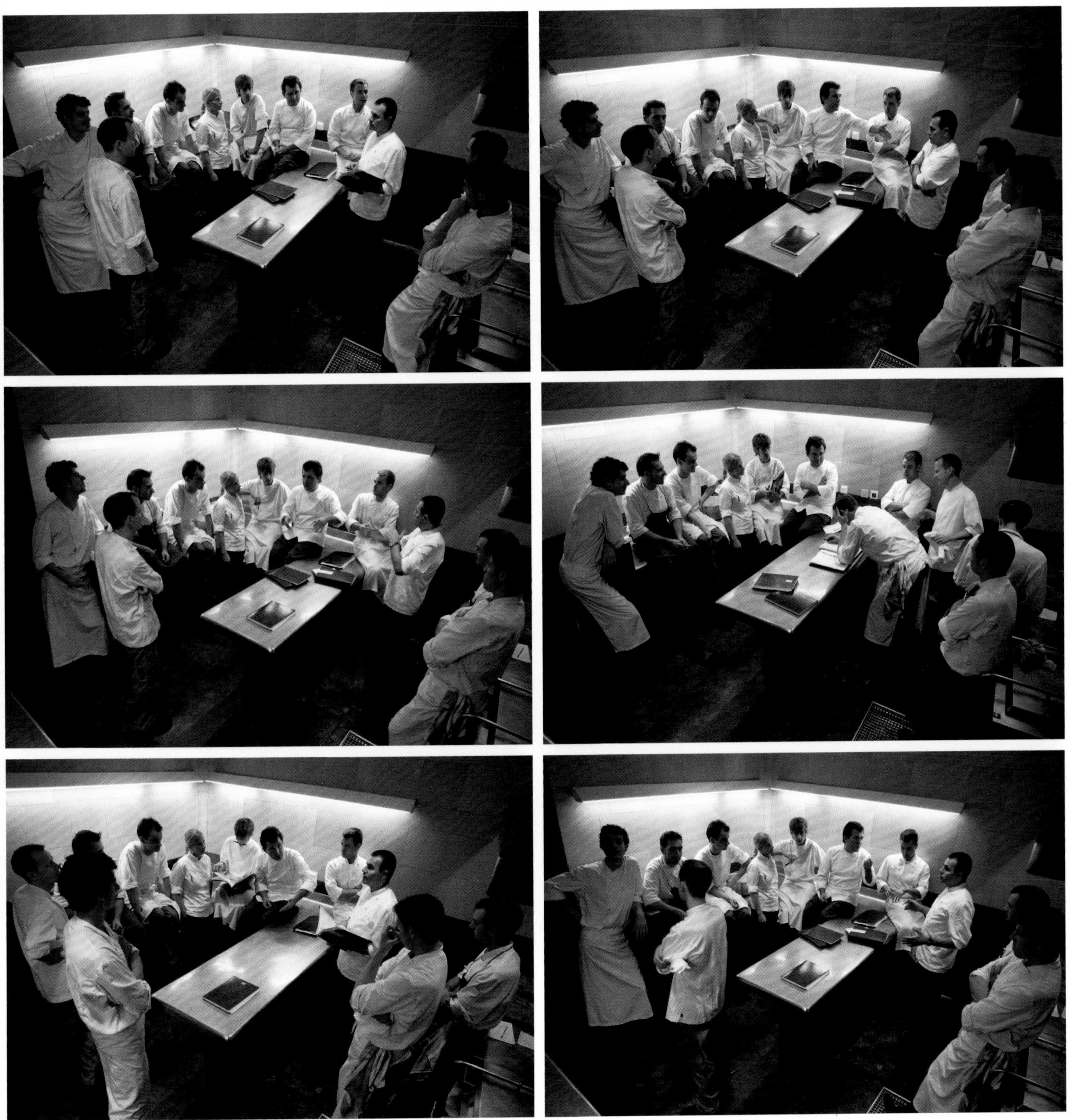

01:20

—

The lights are switched off, but only in the kitchen

02:00

—

The curtain comes down

The creative evolution of elBulli

—

The search for new ideas

The creative evolution chart shown here is the result of a long period of reflection about how to define elBulli's cuisine, and the creative processes instrumental to its development. The first step was to establish what it is that defines any cuisine: the styles and characteristics of its dishes. Then, the creative process was broken down into its key components to provide a structure with which to analyse elBulli's creative evolution.

It is possible to examine any new contribution to the field of high-end restaurant food by using the chart as a whole, or one of its branches. Any new development will fall under one of the headings, and some might fall under several, so it is important to identify which of its creative features are the most significant. For example, when foams were first created in 1994, the technique was included in that year's analysis under the heading 'preparations', but the siphon used to make the foams came under 'technology'.

The chart could also be used to examine the processes behind other creative fields that involve the transformation of raw materials into a functioning product, such as fashion or architecture.

ORGANIZATION AND PHILOSOPHY

A strong creative philosophy and good organization are essential in order to evolve. This might include a set timetable for the creative sessions, clear definitions of the creative methods, or collaborations with experts in other fields and food manufacturers. The scope and variety of these collaborations enriches elBulli's creative development enormously.

The search for new ideas can follow any of these paths:

PRODUCTS

Developments that originate in work with ingredients:

- Analysing products
- Applying new techniques and concepts to products
- Discovering new products
- Combining products in new ways

This section could include products with 'soul' (ingredients that have acquired special significance because of the important role they have played in elBulli's development); 'spin-off' products (the parts of an ingredient that are usually discarded, such as the seeds of peppers or fish skin) or new combinations of ingredients that are identified through the mental palate, or simply by tasting.

TECHNOLOGY

Developments that originate in technological advances:

- Researching and developing new equipment
- Looking for new ways of using existing equipment

Without the accompanying advances in technology, many of elBulli's new concepts and techniques could not have been developed. Technology is divided into two categories: machines (usually electrical) and utensils. Discovering new uses for existing machines or utensils is just as important as finding new equipment.

PREPARATIONS

Developments that originate in new types of dish:

- Looking for new ways of preparing ingredients, which could mean new techniques and concepts, such as hot jellies or frozen powders
- Taking existing preparations out of context or finding new applications for them

A preparation could be a component of dish (an intermediate preparation), or it could be a dish in itself (a final preparation), such as a carpaccio or ravioli. Any type of preparation that has been developed using new techniques or concepts, and which could give rise to future new developments, is included within this category (see next page).

STYLES AND CHARACTERISTICS

Developments that result in the emergence of new styles and characteristics:

- Looking for new styles and characteristics
- Finding new perspectives for existing styles

A set of styles and characteristics is what forms and defines a cuisine.

In elBulli's case the styles and characteristics can also become creative methods (see next page).

The paths may be used singly or together, or in conjunction with techniques from classical and contemporary cuisine to create:

RECIPES

The recipes form a collection of styles and characteristics that will gradually shape elBulli's cuisine.

The search for new ideas: preparations, styles and characteristics

PREPARATIONS

These are the principal categories of preparation that have been developed using new techniques and concepts:

Waters, milks, juices and meat juices, infusions, stocks and consommés

Liquid creams
Soups
Purées

Cold preparations made with gelling agents
Hot preparations made with gelling agents

Spherifications

Airs
Cold foams, cold mousses, clouds and *bavaroises*
Hot foams, hot mousses, soufflés and quenelles
Other light textures

Crème caramels, royales and puddings
Thick creams

Ice creams, sorbets, iced drinks, frappés, compacts and frozen powder
Nitros
Other frozen preparations

Caramels, croquants and liquid croquants
Caramelized fruit and vegetable slices
Other crispy preparations

Caramelized preparations and pralines
Jams, preserves, compotes, jellies *confitado* in syrup and similar preparations

Cocktails

Salads

Carpaccios, sashimi, tartares and marinated preparations

Salted, cured and pickled preparations

Escabeches and confits in fat

Cakes, tarts and similar preparations

Terrines, aspics and *chaud-froids*
Preparations served out of moulds
Individual preparations (such as for spoons or skewers)

Fried food

Dough, pastry, cake mix, batters and preparations made with them

Preparations with fresh and dry pasta
New pastas
New ravioli
Preparations with rice and other cereals

Preparations with cheese and other dairy products
Preparations with eggs as the main element

Slow-cooked meat preparations

Stocks and sauces
Finishing touches (or last-minute additions of a strongly-flavoured ingredient, which are designed to accentuate one or more of the features of a dish)

Preparations with chocolate

Other preparations

STYLES AND CHARACTERISTICS

Many styles have become creative methods, and many creative methods have become styles: there is a symbiotic relationship between them. Styles and characteristics have become more closely connected during elBulli's development.

These are the key styles and creative methods of elBulli's cuisine:

Local cuisine as a style

Influences from other cuisines

Technique-concept search

The senses as a starting point for creativity

The sixth sense

Symbiosis between the sweet and savoury worlds

Commercial products and preparations in high-end cuisine

A new way to serve food

Changes in the structure of dishes

Association

Inspiration

Adaptation and deconstruction

Minimalism

Changes in the structure of the menu

Map of elBulli's cuisine

The map of elBulli's cuisine (next page) summarizes the development of key styles, products, techniques and preparations over the course of elBulli's history. It is updated at the end of every season with the most important new developments, and it is often difficult to decide which ones to include because it is not always immediately apparent which techniques and concepts will prove the most significant in the future. Usually only three or four are added each year.

The map facilitates a measured analysis of each season's creative development, pinpointing the key moments of significant discoveries and the influence they have had on elBulli's creative evolution. It also monitors the restaurant's development, eliminating the possibility of repeating or copying earlier ideas.

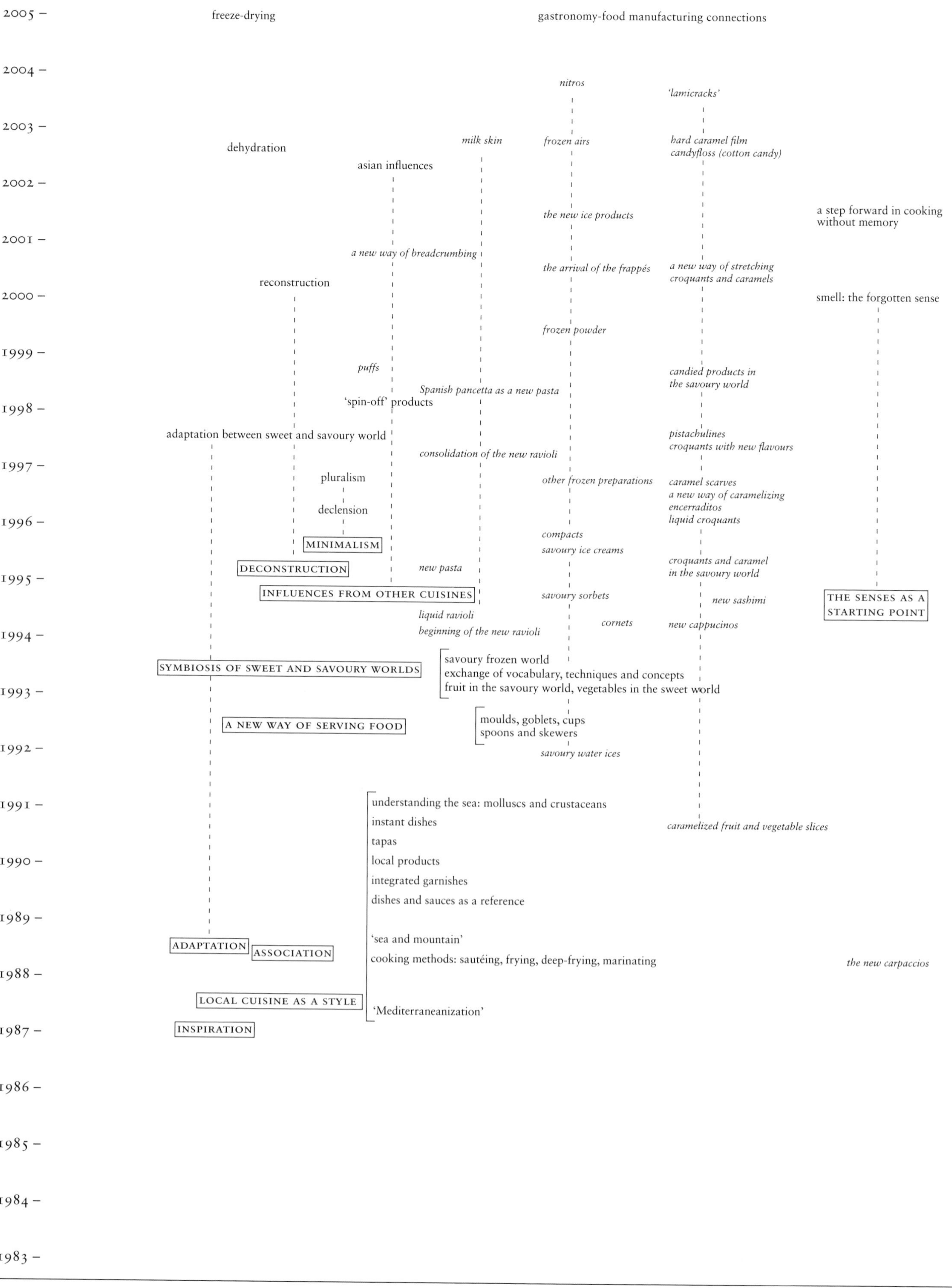
2005 –
freeze-drying
gastronomy-food manufacturing connections
2004 –
nitros
'lamicracks'
2003 –
milk skin
frozen airs
hard caramel film
candyfloss (cotton candy)
dehydration
asian influences
2002 –
the new ice products
a step forward in cooking without memory
2001 –
a new way of breadcrumbing
the arrival of the frappés
a new way of stretching croquants and caramels
reconstruction
2000 –
smell: the forgotten sense
frozen powder
1999 –
puffs
candied products in the savoury world
Spanish pancetta as a new pasta
'spin-off' products
1998 –
adaptation between sweet and savoury world
pistachulines
croquants with new flavours
consolidation of the new ravioli
1997 –
pluralism
other frozen preparations
caramel scarves
a new way of caramelizing
encerraditos
liquid croquants
declension
1996 –
compacts
MINIMALISM
savoury ice creams
DECONSTRUCTION
new pasta
croquants and caramel in the savoury world
1995 –
INFLUENCES FROM OTHER CUISINES
savoury sorbets
new sashimi
THE SENSES AS A STARTING POINT
liquid ravioli
cornets
new cappucinos
1994 –
beginning of the new ravioli
savoury frozen world
SYMBIOSIS OF SWEET AND SAVOURY WORLDS
exchange of vocabulary, techniques and concepts
1993 –
fruit in the savoury world, vegetables in the sweet world
A NEW WAY OF SERVING FOOD
moulds, goblets, cups
spoons and skewers
1992 –
savoury water ices
1991 –
understanding the sea: molluscs and crustaceans
instant dishes
caramelized fruit and vegetable slices
tapas
1990 –
local products
integrated garnishes
dishes and sauces as a reference
1989 –
ADAPTATION
ASSOCIATION
'sea and mountain'
cooking methods: sautéing, frying, deep-frying, marinating
the new carpaccios
1988 –
LOCAL CUISINE AS A STYLE
'Mediterraneanization'
1987 –
INSPIRATION
1986 –
1985 –
1984 –
1983 –

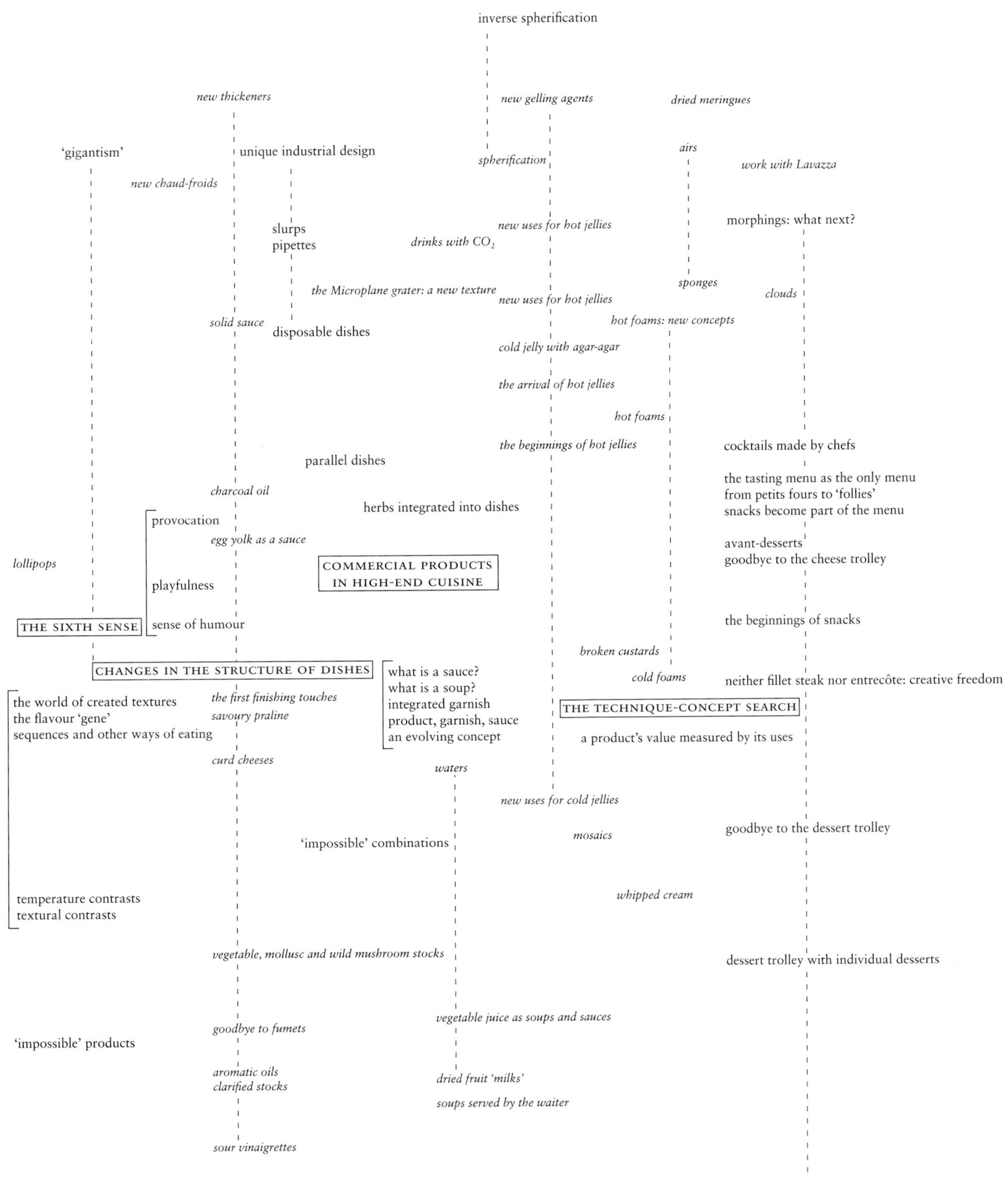

inverse spherification
new thickeners
new gelling agents
dried meringues
'gigantism'
unique industrial design
spherification
airs
work with Lavazza
new chaud-froids
slurps
pipettes
drinks with CO_2
new uses for hot jellies
morphings: what next?
the Microplane grater: a new texture
new uses for hot jellies
sponges
clouds
solid sauce
disposable dishes
hot foams: new concepts
cold jelly with agar-agar
the arrival of hot jellies
hot foams
the beginnings of hot jellies
cocktails made by chefs
parallel dishes
the tasting menu as the only menu
from petits fours to 'follies'
snacks become part of the menu
charcoal oil
herbs integrated into dishes
provocation
egg yolk as a sauce
avant-desserts
goodbye to the cheese trolley
lollipops
COMMERCIAL PRODUCTS IN HIGH-END CUISINE
playfulness
THE SIXTH SENSE
sense of humour
the beginnings of snacks
broken custards
CHANGES IN THE STRUCTURE OF DISHES
what is a sauce?
what is a soup?
integrated garnish
product, garnish, sauce
an evolving concept
cold foams
neither fillet steak nor entrecôte: creative freedom
the world of created textures
the flavour 'gene'
sequences and other ways of eating
the first finishing touches
savoury praline
THE TECHNIQUE-CONCEPT SEARCH
a product's value measured by its uses
curd cheeses
waters
new uses for cold jellies
mosaics
goodbye to the dessert trolley
'impossible' combinations
whipped cream
temperature contrasts
textural contrasts
vegetable, mollusc and wild mushroom stocks
dessert trolley with individual desserts
vegetable juice as soups and sauces
'impossible' products
goodbye to fumets
aromatic oils
clarified stocks
dried fruit 'milks'
soups served by the waiter
sour vinaigrettes

Developing an individual style: 'creativity means not copying'

(Jacques Maximin)

YEARS OF RECREATING AND COPYING CREATE CULINARY 'BAGGAGE'

CHANGES IN THE MENU STRUCTURE

—

elBulli recipes

There is no menu to choose from at elBulli, but not all the guests eat the same thing, and the dishes vary throughout the season.

When elBulli opens in April, the dishes served during the first few days are recipes from the previous year, and then, gradually, the new dishes that are finalized during the morning creative sessions are incorporated. These moments of transition are among the most magical days at elBulli. By the end of April, the menu will be completely different from that of the previous year, and new dishes continue to be incorporated until 30 August. Some are removed because the ingredients go out of season, while others are replaced with better dishes. This does not mean that the menu in September is the most perfect, because at this time of year some ingredients – young pine nuts or asparagus, for example – are no longer available.

The recipes listed here represent a typical August menu at elBulli: thirty dishes, starting with a cocktail, continuing with snacks, tapas-dishes, an avant-dessert, desserts and finally morphings.

The recipes are listed as ingredient combination 'formulas'. These provide a useful record of the flavour and product combinations that have been successful and can be used as a reference tool when developing new dishes.

NOTE ON THE RECIPES

The technical level of elBulli's recipes requires specialist equipment, exact measurements using the metric system and professional experience to achieve good results.

The imperial measures provided are approximate and are intended only as a guide. Very small quantities have not been converted. Liquids are given in metric weight measurements for greater accuracy, and have been converted into rough volume measurements as a guide.

All spoon measurements are level.
1 teaspoon = 5 ml, 1 tablespoon = 15 ml.

I COCKTAIL

Margarita — p. 270

Water
+ sugar
+ lemon
+ tequila
+ Cointreau
+ ice
+ salt
+ Lecite
+ Himalayan crystal salt

12 SNACKS

Spherical-I green olives — p. 282

Algin
+ water
+ green Verdial olives
+ Xantana
+ Calcic
+ extra virgin olive oil
+ garlic
+ lemon
+ orange
+ thyme
+ rosemary
+ black peppercorns

Pine nut marshmallows — p. 284

Virgin pine nut oil
+ gelatine
+ milk
+ pine nuts
+ salt

3Ds with ras-el-hanout and lemon basil shoots — p. 286

3Ds
+ olive oil
+ double (heavy) cream
+ ras-el-hanout
+ lemon basil shoots
+ salt

Cantonese *músico* — p. 288

Sunflower oil
+ water
+ star anise
+ sugar
+ coriander (cilantro)
+ rosemary honey
+ walnuts
+ Szechuan pepper
+ pine nuts
+ green pistachios
+ salt

Mango and black olive discs — p. 290

Olive oil
+ black Aragón olives
+ icing (confectioners') sugar
+ Glice
+ glucose
+ gelatine
+ Isomalt
+ mango purée
+ Sucro

Five pepper melon-CRU/melon-LYO with fresh herbs and green almonds — p. 292

Water
+ basil
+ green almonds
+ sugar
+ five peppers
+ *piel de sapo* melon
+ cantaloupe melon
+ mint

Pumpkin oil sweet — p. 294

Pumpkin seed oil
+ Isomalt
+ gold
+ salt

Thai nymph — p. 296

Basil
+ sugar
+ peanuts
+ coriander (cilantro)
+ coconut
+ Madras curry powder
+ coriander (cilantro) shoots
+ red curry paste
+ tamarind paste
+ cucumber
+ Japanese white sesame seeds

Melon with ham — p. 298

Water
+ Algin
+ Calcic
+ *jamón ibérico*
+ cantaloupe melon
+ black pepper
+ Xantana

Spherical-I mozzarella — p. 300

Water
+ Algin
+ double (heavy) cream
+ buffalo mozzarella
+ single (light) cream
+ salt

Samphire tempura with saffron and oyster cream — p. 302

Olive oil
+ water
+ saffron
+ glutinous rice flour
+ oysters
+ smoked Spanish bacon
+ samphire

Steamed brioche with rose-scented mozzarella — p. 304

Sugar
+ rose essence
+ plain (all-purpose) flour
+ eggs
+ milk
+ Lecite
+ yeast
+ butter
+ sourdough starter
+ buffalo mozzarella
+ salt

Thaw — p. 344

Olive oil
+ ascorbic acid
+ water
+ basil
+ sugar
+ ground coffee
+ powdered egg white
+ pasteurized egg white
+ borage flowers
+ fondant
+ borage shoots
+ glucose
+ gelatine
+ Isomalt
+ liquid nitrogen
+ liquorice paste
+ green pine cones
+ pine nuts
+ salt
+ red shiso
+ green shiso

Carrot-LYO foam with hazelnut foam-air and Córdoba spices — p. 348

Olive oil
+ virgin fennel seed oil
+ water
+ hazelnuts
+ saffron
+ Córdoba spices
+ coriander (cilantro) shoots
+ fennel
+ gelatine
+ milk
+ fermented milk
+ Lecite
+ *mató* cheese
+ single (light) cream
+ hazelnut paste
+ pink grapefruit
+ salt
+ carrots

'Folie' salad — p. 352

Extra virgin olive oil
+ black Aragón olives
+ water
+ garlic
+ artichokes
+ Algin
+ canned tuna
+ hazelnuts
+ Calcic
+ *ficoïde glaciale*
+ bergamot flowers
+ plain (all-purpose) flour
+ strong (bread) flour
+ tuna roe
+ bay leaves
+ milk
+ fermented milk
+ Lecite
+ yeast
+ *mató* cheese
+ mini-cucumber flowers
+ macadamia nuts
+ *pa-ha*
+ bread
+ rosemary
+ salt
+ cat's claw
+ purslane
+ sherry vinegar
+ Xantana
+ goats' milk yoghurt

Rock mussels with seaweed and fresh herbs — p. 356

Water
+ basil
+ dulse
+ nori
+ sugar
+ tarragon
+ rock mussels
+ mint
+ parsley
+ salt
+ samphire
+ *shiraita* kombu
+ red tosaka
+ green tosaka
+ sea grapes
+ rice vinegar
+ wakame
+ Xantana

Baby snails in court bouillon with crab escabeche and amaranth with fennel — p. 358

Olive oil
+ water
+ garlic
+ basil
+ amaranth
+ baby snails
+ onion
+ tarragon
+ fennel flowers
+ bay leaves
+ Lecite
+ mint
+ crab
+ parsley
+ black pepper
+ rosemary
+ salt
+ tomato
+ thyme
+ sherry vinegar

Earthy — p. 360

Water
+ Metil
+ summer truffle
+ single (light) cream
+ white truffle oil
+ salt
+ Venus rice
+ Agar
+ gelatine
+ liquorice stick
+ ascorbic acid
+ liquorice paste
+ ceps (porcini)
+ milk
+ virgin peanut oil
+ peanuts
+ black sesame seeds
+ sunflower oil
+ beetroot shoots
+ white miso paste
+ liquid nitrogen
+ potatoes
+ red cabbage shoots

Monkfish liver fondue with ponzu and white sesame-flavoured kumquat — p. 364

Kombu seaweed
+ water
+ *katsuobushi*
+ lime juice
+ soy sauce
+ Lecite
+ toasted sesame oil
+ rice vinegar
+ *yuzu*
+ monkfish liver
+ ice
+ sugar
+ kumquats
+ toasted Japanese white sesame seeds

Belly of mackerel in chicken escabeche with onions and vinegar caviar — p. 368

Mackerel
+ extra virgin olive oil
+ basil seeds
+ water
+ sherry vinegar
+ Figueres onion
+ chicken
+ onion
+ garlic
+ thyme
+ bay leaf
+ black peppercorns
+ Lecite
+ chives
+ chervil leaves
+ tarragon shoots
+ black pepper

Langoustine with quinoa[3] — p. 370

Olive oil
+ extra virgin olive oil
+ water
+ spring onion
+ langoustine
+ coriander (cilantro)
+ dried chilli
+ kefir
+ Metil
+ quinoa
+ quinoa shoots
+ salt
+ tomato

Tandoori chicken wings with borage shoots, oyster cream and frothy *mató* cheese — p. 374

Toasted almond oil
+ olive oil
+ water
+ green almonds
+ onion
+ Córdoba spices
+ borage shoots
+ milk
+ fermented milk
+ oysters
+ smoked Spanish bacon
+ tandoori paste
+ black pepper
+ chicken wings
+ salt
+ Sucro
+ tandoori powder

1 AVANT-DESSERT

Peach liquid — p. 414

Red peach juice
+ peach liqueur
+ single (light) cream
+ liquid nitrogen

2 DESSERTS

Coulant/soufflé of granadilla with cardamom toffee — p. 416

Sugar
+ cardamom
+ passion fruit
+ granadilla
+ gelatine
+ Metil
+ single (light) cream

Chocolate air-LYO with crisp raspberry sorbet and eucalyptus water ice — p. 418

Water
+ sugar
+ cinnamon
+ chocolate
+ crispy freeze-dried raspberry
+ sorbet stabilizer
+ raspberries
+ glucose
+ eucalyptus leaves
+ Lecite
+ cocoa butter
+ kataifi pastry
+ Piedmont hazelnut praline

4 MORPHINGS

Fruit-LYO in chocolate — p. 440

Rose essential oil
+ citric acid
+ white chocolate
+ freeze-dried strawberry
+ powdered yoghurt

Passion fruit tree — p. 444

Sugar
+ dark brown cane sugar
+ crispy freeze-dried passion fruit

Pineapple/fennel — p. 446

Star anise
+ fennel
+ pineapple

Yoghurt and raspberry *mochi* — p. 448

Citric acid
+ sugar
+ potato starch
+ raspberry
+ glutinous rice flour
+ gelatine
+ rosemary
+ *matcha* tea
+ yoghurt
+ Greek yoghurt

189 DIFFERENT INGREDIENTS

+ water
+ wine
+ coffee
+ liqueurs

Glossary

3D — A cone-shaped potato crisp (chip) made by Lays.

ACKEE — The edible fruit of a tropical West African tree, popularly eaten with salt cod in Jamaican cuisine.

AGAR — A gelling agent derived from seaweed, also known as agar-agar. It retains its gelling properties up to a temperature of 80°C (176°F).

AIR — Very light preparation which forms on the surface of a liquid when it is beaten with an electric whisk.

ALBÓNDIGAS — Spanish meatballs, a popular tapas dish.

ALGIN — A product in the Texturas Ferran y Albert Adrià range of food preparations. It is made from seaweed and used in spherification.

AMARANTH — Cereal originating in South America, found in Mexico and in the Himalayas.

AVANT-DESSERT — A small dish served between the tapas-dishes and the dessert, which provides a gentle transition from the savoury world to the sweet world.

BAVAROIS — French culinary term for a preparation (usually sweet), which is made with cream, set with gelatine and turned out of a mould.

BOQUERIA — A historic food market in central Barcelona.

BORAGE — A herb with a flavour reminiscent of cucumber, usually used fresh.

BORRACHO — A traditional Spanish cake soaked in alcohol.

CALCIC — A product in the Texturas Ferran y Albert Adrià range of food preparations. It is made from calcium salt and used in spherification.

CAT'S CLAW — A creeper native to South America, known for its medicinal properties.

CHAUD-FROID — A classic French dish, usually of cooked meat served cold in aspic.

CHEF DE PARTIE — The professional title for the chef responsible for a particular section of the kitchen.

CHINOIS — A conical, fine-meshed sieve.

CÓRDOBA SPICES — A blend of spices that often includes cinnamon, cardamom, cloves and chilli.

COURT BOUILLON — A stock often used for poaching fish or seafood.

CROQUANT — Preparation made from caramel, to which a dry product is added to give it flavour. Traditionally, this was nuts or dried fruit, but since the mid-1990s elBulli has used other ingredients, such as vegetables.

CROQUANTER — A crunchy preparation made from fruit or vegetable purée which is spread out to create a thin layer and then dehydrated.

-CRU — Denotes a procedure in which a solid substance is infused with a liquid, thus absorbing its flavour.

DULSE — Edible seaweed, bright red in colour and characteristic of Japanese cuisine.

ELBULLICARMEN — The elBulli offices in Barcelona, which manage all the activities not directly related to the restaurant, such as publications.

ELBULLITALLER — The elBulli creative workshop in Barcelona where new techniques and concepts are conceived and developed.

EMPANADILLA — A kind of Spanish pastry resembling a turnover or pasty, usually with a savoury filling.

ENCERRADITO — Product or preparation wrapped in two thin layers of caramel or croquant.

ESCABECHE — A dish that originates in Spain, in which an ingredient (usually cooked fish) is placed in a liquid containing vinegar or citrus juices and other aromatic flavourings. Also refers to the liquid itself.

ESPARDENYES — The Catalan name for sea cucumber and espadrilles (canvas shoes with a woven rope sole).

FATÉMA HAL — A Moroccan chef and food writer.

FICOÏDE GLACIALE — A small edible plant with green fleshy leaves, also known as ice plant.

FIGUERES ONION — A variety of onion native to Catalunya.

FONDANT — A type of sugar paste made by dissolving sugar and glucose in water and boiling it to around 112°C (234°F), then working it on a flat surface until it becomes a smooth white paste.

FUMET — A stock made from fish which is used as a base for cooking.

GARRAPI-NITRO — A term used at elBulli to describe all the preparations which use liquid nitrogen to produce a crunchy outer layer, similar to the results obtained with the traditional method of caramel-coating.

GLICE — A product in the Texturas Ferran y Albert Adrià range of food preparations. It is derived from natural fatty acids and used as an emulsifier.

GOOSE BARNACLE — A thick-stemmed crustacean found on rocks and cliffs, widely eaten in Spain and Portugal.

GRANADILLA — A round orange fruit with black spots and juicy seeds native to South and Central America, related to the passion fruit.

ISI SIPHON — A pressurized container in which foams can be created by aerating a liquid under pressure.

ISOMALT — A crystalline sugar substitute often used in place of sucrose.

JAMÓN IBÉRICO — Fine quality Spanish cured ham made from the *cerdo negro*, or black pig.

JULIENNE — Slice thinly into matchstick-sized pieces.

KAISEKI — A style of formal Japanese cuisine, which involves many carefully balanced courses prepared with seasonal ingredients.

KATAIFI — A type of pastry in long, thin threads.

KATSUOBUSHI — Dried, smoked and cured Japanese bonito.

KEFIR — A fermented dairy product, originally from the Caucasus region.

—

LECITE — A product in the Texturas Ferran y Albert Adrià range of food preparations, made from soy lecithin and used as an emulsifier to create airs.

LONGUEIRONES — Shellfish similar to the razor-shell clam, originating in Galicia.

-LYO — Indicates that a product has been freeze-dried at elBulli.

MAÍZ FRITO — Fried and toasted corn kernels commonly sold as a snack in Spain.

MANGOSTEEN — A tropical fruit with a dark purplish skin and white interior.

MANTECADO — A crumbly Spanish cake made with lard and traditionally eaten at Christmas.

MASTIC — A clear resin, yellowish in colour and slightly aromatic, which is extracted from the Lentisc or Mastic tree and used to provide aroma. Also known as mastic resin.

MATCHA TEA — Japanese powdered green tea.

MATÓ — A fresh, soft cows' or goats' milk cheese from Catalunya.

MENTAIKO — Marinated pollack roe, Korean in origin and typical in Japanese cuisine.

MERCABARNA — A large wholesale food market on the outskirts of Barcelona.

METIL — A product in the Texturas Ferran y Albert Adrià range of food preparations. It is made from vegetable cellulose and acts as a thickener when cold and a gelling agent when heated.

MICROPLANE GRATER — A type of high-quality grater often used in professional kitchens.

MIRACULIN — A naturally occurring plant protein derived from an African shrub that can make acidic foods taste sweet.

MISE EN PLACE — The culinary procedures and preparations that take place in a restaurant kitchen before service begins, such as preparing sauces and chopping vegetables.

MORPHINGS — Sweet preparations served at elBulli after the desserts, with the coffee.

MOCHI — Little filled glutinous rice cakes, typical in Japan.

MÚSICO — Nuts and dried fruit served with a glass of wine at the end of a traditional Catalan meal. The name originates from the fact that travelling musicians would take a handful of dried fruit and nuts at the end of the meal to snack on after the performance, as they were usually the first to leave the table.

NAPOLEON OYSTER — A variety of large oyster from Galicia.

-NITRO — Suffix which indicates that the dish in question has been prepared using liquid nitrogen.

PACOJET — A machine used to make sorbets with a very fine texture, as well as other creations such as frozen powders.

PA-HA — A long, thick-stemmed Asian vegetable with a porous interior.

PALET — French culinary term for a dessert presented in a flat shape.

PAUPIETTE — French culinary term for a piece of meat that has been beaten out thinly and stuffed.

PAVÉ — French culinary term for a savoury dish, usually in a square, flat shape like a paving stone.

PIPETTE — A laboratory utensil used at elBulli to serve preparations which consist of a solid element, which is speared on the rod or skewer, and a liquid one, that is introduced in the round part of the pipette. Similar to a brochette, in which the sauce is incorporated.

PISTACHULINE — Preparation comprising one ingredient, usually a nut or dried fruit, wrapped in a croquant of the same ingredient.

POLVORONE — Rich, crumbly Spanish almond biscuit dusted with sugar and traditionally eaten at Christmas.

PURPLE GLASSWORT — An annual plant that grows in saline soils. A variety of samphire.

PURSLANE — A small green plant with edible fleshy leaves.

PX — Pedro Ximénez, a Spanish variety of white grape which produces a dark-coloured, liqueur-like wine of the same name.

QUENELLE — A small portion of food shaped with two spoons into an elongated sphere like a rugby ball (American football).

QUINOA — A cereal originating from South America.

RAS-EL-HANOUT — A North African blend of spices, which usually includes cumin, coriander, turmeric, ginger and cardamom.

REYPENAER — A hard Dutch cheese.

RONER — A machine often used in professional kitchens to poach foods in liquid for long periods at a low and constant temperature.

SALAZONES — A Spanish term for salted and dried products, especially fish or meat.

SAMPHIRE — A green plant with long, fleshy stems that grows in saline soils close to the sea.

SEA GRAPES — A vibrant green seaweed, known as *umi budo* in Japan, which has a crisp texture with tiny liquid-filled globules along the stem.

SEA SPAGHETTI — A long, thin seaweed known as *judia de mar* in Spain.

SHIRAITA KOMBU — Sheets made from kombu seaweed.

SHISO — Aromatic herb of Asian origin, reminiscent of mint or basil. There are two varieties: purple shiso and green shiso.

SILPAT — Non-stick baking sheet, often used for confectionery.

SIPHON — Utensil designed to whip cream and which, in the mid-1990s, enabled the creation of foams at elBulli.

SLURPS — The name given by elBulli to the wide glass straws that were developed for serving snacks.

SNIFF — Utensil consisting of a little straw containing a loosely-set gelatine. It is eaten by sucking the straw.

SOURDOUGH STARTER — A paste of flour and water that is left to ferment and collect natural yeasts for a few days, and is then used as the raising (rising) agent in sourdough bread.

SPHERIFICATION — Controlled setting of a liquid which, through the action of hydrocolloids, facilitates the creation of spheres covered in a membrane of gelatine with a liquid centre.

STAGE — A temporary work experience placement in a restaurant (those participating are known as 'stagers').

SUCRO — A product in the Texturas Ferran y Albert Adrià range of food preparations. It is derived from sucrose and fatty acids and is used as an emulsifier, as well as for its aerating properties.

SUPERBAG — A very fine mesh bag through which liquids can be strained and clarified.

TAGETE FLOWER — A variety of edible marigold native to South America

TAPAS-DISHES — The main savoury dishes at elBulli, served after the snacks and before the avant-desserts.

THERMOMIX — A food processor that can blend foods at different temperatures.

TONKA BEAN — The fruit of a South American tree, which has a vanilla-like flavour.

TOSAKA — A type of seaweed used in Japanese cooking. It comes in white, green and red varieties.

VENUS RICE — A variety of black rice from Italy.

VERDIAL — A variety of green olive from southern Spain, often served as part of tapas.

XANTANA — A product in the Texturas Ferran y Albert Adrià range of food preparations. Derived from fermented starch, it is used as a thickening agent and to maintain solids in suspension within a liquid.

YUZU — An Asian citrus fruit, which tastes like a cross between mandarin and lemon. It is used particularly for its aromatic zest.

—

The authors would like to thank Richard Schlagman, Emilia Terragni, Laura Gladwin and Julia Hasting at Phaidon Press for the passion and enthusiasm they have brought to this project. They would also like to thank Josep Maria Pinto and Marta Méndez Blaya in Barcelona for their invaluable assistance in preparing this book.

Phaidon Press Limited
Regent's Wharf
All Saints Street
London N1 9PA

Phaidon Press Inc.
180 Varick Street
New York, NY 10014

www.phaidon.com

First published 2008
Reprinted in paperback 2010

ISBN 978 0 7148 5674 2

A CIP catalogue record of this book is available from the British Library.

Translated from the Spanish by Equipo de Edicion and Cillero & De Motta

Photographs by Maribel Ruiz de Erenchun, except pages 270, 282–304, 344–74, 414–18 and 440–48 by Francesc Guillamet

Designed by Julia Hasting
Printed in China